The Definitive Guide to JasperReports™

Teodor Danciu and Lucian Chirita

Apress®

The Definitive Guide to JasperReports™

ISBN-13 (pbk): 978-1-59059-927-3

ISBN-10 (pbk): 1-59059-927-6

Printed and bound in the United States of America 9 8 7 6 5 4 3 2 1

Lead Editor: Steve Anglin
Editorial Board: Steve Anglin, Ewan Buckingham, Gary Cornell, Jonathan Gennick, Jason Gilmore, Jonathan Hassell, Chris Mills, Matthew Moodie, Jeffrey Pepper, Ben Renow-Clarke, Dominic Shakeshaft, Matt Wade, Tom Welsh
Project Manager: Kylie Johnston
Copy Editor: Damon Larson
Assistant Production Director: Kari Brooks-Copony
Production Editor: Kelly Winquist
Compositor: Molly Sharp
Proofreader: Lori Bring
Indexer: Julie Grady
Artist: April Milne
Cover Designer: Kurt Krames
Manufacturing Director: Tom Debolski

Distributed to the book trade worldwide by Springer-Verlag New York, Inc., 233 Spring Street, 6th Floor, New York, NY 10013. Phone 1-800-SPRINGER, fax 201-348-4505, e-mail `orders-ny@springer-sbm.com`, or visit `http://www.springeronline.com`.

For information on translations, please contact Apress directly at 2855 Telegraph Avenue, Suite 600, Berkeley, CA 94705. Phone 510-549-5930, fax 510-549-5939, e-mail `info@apress.com`, or visit `http://www.apress.com`.

The source code for this book is available to readers at `http://www.apress.com` in the Source Code/Download section.

To my wife and daughter.
—Teodor Danciu

To my parents and my wife.
—Lucian Chirita

Contents at a Glance

Contents

CHAPTER 10 Report Elements

Foreword

I can still remember the first time I used JasperReports™. I was in charge of finding a way to generate PDF reports from a large web application we were working on. The job was initially started by another developer: his solution was to use iText, a powerful Java library to generate PDF files, and it's still used today by JasperReports. The effort to create just a single report was really considerable, having to write Java code—a *lot* of Java code—and the performance was terrible, especially when working with a large amount of data.

When you have several people working on designing reports, a lot of reports to design, and only a few Java developers, you need a different way to generate your reports.

JasperReports was the answer to all my needs: it requires just a few lines of code to generate a report (and in several output formats, not only PDF); it can be easily integrated in a Java application; the people who design reports can work independently from the developers, so they can run and test the reports without the intervention of a Java programmer; the engine is fast; there are a lot of ways to supply data to the report, included using SQL and HQL queries, collections of JavaBeans, and custom data sources; and finally, it is open source.

Over the years, more than a million people have downloaded this library, and many of them have come to appreciate its simplicity of use and smart design. It is used everywhere; it represents the perfect choice to report data if you are using JDBC, XML, Hibernate, and so on; it has been integrated with the Spring Framework; and the support for EJBQL and MDX (to query OLAP databases) inducts the library as a cutting-edge Java technology.

JasperReports is the core of the JasperSoft® Business Intelligence Suite, a comprehensive set of tools for integrated reporting, analysis, and data integration. The suite is comprised of iReport™, an easy-to-use designer for JasperServer™, JasperReports, and Jasper4Salesforce™; JasperServer, a high-performance business intelligence and report server; JasperAnalysis™, an OLAP engine to drill down and slice and dice data to explore causes, trends, patterns, anomalies, and correlations using a standard web browser; and JasperETL™, a ready-to-run data integration platform providing data extract-transform-load (ETL) capabilities.

JasperReports comes with a lot of samples, so getting started with it is really easy, but this library has much more to offer, and it is here where this book becomes a irreplaceable source of knowledge: it is not just a detailed reference for the JRXML report design language, but a rich collection of tips and tricks, suggestions, and solutions to both simple and complex problems, such as how to effectively implement your own custom data source, how to write a personalized query executer to support a new query language, how to modify the JasperReports default properties using Java code, and much more. You have the unique possibility to deeply understand each architectural choice and acquire the full control to really leverage the power of JasperReports.

Teodor Danciu and Lucian Chirita have worked on JasperReports for years. Teodor founded the project in 2001, and both authors are the ultimate experts on the topic this book covers; in addition, being two expert Java engineers with a lot of experience and incredible skills, they represent the best guarantee for the quality of this guide, and this book is the essence of their knowledge.

Giulio Toffoli
iReport Founder and Senior Software Engineer, JasperSoft

About the Authors

TEODOR DANCIU is the founder and architect of the JasperReports library, the most popular open source reporting tool, and is now working for JasperSoft. Before joining JasperSoft, Teodor worked for almost 8 years with several French IT companies as a software engineer and team leader on ERP and other medium-to-large database-related enterprise applications using mainly Java technologies and the J2EE platform.

Teodor holds a B.S. in computer science from the Academy of Economic Studies in Bucharest.

LUCIAN CHIRITA joined Teodor Danciu at JasperSoft in the development of JasperReports library back in 2005, and he quickly became one of the main contributors to the project. Prior to joining JasperSoft, Lucian had 3 years of software engineering experience on several Java/J2EE products and applications. His contributions to JasperReports include support for crosstabs and integration with data query technologies such as Hibernate and OLAP.

Lucian holds an M.S. in computer science from the University of Bucharest.

Acknowledgments

We'd like to recognize the entire JasperSoft community for their support and input, which has helped to make JasperReports the leading open source Java reporting engine. In particular, we'd like to thank Sanda Zaharia and Ionut Nedelcu for their contributions to the JasperReports project and *The Definitive Guide to JasperReports*.

Introduction

The JasperReports library is a very powerful and flexible report-generating tool that delivers rich content to the screen, printer, or file in PDF, HTML, RTF, XLS, ODT, CSV, or XML format.

The library is written entirely in Java and can be used in a variety of Java-enabled applications, including J2EE or web applications, to generate dynamic content. Its main purpose is to help to create page-oriented, ready-to-print documents in a simple and flexible manner.

JasperReports, like most reporting applications, uses report templates structured in multiple sections, such as title, summary, detail, and page and group headers and footers. Each section has a free-form layout in which you can place various types of elements, including images, static and dynamic text fields, lines, and rectangles. The reporting engine uses this template to organize data in an XML file (JRXML) or to create it programmatically using the library's API. This data may come from various data sources, including relational databases, collections, or arrays of Java objects or XML data. Users can plug the reporting library into custom-made data sources by implementing a simple interface.

To fill a report with data, you must first compile the initial XML report template. Compilation validates the report template and attaches some compiler-related data to it. This data is used to evaluate the report expressions at runtime. The compiled report template can be serialized to store it on disk or sent over the network. This serialized object is then used when the application fills the specified report template with data. In fact, compiling a report template involves compiling all report expressions. Various verifications are made at compilation time to check report design consistency. The result is a ready-to-fill report template that is then used to generate documents on different sets of data.

To fill a report template, the engine must receive the report data. This data may come in various forms. Some of this data can be passed in as report parameters, but most of it comes from the report's data source. The reporting engine can directly receive special data source objects that provide the information for the report, or it can use a supplied JDBC connection object if the data is in a relational database.

The result of the report-filling operation is a new object that represents the ready-to-print document. This object can also be serialized for storage on disk or network transfer. It can be viewed directly using the JasperReports built-in viewer or can be exported to other, more popular formats such as PDF, HTML, RTF, XLS, ODT, CSV, and XML.

JasperReports is part of the JasperSoft Business Intelligence Suite, which is a comprehensive set of tools for integrated reporting, analysis, and data integration. In addition to JasperReports, the suite is comprised of iReport, an easy-to-use designer for JasperServer, JasperReports, and Jasper4Salesforce; JasperServer, a high-performance business intelligence and report server; JasperAnalysis, an OLAP engine to drill down and slice and dice data to explore causes, trends, patterns, anomalies, and correlations using a standard web browser; and JasperETL, a ready-to-run data integration platform providing data extract-transform-load (ETL) capabilities.

The JasperSoft Business Intelligence Suite began as a complete open source reporting and BI solution. Today, JasperSoft offers both open source and professional versions of the suite. The professional version includes JasperStudio™, the professional edition of iReport.

Who This Book Is For

The JasperReports library has a simple and straightforward API that should be easy to understand when you start working with it. JasperReports is also a very flexible and configurable tool that can adapt to various needs when embedded into your Java application. This is not immediately apparent when you first look at the high-level API it exposes, so having a complete reference to all its functionality, as we've put together in this book, might prove to be very helpful to developers wanting to make the best of this library.

Because JasperReports is mainly a developer tool, this book is mainly for Java developers who want to better understand how the content-rendering engine works and how it could be plugged into their applications.

How This Book Is Structured

The book starts with a high-level presentation of the JasperReports library including installation, requirements, and building from source code. It then presents the main processes involved when working with the library, such as report template creation, filling reports with data, and handling of generated documents. After completing the JasperReports API overview, the book delves into the detailed structure of the report templates, explaining how the engine works with the data it receives and how it performs calculations during report filling. Chapters in the second half of the book present the more advanced features of the JasperReports engine, such as the use of subreports, scriptlets, crosstabs, and charts, and provide a complete reference for all the parameters supported by the built-in exporters.

Prerequisites

JasperReports is a content-rendering library that cannot run on its own and has to be embedded into another Java application that needs reporting capabilities. This is why you should be familiar with the Java language and platform. To make the best of this book, you should also be familiar with XML and other Java-related technologies such as JDBC and JavaBeans.

JasperReports integrates with higher-level technologies such as Hibernate, EJB, XPath, and others, and if you want to leverage any of those, you should be familiar with these third-party technologies before reading the corresponding chapters of this book.

Support and Training

JasperSoft Corporation offers support services and training for JasperReports. You can learn more about these at the following location:

`www.jaspersoft.com/ss_overview.html`

Discussion Forums

If you need help using the JasperReports library or you want to share your experience and help others, you can log in to these public forums and post your messages here:

`www.jasperforge.org/index.php?option=com_joomlaboard&Itemid=215&func=showcat&catid=8`

Articles

Throughout the years, the community created around JasperReports has contributed to the project by providing not only feedback, bug fixes, and patches, but also helpful documentation in the form of public articles that describe the various ways to work with the library and integrate it with third-party technologies. The complete list of articles can be found at the following location:

`http://jasperforge.org/sf/wiki/do/viewPage/projects.jasperreports/wiki/HomePage`

Downloading the Code

The source code for this book is available to readers at `www.apress.com` in the Source Code/Downloads section of this book's home page. Please feel free to visit the Apress web site and download all the code there. You can also check for errata and find related titles from Apress.

Contacting the Authors

You can contact the authors of this book at the following e-mail addresses:

`teodord@users.sourceforge.net`
`lucianc@users.sourceforge.net`

Both authors are active members on the public discussion forums mentioned previously, so you are encouraged to use these forums if you have questions about JasperReports. You can also use the JasperForge web site (`www.jasperforge.org`) to get in touch with the authors of this book and the team behind the JasperReports project.

CHAPTER 1

Getting Started

This chapter is for those who have never used JasperReports. If you have already installed JasperReports and used the samples, skip to Chapter 2.

Installing JasperReports

JasperReports is a content-rendering library, not a standalone application. It cannot run on its own and must be embedded in another client- or server-side Java application. JasperReports is a pure Java library and can be used on any platform that supports Java. Being a library, JasperReports is completely agnostic about the environment in which it is used for generating reports.

All JasperReports functionality is concentrated in a single JAR file, `jasperreports-x.x.x.jar`, available for download at the following URL:

```
http://sourceforge.net/project/showfiles.php?group_id=36382&package_id=28579
```

Even though all its reporting functionality is available in this single JAR file, JasperReports relies on other third-party libraries for related required functionality like XML parsing, logging, and PDF and XLS generation.

Because JasperReports is a library and cannot run on its own, you do not really install it. “Installing” JasperReports simply means downloading its JAR file and putting it into the classpath of your application along with the other required JAR files.

Requirements

JasperReports handles only reporting. It relies on third-party libraries and APIs to perform needed functionality like XML parsing, database connectivity, PDF or XLS output, and so on.

This section contains all the libraries that JasperReports may require, depending on the functionality required by JasperReports's parent application.

The two types of requirements for using JasperReports are the following:

- Absolute requirements, needed regardless of the module of JasperReports that is actually used.
- Optional requirements, needed only for a specific JasperReports function. (If a certain function of JasperReports is not used by the parent application, then the required libraries needed by that module can be skipped at deployment time.)

The following list details the requirements for using JasperReports:

- Java Virtual Machine (JVM), JRE 1.3 or higher
- One of the following for report compilation, depending on the report compiler used:
    - Eclipse JDT Java compiler (`www.eclipse.org/jdt/index.php`)
    - JDK 1.3 or higher
    - Jikes (`http://jikes.sourceforge.net`)
    - Groovy (`http://groovy.codehaus.org`)
    - BeanShell (`www.beanshell.org`)
- JAXP 1.1 XML Parser
- Jakarta Commons Javaflow, sandbox version (`http://jakarta.apache.org/commons/sandbox/javaflow`)
- Jakarta Commons Digester component, version 1.7 or later (`http://jakarta.apache.org/commons/digester`)
- Jakarta Commons BeanUtils component, version 1.4 or later (`http://jakarta.apache.org/commons/beanutils`)
- Jakarta Commons Collections component, version 2.1 or later (`http://jakarta.apache.org/commons/collections`)
- Jakarta Commons Logging component, version 1.0 or later (`http://jakarta.apache.org/commons/logging`)
- JDBC 2.0 driver
- iText (free Java PDF library by Bruno Lowagie and Paulo Soares), version 1.01 or later (`www.lowagie.com/iText`)
- The following APIs for XLS:
    - Jakarta POI, version 2.0 or later (`http://jakarta.apache.org/poi`)
    - JExcelApi, version 2.6 or later (`http://jexcelapi.sourceforge.net`)
- JFreeChart (free Java chart library), version 1.0.0 or later (`www.jfree.org/jfreechart`)

X11/Headless Java

JasperReports relies on AWT rendering when generating reports, so it might not work if you are using it in a server environment running UNIX/Linux without graphics support.

The application might raise errors such as "Can't connect to X11 window server using ':0.0'."

To solve this problem for JVM releases prior to 1.4, provide a pseudo–X server to emulate a display environment. Following are some of these emulators:

- X Virtual Frame Buffer (Xvfb)
- Pure Java AWT (PJA)
- Virtual Network Computing (VNC)

The preferred solution for JRE 1.4 or higher is to use the new headless AWT toolkit. This new feature allows you to use the J2SE API in a server-side Java application without a GUI environment.

To specify the headless environment when using the Sun Microsystems reference implementation, run your application with this property:

```
-Djava.awt.headless=true
```

Building the Source Files and Running the Samples

The best way to start working with JasperReports is to download the full project package from the following SourceForge.net location:

```
http://sourceforge.net/project/showfiles.php?group_id=36382&package_id=28579
```

The `jasperreports-x.x.x-project.zip` file available at this location contains all the source files, required libraries, and freely available documentation, as well as a complete set of sample applications and reports.

Download the archive and extract its contents to the directory of your choice on your local machine. You'll be able to see JasperReports in action without having to create a Java application to embed JasperReports in.

Ant Build Tool

Before using the JasperReports distribution files and samples, install the Ant tool on your machine.

JasperReports relies heavily on the Ant build tool from the Apache Foundation (`http://ant.apache.org`) to compile the source files, build the distribution files, generate the Javadoc documentation, and run the samples. The Ant build tool will make working with the JasperReports library easier. Please refer to the Ant documentation for installation instructions.

Building the Project from Source Files

Once you have installed Ant, you can compile the source files, generate the Javadoc API documentation, or build the distribution JAR files. To do this, execute the Ant tasks declared in the `build.xml` file found in the root directory of the project tree.

To see details of each available task, launch the `ant -p` command from the command prompt inside this root directory.

Running the Samples

The JasperReports distribution package comes with a complete set of sample applications and reports that show how each individual feature of the library can be used.

The samples are in the `/demo/samples` directory inside the project tree.

HSQLDB Demo Database

Some of the samples use data from an HSQLDB demo database supplied in the `/demo/hsqldb` directory of the JasperReports distribution (`www.hsqldb.org`).

Before running those samples, start the HSQLDB database by going to the `/demo/hsqldb` directory and launching `ant runServer` from the command prompt. To look into the database content using a simple SQL client tool, launch the HSQLDB Manager application by invoking `ant runManager` in the same directory after starting the database.

To test a particular sample in the `/demo/samples` directory, go to the corresponding sample subfolder and launch `ant -p` from the command line.

This displays a short description of what that sample demonstrates as well as a complete list of Ant tasks available for use on the sample's source files.

The following list gives the typical steps for running a sample:

1. Compile the sample's Java source files by calling `ant javac`.
2. Compile the JRXML report templates used by the sample application with `ant compile`.
3. Fill those report templates with data by calling `ant fill`.
4. View the result with `ant view`.

To export to other formats, simply use commands like `ant pdf` or `ant html`.

These samples are used throughout this guide to illustrate features of the library. Therefore make sure you can run the samples before reading the rest of this guide.

CHAPTER 2

Working with Report Templates

Report templates are standard in reporting applications. They define the layout of the documents that the report-filling process produces.

Like other reporting engines, JasperReports uses report templates structured in multiple sections. Each section type has its own characteristics and behavior. Section types include title, summary, page and column headers and footers, group headers and footers, and details. Each section is made of individual elements like lines, rectangles, static and dynamic text fields, images, and charts.

Creating a report template is a two-phase process because of how JasperReports evaluates report expressions, also known as *formulas*. The phases are as follows:

1. The initial report templates are compiled into a more digestible form before being filled with data.

2. Various consistency checks are performed and information for evaluating expressions at runtime is added.

The entry point into the JasperReports object model is the `net.sf.jasperreports.engine.design.JasperDesign` class, whose instances represent the source report templates, also called the *raw material*. These objects are created by using the JasperReports API directly, through parsing of a JRXML file edited by hand, or by using an UI design tool. Once compiled, these report-design objects are transformed into compiled report templates in the form of `net.sf.jasperreports.engine.JasperReport` objects.

Through compilation, the report templates are validated and put into a more read-only form containing attached compiler data that will be used for expression evaluation during the filling process.

Creating Report Templates

There are two ways to create report templates:

- Creating `net.sf.jasperreports.engine.design.JasperDesign` objects directly using the API

- Editing JRXML files using either a simple text editor, an XML editor, or a specialized GUI tool

The first option is recommended only in case the parent application that uses JasperReports inside the reporting module needs to create report templates at runtime.

In most cases this is not needed because the report templates do not need to change with every report execution, and hence static report templates could be used. Only the data used to fill these static report templates is dynamic.

However, there are cases when the actual report template is the result of some user input. The parent application might supply its users with a set of options when launching the reports that might take the form of some simplified report designer or wizard. In such cases, the actual report layout is not known or is not complete at design time, and can only be put together after the user's input is received.

The most common use case scenario that requires dynamically built or *ad hoc* report templates (as we call them) is one in which the columns that are going to be present in a table-like report layout are not known at design time. Instead, the user will give the number of columns and their order inside the desired report at runtime.

Developers have to make sure that the applications they create really need ad hoc reports and cannot rely solely on static report templates. Since dynamically built report templates have to be compiled on the fly at runtime, they can result in a certain loss of performance.

The second option for creating report templates is to edit JRXML files and use those with the `net.sf.jasperreports.engine.JasperCompileManager` to prepare them for filling with data. Because they are well structured and are validated against a public DTD when parsed, these files can be easily edited using simple editors or specialized XML editors.

Report Design Preview

The JasperReports library does not ship with an advanced GUI tool to help design reports. At this time, there are several third-party projects that provide such a tool. Please refer to Chapter 20 for a complete list of GUI tools available for JasperReports.

However, the library contains a very helpful visual component that lets you preview the report designs as you build them.

The `net.sf.jasperreports.view.JasperDesigner` class is a simple Swing-based Java application that can load and display a report template either in its JRXML form or its compiled form. Even though it is not a complex GUI application and lacks advanced functionality like dragging and dropping visual report elements, it is a very helpful tool. All the supplied samples were initially created using this design viewer.

All the supplied samples already have Ant tasks in their `build.xml` files that will launch this design viewer to display the report templates.

There are two Ant tasks for each sample report: `viewDesign` and `viewDesignXML`. The first one loads the compiled report template that is normally found in the `*.jasper` file. The second one loads the JRXML report template, which is more useful since you can edit the JRXML file and click the Reload button to immediately see the modification on the screen.

To preview a sample report template if you have the Ant build tool installed on your system, simply go to the desired sample directory and enter something like the following from the command line:

```
>ant viewDesignXML
```

or

```
>ant viewDesign
```

By launching this command, you should see the window shown in Figure 2-1.

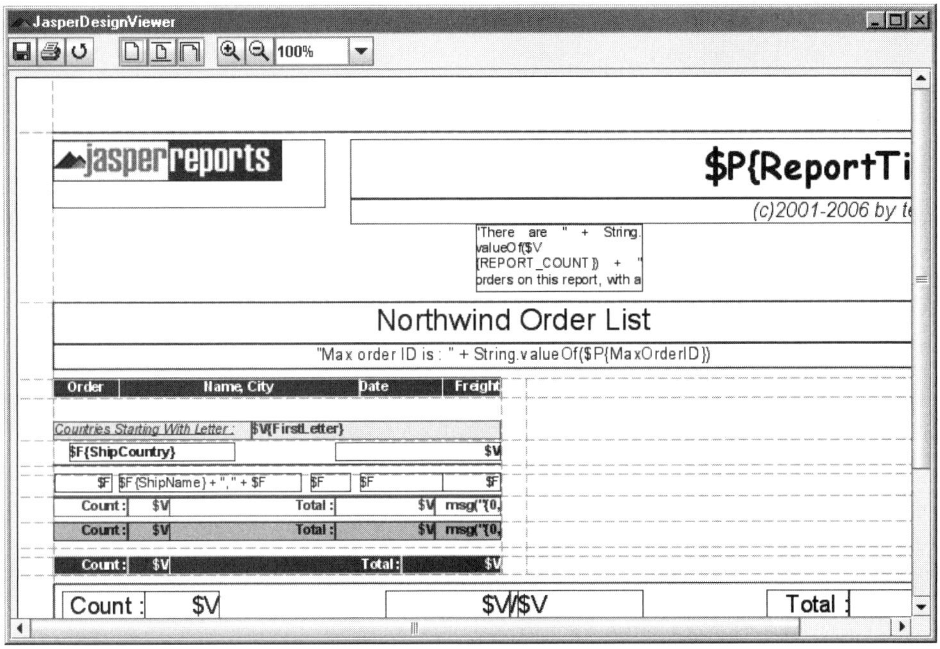

Figure 2-1. *Report design preview tool*

Loading and Storing Report Template Files

Both the `net.sf.jasperreports.engine.design.JasperDesign` and `net.sf.jasperreports.engine.JasperReport` classes implement the `java.io.Serializable` interface. This allows users to store their report templates as serialized objects either in their fully modifiable state (`JasperDesign` objects) or in their compiled form (`JasperReport` objects).

The preferred file extension for storing `net.sf.jasperreports.engine.JasperReport` objects in files is `*.jasper`. Throughout the documentation we'll often mention the `*.jasper` file when referring to a compiled report template. There is no preferred file extension for storing `net.sf.jasperreports.engine.design.JasperDesign` objects because this is not done very often.

For serializing objects to files or output streams, the JasperReports library offers a utility class named `net.sf.jasperreports.engine.util.JRSaver`.

To load serialized objects, you can rely on the supplied `net.sf.jasperreports.engine.util.JRLoader` utility class, which exposes various methods for loading objects from files, input streams, URLs, or classpath resources. This utility class has a method called `loadObjectFromLocation(String location)`, with built-in logic to load a serialized object from a specified `java.lang.String` location received as parameter. If this method is called, the program first tries to see if the specified location is a valid URL. If it is not, it then tries to determine whether the location points to an existing file on disk. If that also fails, the program tries to load the serialized object from the classpath using the specified location as a classpath resource name.

The library also exposes methods for parsing JRXML content into `JasperDesign` objects or for producing JRXML content out of a `JasperDesign` or `JasperReport` object.

The functionality is located in the `net.sf.jasperreports.engine.xml.JRXmlLoader` and `net.sf.jasperreports.engine.xml.JRXmlWriter` classes.

In certain cases in your application, you might want to manually load the JRXML report template into a `net.sf.jasperreports.engine.design.JasperDesign` object without immediately compiling it. You might do this for applications that programmatically create report designs and use the JRXML form to store them temporarily or permanently.

You can easily load `net.sf.jasperreports.engine.design.JasperDesign` objects from JRXML report designs by calling one of the public static `load()` methods exposed by the `net.sf.jasperreports.engine.xml.JRXmlLoader` class. This way, report design objects can be loaded from JRXML content stored in a database field or other input stream sources.

The library contains utility methods for parsing JRXML into report design objects and vice versa. You can generate JRXML from an in-memory report design object.

As shown, sometimes report designs are created programmatically using the JasperReports API. Report design objects obtained this way can be serialized for disk storage or transferred over the network, but they also can be stored in JRXML format.

You can obtain the JRXML representation of a given report design object by using one of the public static `writeReport()` methods exposed by the `net.sf.jasperreports.engine.xml.JRXmlWriter` utility class.

Compiling Report Templates

Source report templates, created either by using the API or by parsing JRXML files, are subject to the report compilation process before they are filled with data.

This is necessary to make various consistency validations and to incorporate into these report templates data used to evaluate all report expressions at runtime.

The compilation process transforms `net.sf.jasperreports.engine.design.JasperDesign` objects into `net.sf.jasperreports.engine.JasperReport` objects. Both classes are implementations of the same basic `net.sf.jasperreports.engine.JRReport` interface. However, `JasperReport` objects cannot be modified once they are produced, while `JasperDesign` objects can. This is because some modifications made on the report template would probably require revalidation, or if a report expression is modified, the compiler-associated data stored inside the report template would have to be updated.

`JasperDesign` objects are produced when parsing JRXML files using the `net.sf.jasperreports.engine.xml.JRXmlLoader` or created directly by the parent application if dynamic report templates are required. The GUI tools for editing JasperReports templates also work with this class to make in-memory modifications to the report templates before storing them on disk.

A `JasperDesign` object must be subject to the report compilation process to produce a `JasperReport` object.

Central to this process is the net.sf.jasperreports.engine.design.JRCompiler interface, which defines two methods, one being the following:

```
public JasperReport compileReport(JasperDesign design) throws JRException;
```

There are several implementations for this compiler interface depending on the language used for the report expressions or the mechanism used for their runtime evaluation.

Expressions Scripting Language

The default language for the report expressions is Java (see the discussion of the language property in the "Report Template Properties" section of Chapter 7), but report expressions can be written in Groovy or any other scripting language as long as a report compiler implementation that can evaluate them at runtime is available.

JasperReports currently ships a report compiler implementation for the Groovy scripting language (http://groovy.codehaus.org) and another one for the BeanShell scripting library (http://www.beanshell.org).

The Groovy-based report compiler is implemented by the net.sf.jasperreports.compilers.JRGroovyCompiler class, which is now part of the core library, while the BeanShell one is shipped as a separate sample.

For more details about those two report compilers, check the /demo/samples/beanshell and /demo/samples/groovy samples distributed with the project source files.

Report Compilers

The report templates can be compiled using the desired report compiler implementation by instantiating it and calling the compileReport() method mentioned previously.

Since the most common scenario is to use the Java language for writing report expressions, default implementations of the report compiler interface are shipped with the library and are ready to use. They generate a Java class from the report expressions and store bytecode in the generated net.sf.jasperreports.engine.JasperReport object for use at report-filling time.

The Java report compilers come in different flavors depending on the Java compiler used to compile the class that is generated on the fly:

```
net.sf.jasperreports.engine.design.JRJdtCompiler
net.sf.jasperreports.engine.design.JRJdk13Compiler
net.sf.jasperreports.engine.design.JRJdk12Compiler
net.sf.jasperreports.engine.design.JRJavacCompiler
net.sf.jasperreports.engine.design.JRJikesCompiler
```

To simplify the report-compilation process, the JasperReports API offers a façade class (net.sf.jasperreports.engine.JasperCompileManager) for compiling reports. This class has various public static methods for compiling report templates that come from files, input streams, or in-memory objects. The façade class relies on a special report compiler implementation that has a built-in fallback mechanism that tries to pick up the best Java-based report compiler available in the environment where it runs.

The `net.sf.jasperreports.engine.design.JRDefaultCompiler` first reads the configuration property called `net.sf.jasperreports.compiler.class` to allow users to override its built-in compiler-detection logic by providing the name of the report compiler implementation to use directly. More on configuration properties for customizing report compilation can be found later in this chapter.

This default implementation first tries to see if the JDT compiler from the Eclipse Foundation is available in the application's classpath. If it is, the `net.sf.jasperreports.engine.design.JRJdtCompiler` implementation is used. The current JasperReports distribution ships the JDT compiler packed in the `/lib/jdt-compiler.jar` file.

If the JDT compiler is not available, it then tries to locate the JDK 1.3–compatible Java compiler from Sun Microsystems. This is normally found in the `tools.jar` file that comes with the JDK installation.

If the JDK 1.3–compatible Java compiler is not in the classpath, the fallback search mechanisms look for the JDK 1.2–compatible Java compiler, also from Sun Microsystems, in case the application is running in an environment that has a JDK version prior to 1.3 installed. This is also found in the `tools.jar` file from the JDK installation.

If all these fail, the last thing the default Java compiler does is to try to launch the `javac.exe` program from the command line in order to compile the temporarily generated Java source file on the fly.

A Brief History of Report Compilation

All these report compiler implementations are included for historical reasons. In the beginning, JasperReports started with only the JDK 1.2–compatible report compiler. Then the JDK 1.3–compatible report compiler was introduced. But both were slow. This is why the `net.sf.jasperreports.engine.design.JRJikesCompiler` was created, because the Jikes compiler proved to be up to ten times faster than the JDK-based Java compiler.

However, compiling reports on the fly (in the cases in which dynamic report templates were required) proved to be problematic, especially in a web environment, because all the aforementioned compilers worked only with files on disk and required a temporary working directory to store the generated Java source files and the corresponding class files during the report-compilation process. This is why a new implementation was added—one that relied on the BeanShell library for runtime expression evaluation. BeanShell does not produce Java bytecode and can work with in-memory scripts that it interprets at runtime. With the `net.sf.jasperreports.engine.design.JRBshCompiler`, deployment was simpler, but expression evaluation was slower and loss in performance was noticeable.

The addition of the JDT-based report compiler makes the whole process both faster and simpler to deploy, as it does not require files on disk and its performance is comparable to Jikes. Runtime report compilation is not an issue anymore, and simply putting the supplied `/lib/jdt-compiler.jar` file in the application's classpath allows dynamic report template creation without requiring any further settings.

Now the BeanShell report compiler has been removed from the core library and is shipped only as a sample, since the advantages it offered are part of the JDT-based compiler, which is now the recommended one.

Configuration Properties to Customize Report Compilation

Because it is a library, JasperReports offers various mechanisms for letting users customize its behavior. One of these mechanisms is a complete set of configuration properties. The following paragraphs list all the configuration properties that customize report compilation. You can learn more about how JasperReports can be configured using configuration files in Chapter 18.

net.sf.jasperreports.compiler.class

Formerly known as the `jasper.reports.compiler.class` system property, this is used for indicating the name of the class that implements the `JRCompiler` interface to be instantiated by the engine when the default compilation is used through the `JasperCompileManager` and its corresponding `JRDefaultCompiler` implementation. The value for this configuration property can be the name of one of the five built-in implementations of this interface shipped with the library as listed previously, or the name of the custom-made implementing class.

Note that the classes implementing the `JRCompiler` interface can also be used directly in the programs without having to call them through the façade `JasperCompilerManager` class.

net.sf.jasperreports.compiler.xml.validation

This was formerly known as the `jasper.reports.compile.xml.validation` system property.

The XML validation, which is on by default, can be turned off by setting the `net.sf.jasperreports.compiler.xml.validation` configuration property to `false`. When turned off, the XML parser no longer validates the supplied JRXML against its associated DTD. This might prove useful in some environments, although it is not recommended.

When working with a Java class generating the type of a report compiler, further customizations can be made using the following system properties, which only apply to them.

net.sf.jasperreports.compiler.classpath

Formerly known as the `jasper.reports.compile.class.path` system property, this supplies the classpath. JDK-based and Jikes-based compilers require that the classpath be supplied as a parameter. They cannot use the current JVM classpath. The supplied classpath resolves class references inside the Java code they are compiling.

This property is not used by the JDT-based report compiler, which simply uses the parent application's classpath during Java source file compilation.

net.sf.jasperreports.compiler.temp.dir

This was formerly known as the `jasper.reports.compile.temp` system property.

The temporary location for the files generated on the fly is by default the current working directory. It can be changed by supplying a value to the `net.sf.jasperreports.compiler.temp.dir` configuration property. This is used by the JDT-based compiler only when it is requested that a copy of the on-the-fly generated Java class be kept for debugging purposes as specified by the next configuration property, because normally this report compiler does not work with files on disk.

net.sf.jasperreports.compiler.keep.java.file

This was formerly known as the `jasper.reports.compile.keep.java.file` system property.

Sometimes, for debugging purposes, it is useful to have the generated `*.java` file or generated script in order to fix compilation problems related to report expressions. By default, the engine deletes this file after report compilation, along with its corresponding `*.class` file. To keep it, however, set the configuration property `net.sf.jasperreports.compiler.keep.java.file` to `true`.

JDT Compiler–Specific Configuration Properties

The `JRJdtCompiler` report compiler can use special JasperReports configuration properties to configure the underlying JDT Java compiler. This report compiler collects all the JasperReports configuration properties (the ones usually set in the `jasperreports.properties` file) that start with the `org.eclipse.jdt.core.` prefix and passes them to the JDT Java compiler when compiling the generated Java class to evaluate report expressions.

One of the uses of this mechanism is to instruct the JDT compiler to observe Java 1.5 code compatibility. To do so, the following properties should be set:

```
org.eclipse.jdt.core.compiler.source=1.5
org.eclipse.jdt.core.compiler.compliance=1.5
org.eclipse.jdt.core.compiler.codegen.TargetPlatform=1.5
```

This is demonstrated in the `/demo/samples/java1.5` sample distributed with JasperReports.

Ant Tasks for Compiling Reports

Since report template compilation is more like a design-time job than a runtime one, a custom Ant task has been provided with the library to simplify application development.

This Ant task is implemented by the `net.sf.jasperreports.ant.JRAntCompileTask` class. Its syntax and behavior are very similar to the built-in `<javac>` Ant task.

The report template compilation task can be declared like this, in a project's `build.xml` file:

```
<taskdef name="jrc"
      classname="net.sf.jasperreports.ant.JRAntCompileTask">
  <classpath>
    <fileset dir="./lib">
      <include name="**/*.jar"/>
    </fileset>
  </classpath>
</taskdef>
```

In the preceding example, the `lib` should contain the `jasperreports-x.x.x.jar` file along with its other required libraries.

You can then use this user-defined Ant task to compile multiple JRXML report template files in a single operation by specifying the root directory that contains those files or by selecting them using file patterns.

Attributes of the Report Template Compilation Task

Following is the list of attributes that can be used inside the Ant report compilation task to specify the source files, the destination directory, and other configuration properties:

`srcdir`: Location of the JRXML report template files to be compiled. Required unless nested `<src>` elements are present.

`destdir`: Location to store the compiled report template files (the same as the source directory by default).

`compiler`: Name of the class that implements the `net.sf.jasperreports.engine.design.JRCompiler` interface to be used for compiling the reports (optional).

`xmlvalidation`: Flag to indicate whether the XML validation should be performed on the source report template files (`true` by default).

`tempdir`: Location to store the temporarily generated files (the current working directory by default).

`keepjava`: Flag to indicate if the temporary Java files generated on the fly should be kept and not deleted automatically (`false` by default).

The report template compilation task supports nested `<src>` and `<classpath>` elements, just like the Ant `<javac>` built-in task.

To see this in action, check the `/demo/samples/antcompile` sample provided with the project's source files.

CHAPTER 3

Filling Report Templates

The report-filling process is the most important piece of JasperReports library functionality, because it manipulates sets of data to produce high-quality documents. This is the main purpose of any reporting tool.

The following things should be supplied to the report-filling process as input:

- Report template (in the compiled form)
- Parameters
- Data source

The output is always a single, final document ready to be viewed, printed, or exported to other formats.

The `net.sf.jasperreports.engine.JasperFillManager` class is usually used for filling a report template with data. This class has various methods that fill report templates located on disk, come from input streams, or are supplied directly as in-memory `net.sf.jasperreports.engine.JasperReport` objects.

The output produced always corresponds to the type of input received. That is, when receiving a file name for the report template, the generated report is also placed in a file on disk. When the report template is read from an input stream, the generated report is written to an output stream, and so forth.

The various utility methods for filling the reports may not be sufficient for a particular application—for example, loading report templates as resources from the classpath and outputting the generated documents to files on disk at a certain location.

In such cases, consider manually loading the report template objects before passing them to the report-filling routines using the `net.sf.jasperreports.engine.util.JRLoader` utility class. This way, you can retrieve report template properties, such as the report name, to construct the name of the resulting document and place it at the desired disk location.

The report-filling manager class covers only the most common scenarios. However, you can always customize the report-filling process using the library's basic functionality just described.

Reporting Data

The JasperReports library is completely agnostic and makes no assumptions about where the data it uses for filling the reports comes from. It is the responsibility of JasperReports's parent application to supply this data and handle the output generated by the library.

JasperReports can make use of any data that the parent application might have for generating reports because it relies on two simple things: the report parameters and the report data source.

Report parameters are basically named values that are passed to the engine at report-filling time. The report parameter values are always packed in a `java.util.Map` object, which has the parameter names as its keys.

As for the data source, there are two different scenarios:

Normally, the engine works with an instance of the `net.sf.jasperreports.engine.JRDataSource` interface, from which it extracts the data when filling the report.

The façade class `net.sf.jasperreports.engine.JasperFillManager` has a full set of methods that receive a `net.sf.jasperreports.engine.JRDataSource` object as the data source of the report that is to be filled.

But there is another set of report-filling methods in this manager class that receive a `java.sql.Connection` object as a parameter, instead of an expected data source object.

This is because reports are usually generated using data that comes from tables in relational databases.

Users can put the SQL query needed to retrieve the report data from the database in the report template itself. At runtime, the only thing the engine needs is a JDBC connection object to connect to the desired relational database, execute the SQL query, and retrieve the report data.

Behind the scenes, the engine still uses a special `net.sf.jasperreports.engine.JRDataSource` object, but this is performed transparently for the calling program.

The main difference between parameters and the data source is that parameters are single-named values used inside report expressions for calculations or display, while the data source represents tabular data made of virtual rows and columns that the engine uses for iteration during the report-filling process.

JasperReports can make use of any application data because the `JRDataSource` interface is very simple and easy to implement. It only has two methods:

- The `next()` method, which moves the record pointer to the next record in the virtual tabular data
- The `getFieldValue()` method, which retrieves the value for each column in the current virtual record of the data source

The library ships with several implementations for the `JRDataSource` interface that cover the most commonly used sources for filling reports using Java, such as collections or arrays of JavaBeans, XML data, Swing table models, or JDBC result sets.

Provided with the project are several sample applications that fill the reports using data from the supplied HSQLDB database server. Additionally, the `/demo/samples/datasource` sample shows how to create custom data source implementations and how to use some of the supplied data source implementations. Also check the `/demo/samples/xmldatasource` to see how to use the XPath-based data source implementation shipped with the library for reporting.

Generated Reports

The output of the report-filling process is always a pixel-perfect document, ready for viewing, printing, or exporting to other formats. These documents come in the form of `net.sf.jasperreports.engine.JasperPrint` objects, which are serializable. This allows the parent application to store them or transfer them over the network if needed.

At the top level, a `JasperPrint` object contains some document-specific information, like the name of the document, the page size, and its orientation (portrait or landscape). Then it points to a collection of page objects (`net.sf.jasperreports.engine.JRPrintPage` instances), each page having a collection of elements that make up its content. Elements on a page are absolutely positioned at x and y coordinates within that page and have a specified width and height in pixels. They can be lines, rectangles, ellipses, images, or text, with various style settings corresponding to their type.

Filling Order (Vertical/Horizontal Filling)

JasperReports templates allow the detail section to be smaller than the specified page width so that the output can be structured into multiple columns, like a newspaper.

When multiple-column report templates are used, the order used for filling those columns is important (see Figure 3-1).

There are two possible column orders (see the `columnCount` and `printOrder` properties presented in the "Report Template Properties" section of Chapter 7):

- *Vertical*, meaning that they run from top to bottom and then from left to right
- *Horizontal*, meaning that they first run from left to right and then from top to bottom

When filling report templates horizontally, dynamic text fields inside the detail section do not stretch to their entire text content, because this might cause misalignment on the horizontal axis of subsequent detail sections. The detail band actually behaves the same as the page and column footers, preserving its declared height when horizontal filling is used.

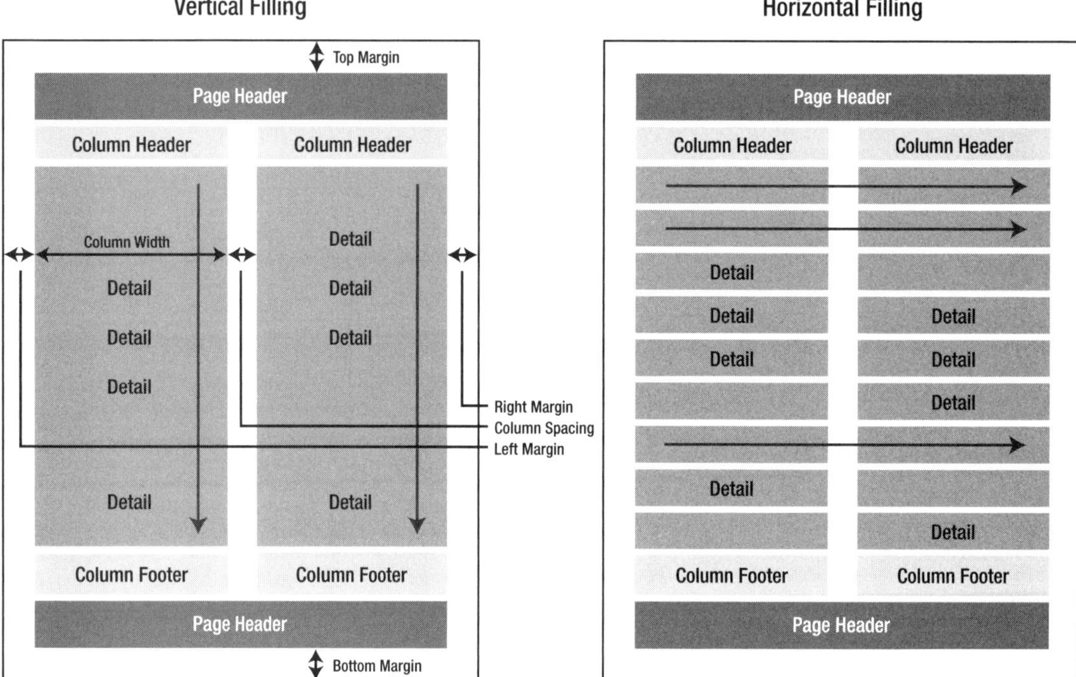

Figure 3-1. *Multicolumn report print order*

Asynchronous Report Filling

JasperReports provides the `net.sf.jasperreports.engine.fill.AsynchronousFillHandle` class to be used for asynchronous report filling. The main benefit of this method is that the filling process can be canceled if it takes too much time. This can be useful, for example, in GUI applications where the user would be able to abort the filling after some time has elapsed and no result has been yet produced.

When using this method, the filling is started on a new thread. The caller is notified about the progress of the filling process by way of listeners implementing the `net.sf.jasperreports.engine.fill.AsynchronousFillListener` interface. The listeners are notified of the outcome of the filling process, which can be success, failure, or user cancellation. The handle is used to start the filling process, register listeners, and cancel the process if wanted.

A typical usage of this handle is the following:

- The handle is created by calling the static `AsynchronousFillHandle.createHandle()` methods that take as arguments the report object, the parameter map, and the data source or the database connection to be used.
- One or more listeners are registered with the handle by calling the `addListener()` method. In a GUI application, the listener could perform some actions to present to the user the outcome of the filling process.

- The filling is started with a call to the `startFill()` method. In a GUI application, this could be the result of some user action; the user can also be notified that the filling has started and is in progress.
- The filling can be canceled by calling `cancellFill()` on the handle. In a GUI, this would be the result of a user action.
- The listeners are notified when the process finishes. There are three events defined for the listeners, only one of which will be called, depending on the outcome of the filling:
  - `reportFinished()`: Called when the filling has finished successfully; the filled report is passed as a parameter. In a GUI, the user would be presented the filled report or would be able to save/export it.
  - `reportFillError()`: Called when the filling ends in error; the exception that occurred is passed as a parameter.
  - `reportCancelled()`: Called when the filling is aborted by the user.

CHAPTER 4

Handling Generated Reports

The output of the report-filling process is a pixel-perfect document made of multiple pages, each containing a series of absolutely positioned and sized visual elements. The document is an instance of the `net.sf.jasperreports.engine.JasperPrint` class, and it is the responsibility of the parent application to make use of it once generated by JasperReports.

`JasperPrint` objects can be serialized for storage or transfer over the network, viewed using a built-in viewer component, or printed or exported to more popular document formats like PDF, HTML, RTF, XLS, ODT, CSV, or XML.

Loading and Saving Generated Reports

Once a `net.sf.jasperreports.engine.JasperPrint` object has been created as a result of the report-filling process, you can serialize it and store it on disk, normally in a `*.jrprint` file. We could say that this is the proprietary format in which JasperReports stores its generated documents.

You can easily save and load `JasperPrint` objects to and from `*.jrprint` files or other byte streams using the `net.sf.jasperreports.engine.util.JRSaver` and `net.sf.jasperreports.engine.util.JRLoader` utility classes that the library offers. The `JRLoader` has various methods for loading serialized objects from files, URLs, input streams, or classpath resources. Its `loadObjectFromLocation(String)` method is the most flexible because it has a built-in fallback mechanism that tries to understand if the supplied `java.lang.String` location is a URL, file name, or classpath resource; only after all these fail will it raise an error.

Sometimes it is more convenient to store generated documents in a text-based format like XML instead of serialized `JasperPrint` objects. This can be achieved by exporting those documents to XML using the `net.sf.jasperreports.engine.export.JRXmlExporter` implementation. The recommended file extension for these is `*.jrpxml`. The documents can be parsed back into in-memory `JasperPrint` objects using the `net.sf.jasperreports.engine.xml.JRPrintXmlLoader` utility class.

Exporting to XML is explained in detail in the "XML Exporter" section of Chapter 17.

Viewing Reports

JasperReports provides a built-in viewer for viewing the generated reports in its proprietary format or in the proprietary XML format produced by the internal XML exporter. It is a Swing-based component. Other Java applications can easily integrate this component without having to export the documents into more popular formats in order to be viewed or printed. The `net.sf.jasperreports.view.JRViewer` class represents this visual component. It can be customized to respond to a particular application's needs by subclassing it. For example, you could add or remove buttons from the existing toolbar.

This is illustrated in the supplied `/demo/samples/webapp` sample, where the `JRViewerPlus` class adds a new button to the existing toolbar of this report viewer component. More details about how to extend the viewer component are provided in the "Customizing Viewers" section of the Chapter 19.

JasperReports also comes with a simple Swing application that uses the visual component for viewing the reports. This application helps view reports stored on disk in the JasperReports `*.jrprint` proprietary format or in the JRPXML format produced by the default XML exporter.

This simple Java Swing application is implemented in the `net.sf.jasperreports.view.JasperViewer` class. It is used in almost all the provided samples for viewing the generated reports.

To view a sample report if you have the Ant build tool installed on your system, go to the desired sample directory and launch the following from the command line:

```
>ant view
```

or

```
>ant viewXML
```

You should see the window shown in Figure 4-1.

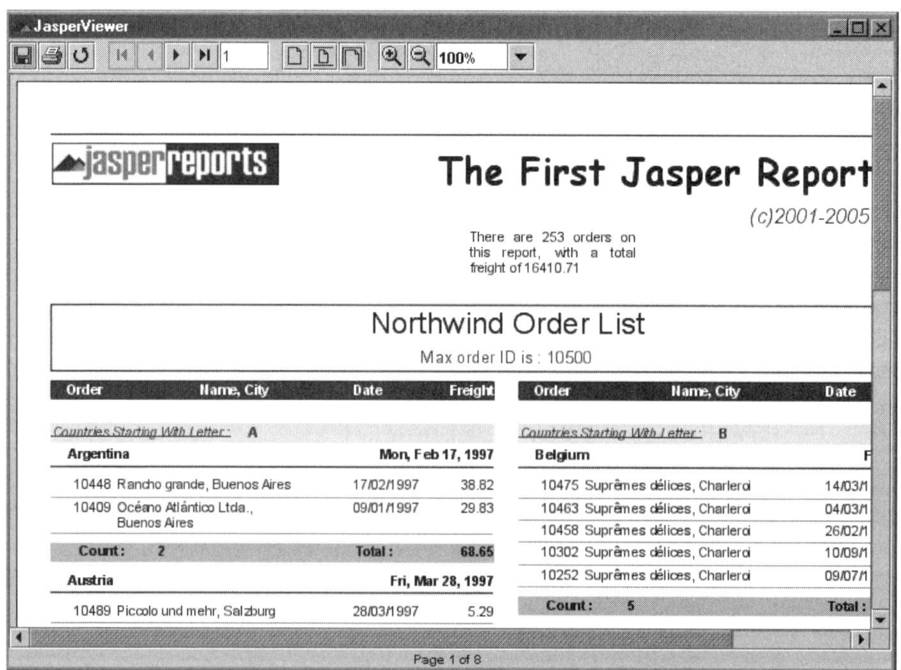

Figure 4-1. *Report viewer*

■ **Note** The viewer application implemented in the `net.sf.jasperreports.view.JasperViewer` class should be considered a demo application that shows how the `net.sf.jasperreports.view.JRViewer` component can be used in Swing applications to display reports.

If you use it directly in your application by calling the public and static `viewReport()` methods it exposes, when you close the report viewer frame, the application will unexpectedly terminate. This is because the `JasperViewer` class makes a call to `System.exit(0)`. A workaround is to subclass it and remove the `java.awt.event.WindowListener` it has registered by default.

Printing Reports

The main objective of the JasperReports library is to create ready-to-print documents. Most reports that are generated by applications end up (or are supposed to end up) on paper.

The printing functionality built into JasperReports at this time reflects the evolution of printing capabilities within the Java platform.

JDK 1.2 introduced a new API called the Java 2 Printing API to allow Java applications to render all Java 2D graphics on any platform even though the host and printer capabilities are overmatched by Java 2D. This requirement meant that the Printing API in some situations would have had to rasterize Java 2D graphics on the host computer.

The SDK 1.2 Printing API primarily supplies the "imaging" portion of the print subsystem and allows applications to format pages and draw their contents; however, printer discovery is not supported by the SDK 1.2 Printing API. An application can obtain information about the current printer and print to it by using the Printing API. The printing dialog supplied by the Printing API also allows a user to change the current printer, but the application cannot do this programmatically.

Starting with JDK 1.4, a new Java print API called the Java Print Service API was introduced to allow applications to print on all Java platforms (including platforms requiring a small footprint, such as a J2ME profile) and still support the existing Java 2 Printing API. The Java Print Service API includes an extensible print attribute set based on the standard attributes specified in the Internet Printing Protocol (IPP) 1.1 from the Internet Engineering Task Force (IETF). With these attributes, client and server applications can discover and select printers that have the capabilities specified by the attributes.

You can print the documents generated by the JasperReports library using the `net.sf.jasperreports.engine.JasperPrintManager` class, which is a façade class that relies on the former Java 2 Printing API. Of course, documents can also be printed after they are exported to other formats such as HTML or PDF. However, here we will explain how to use the specialized manager class mentioned to print documents that are stored or transferred in the JasperReports proprietary format (`net.sf.jasperreports.engine.JasperPrint` objects).

Among the various methods that the `net.sf.jasperreports.engine.JasperPrintManager` class exposes, some allow printing a whole document, a single page, or a page range, with and without displaying the print dialog.

Here's how you can print an entire document without displaying the standard print dialog:

```
JasperPrintManager.printReport(myReport, false);
```

Here's how to print all the pages from 5 to 11 of your document, after having displayed the standard print dialog:

```
JasperPrintManager.printPages(myReport, 4, 10, true);
```

Making use of the much more flexible Java Print Service API introduced with JDK 1.4 requires a special exporter implementation. This implementation uses this new API to allow applications to print JasperReports documents to printing services searched for using attributes such as the network printer name and/or page size.

This is the `net.sf.jasperreports.engine.export.JRPrintServiceExporter` class. More details about using it can be found in the "Java Print Service Exporter" section of Chapter 17.

An exporter implementation is well suited for sending documents to the printer through the Java Print Service API, because in some ways printing is similar to document exporting; both printing and exporting store generated reports in some other format (paper).

Exporting Reports

In some application environments, it is useful to transform the JasperReports–generated documents from the proprietary format into other, more popular formats like PDF, HTML, RTF, or XLS. This way, users can view those reports without having to install special viewers on their systems, which is especially important in the case of documents sent over a network.

There is a façade class in JasperReports for this type of functionality: `net.sf.jasperreports.engine.JasperExportManager`; it can be used to obtain PDF, HTML, or XML content for the documents produced by the report-filling process.

Exporting means taking a `net.sf.jasperreports.engine.JasperPrint` object, which represents a JasperReports document, and transforming it into a different format. The main reason to export reports into other formats is to allow more people to view those reports. HTML reports can be viewed by anybody these days, since at least one browser is available on any system. Viewing JasperReports documents in their proprietary form would require the installation of special software on the target platform (at least a Java applet, if not more).

With time, more and more output formats will be supported by the JasperReports library. For the moment, the various exporter implementations shipped with the library produce only PDF, HTML, RTF, XLS, ODT, CSV, and XML output. These implementations are found in the `net.sf.jasperreports.engine.export` package.

The `JasperExportManager` class offers easy access for only the PDF, HTML, and XML implementations, as these have historically been the most common formats or required the least export configuration.

Here's how you can export your report to HTML format using the façade export manager class:

```
JasperExportManager.exportReportToHtmlFile(myReport);
```

To avoid excessive utility methods, this class was originally written such that the default settings only offer easy access to the most common export formats. When new exporters were added to the library, the export manager class was not extended, and users were encouraged to use the exporter classes directly. Only by doing that could they fully customize the behavior of that particular exporter using specific exporter parameters.

Chapter 17 explains in detail how to use each exporter implementation currently shipped with the JasperReports library.

Note To export reports into other formats not supported by JasperReports, you must implement a special interface called `net.sf.jasperreports.engine.JRExporter` or extend the corresponding `net.sf.jasperreports.engine.JRAbstractExporter` class.

CHAPTER 5

Large File Support

When filling report templates with data, the engine takes a `JasperReport` object along with the supplied parameters and data source and generates an in-memory `JasperPrint` object. If very large datasets are used for report filling, the size of the resulting `JasperPrint` object could also be very large and might cause the JVM to run out of memory.

To increase the memory available for the Java application, first use the `-Xmx` option when launching the JVM, since the default value for this parameter is fairly small. However, if you do this with large datasets (e.g., containing tens of thousands or more records and resulting in documents that have thousands or more pages), the JVM may run out of memory.

Recent versions of JasperReports offer a simple solution to the problem by introducing the *report virtualizer*. The virtualizer is a simple interface (`net.sf.jasperreports.engine.JRVirtualizer`) that enables the reporting engine to optimize memory consumption during report filling by removing parts of the JasperPrint object from memory and storing them on disk or in other temporary locations. If a report virtualizer is used during filling, the engine keeps only a limited number of pages from the generated `JasperPrint` object at a time and serializes all the other pages to a temporary storage location, usually the file system.

Using a report virtualizer is very simple. You supply an instance of the `net.sf.jasperreports.engine.JRVirtualizer` interface as the value for the built-in `REPORT_VIRTUALIZER` parameter when filling the report.

In virtualized form, a generated `JasperPrint` document still behaves normally and can be subject to exporting, printing, or viewing processes, and the impact on memory consumption is minimal even when dealing with very large documents.

When produced using a virtualizer (which itself performs partial document serialization into temporary files), once completed, a `JasperPrint` document can itself be serialized normally without any loss of information. During the serialization of a virtualized `JasperPrint` object, the program puts back together all the pieces and a single serialized file is produced. However, because this single file is probably very large, simple deserialization would not make sense (in fact, it wouldn't be possible, as the JVM would run out of memory, which is the reason for using virtualization in the first place). So in order to reload into memory a virtualized document that was serialized to a permanent storage facility, a report virtualizer is needed. This would be set using a local thread variable by calling the following:

```
JRVirtualizationHelper.setThreadVirtualizer(JRVirtualizer virtualizer)
```

For details about how report virtualization can be used for generating large reports, check the supplied `/demo/samples/virtualizer` sample.

File Virtualizer

The library ships with a ready-to-use implementation of this interface called `net.sf.jasperreports.engine.fill.JRFileVirtualizer`, which stores document pages on disk during the filling process to free up memory. Once a `JasperPrint` object is produced using a report virtualizer, it can be exported to other formats or viewed directly using the library's built-in viewer component, even though this document is not fully loaded at any one time. The virtualizer ensures that pages are deserialized and loaded from their temporary storage location as needed during exporting or display.

A single `JRFileVirtualizer` instance can be shared across multiple report-filling processes so that the number of document pages kept in-memory at any one time will be limited by the virtualizer `maxSize` property, regardless of the number of reports that are generated simultaneously.

Because it works with temporary files on disk, the file virtualizer has a built-in mechanism to remove those files after they are no longer needed (i.e., after the generated document or the virtualizer itself have been disposed of by the JVM). The `cleanup()` method exposed by this virtualizer implementation can be also called manually so that the temporary files are removed from disk right away instead of after the finalization of the entities involved.

To ensure that no virtualization files are left over on disk by the application that uses the file virtualizer, all these temporary files are registered with the JVM so that they are deleted automatically when the JVM exits normally.

But using `File.deleteOnExit()` will accumulate JVM process memory on some virtual machine implementations (see `http://bugs.sun.com/bugdatabase/view_bug.do?bug_id=4513817`); you should avoid using this feature in long-running applications by turning it off using the `net.sf.jasperreports.virtualizer.files.delete.on.exit` configuration property.

Swap File Virtualizer

On some platforms, working with a large number of files in a single folder, or even the file manipulating processes themselves, may have a significant impact on performance or pose additional problems. This makes the use of the `JRFileVirtualizer` implementation less effective.

Fortunately, there is another implementation of a file-based report virtualizer that uses a single swap file and can also be shared among multiple report-filling processes. Instead of having one temporary file per virtualized page, we create a single file into which all virtualized pages are stored to and then retrieved from.

This swap file virtualizer implementation is represented by the `net.sf.jasperreports.engine.fill.JRSwapFileVirtualizer` class that is now part of the JasperReports library core functionality, and works in combination with a `net.sf.jasperreports.engine.util.JRSwapFile` instance representing the target swap file.

The `JRSwapFile` instance has to be created and configured prior to being passed to the swap virtualizer. You can create such an instance by specifying the target directory where the swap file will be created, the size of the blocks allocated by the swap file, and the minimum number of blocks by which the swap file will grow when its current size becomes insufficient.

The `net.sf.jasperreports.engine.util.JRConcurrentSwapFile` class represents an enhanced implementation of the `JRSwapFile` that only works with JRE version 1.4 or later, because it uses a `java.nio.channels.FileChannel` to perform concurrent I/O on the swap file.

In-Memory GZIP Virtualizer

The `net.sf.jasperreports.engine.fill.JRGzipVirtualizer` is a convenient report virtualizer implementation that does not rely on the file system to temporarily store unused/virtualized document pages during the report filling. Rather, it optimizes memory consumption by compressing those pages in-memory using a GZIP algorithm.

Tests indicate that memory consumption during large report-generating processes is reduced up to a factor of ten when the in-memory GZIP report virtualizer is used.

CHAPTER 6

API Overview

Usually you will work only with a few JasperReports library classes and won't have to get to know the entire API.

This section addresses the classes and interfaces that are significant when using the library, and shows you how to use them in applications that require reporting functionality (see Figure 6-1).

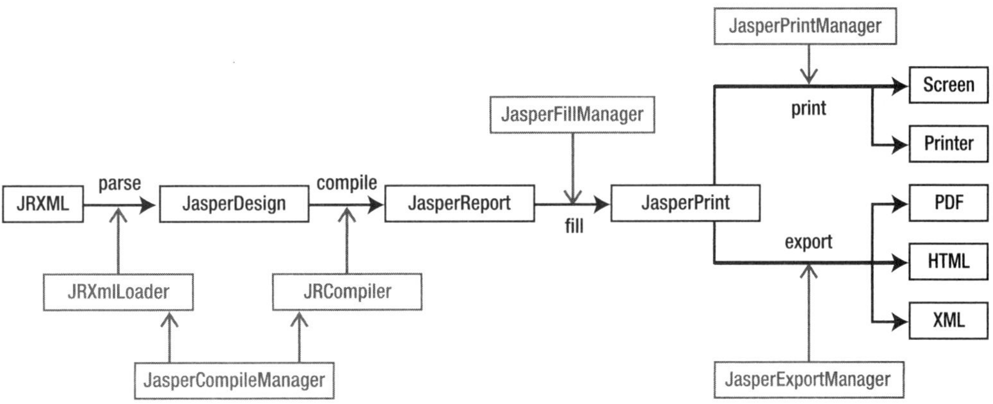

Figure 6-1. *JasperReports API overview*

net.sf.jasperreports.engine.design.JasperDesign

Instances of this class are the raw material that the JasperReports library uses to generate reports. Such instances are usually obtained by parsing the JRXML report template files using the library's internal XML-parsing utility classes. But they can also be built programmatically by the application that uses JasperReports through API calls if working with JRXML files is not an option. Third-party GUI design tools use the JasperReports API to create these report template objects. Among the supplied samples that come with the project source files, there is one inside `/demo/samples/noxmldesign` that you can check to see how to dynamically create a `JasperDesign` object without editing a JRXML report design file.

All instances of the `JasperDesign` class are subject to compilation before being used for filling and report generation. This is why they are considered the raw material for the library.

net.sf.jasperreports.engine.JasperReport

Instances of this class represent compiled report template objects. They are obtained only through the JasperReports report compilation process and are ready to use for filling with data and report generation.

Through compilation, along with various consistency checks and rearrangements of the report elements for more rapid performance in the application, the library creates an on-the-fly class file (or a script, depending on the type of the report compiler used) containing all the report expressions (such as report variables expressions, text field and image expressions, and group expressions). This class or script is used to evaluate report expressions during the report-filling process at runtime.

net.sf.jasperreports.engine.JasperCompileManager

This is the class that exposes all the library's report compilation functionality. It has various methods that allow the users to compile JRXML report templates found in files on disk or that come from input streams. It also lets you compile in-memory report templates by directly passing a `net.sf.jasperreports.engine.design.JasperDesign` object and receiving the corresponding `net.sf.jasperreports.engine.JasperReport` object.

Other utility methods include report template verification and JRXML report template generation for in-memory constructed `net.sf.jasperreports.engine.design.JasperDesign` class instances. These instances are especially useful in GUI tools that simplify report design work.

net.sf.jasperreports.engine.JasperPrint

After a compiled report template is filled with data, the resulting document comes in the form of a `net.sf.jasperreports.engine.JasperPrint` instance. Such an object can be viewed directly using the built-in JasperReports report viewer, or can be serialized for disk storage and later use or sending over the network.

The instances of this class are the output of the report-filling process of the JasperReports library, and represent its proprietary format for storing full-featured, page-oriented documents. You can transform them into other more popular formats (such as PDF, HTML, RTF, XLS, ODT, CSV, or XML) by using the library's export functionality.

net.sf.jasperreports.engine.JRDataSource

JasperReports is very flexible as to the source of the report data. It lets people use any kind of data source they want, as long as they can provide an appropriate implementation of this interface.

Normally, every time a report is filled, an instance of this interface is supplied or created behind the scenes by the reporting engine.

net.sf.jasperreports.engine.JRResultSetDataSource

This is a default implementation of the `net.sf.jasperreports.engine.JRDataSource` interface. Since most reports are generated using data from a relational database, JasperReports includes by default this implementation that wraps a `java.sql.ResultSet` object.

This class can be instantiated intentionally to wrap already loaded result sets before passing them to the report-filling routines, but it is also used by the reporting engine to wrap the data retrieved from the database after having executed the report query (if present) through JDBC.

net.sf.jasperreports.engine.data.JRBeanArrayDataSource and net.sf.jasperreports.engine.data.JRBeanCollectionDataSource

It is now common to access application data through object persistence layers like EJB, Hibernate, or JDO. Such applications may need to generate reports using data they already have available as arrays or collections of in-memory JavaBean objects.

JasperReports ships with two JavaBean-compliant data source implementations that can wrap either an array or a collection of JavaBean objects.

This can be seen in the supplied `/demo/samples/datasource` sample, where instances of a custom JavaBean class are used to fill a report with data.

net.sf.jasperreports.engine.data.JRXmlDataSource

If application data resides inside XML files, and you need this data to generate reports, the built-in XPath-based implementations of the `JRDataSource` interface are useful. With the help of an XPath query, the XML data can take a tabular form and be fed into the report-filling process to generate documents.

The `/demo/samples/xmldatasource` sample in the distribution package shows how this special data source implementation can be used with XML data.

net.sf.jasperreports.engine.JREmptyDataSource

The simplest implementation of the `net.sf.jasperreports.engine.JRDataSource` interface, this class can be used in reports that do not display data from the supplied data source, but rather from parameters, and when only the number of virtual rows in the data source is important.

Many of the provided samples found in the `/demo/samples` directory of the project's distribution (such as `fonts`, `images`, `shapes`, and `unicode`) use an instance of this class when filling reports to simulate a data source with one record in it, but with all the fields in this single record being `null`.

net.sf.jasperreports.engine.JasperFillManager

This class is the façade to the report-filling functionality of the JasperReports library. It exposes a variety of methods that receive a report template in the form of an object, file, or input stream, and also produces a document in various output forms (object, file, or output stream).

Along with the report template, the report-filling engine must also receive data from the data source, as well as the values for the report parameters, to generate the documents.

Parameter values are always supplied in a `java.util.Map` object, in which the keys are the report parameter names.

The data source can be supplied in two different forms, depending on the situation.

Normally, it is supplied as a `net.sf.jasperreports.engine.JRDataSource` object, as just mentioned.

However, since most reports are filled with data from relational databases, JasperReports has a built-in default behavior that lets people specify an SQL query in the report template itself. This SQL query is executed to retrieve the data for filling the report at runtime.

In such cases, the only thing JasperReports needs is a `java.sql.Connection` object, instead of the usual data source object. It needs this connection object to connect to the relational database management system through JDBC and execute the report query.

It automatically creates a `net.sf.jasperreports.engine.JRResultSetDataSource` behind the scenes to wrap the `java.sql.ResultSet` object returned after the execution of the query and passes it to the normal report-filling process.

net.sf.jasperreports.engine.JRAbstractScriptlet

Scriptlets are a very powerful feature of the JasperReports library. They allow users to write custom code to be executed by the reporting engine during the report-filling process. This user code can manipulate report data and gets executed at well-defined moments such as page, column, or group breaks.

net.sf.jasperreports.engine.JRDefaultScriptlet

This is a convenient subclass of the `net.sf.jasperreports.engine.JRAbstractScriptlet` class. You will usually subclass this when working with scriptlets so that they don't have to implement all the abstract methods declared in the abstract class.

net.sf.jasperreports.engine.JasperPrintManager

After having filled a report, you have the option of viewing it, exporting it to a different format, or (most commonly) printing it.

In JasperReports, you can print reports using this manager class, which is a façade to the printing functionality exposed by the library. This class contains various methods that can send entire documents or portions of them to the printer. It also allows you to choose whether to display the print dialog. You can display the content of a page from a JasperReports document by generating a `java.awt.Image` object for it using this manager class.

net.sf.jasperreports.engine.JasperExportManager

As already mentioned, JasperReports can transform generated documents from its proprietary format into more popular documents formats such as PDF, HTML, or XML. Over time, this part of the JasperReports functionality has been extended to support other formats, including RTF, XSL, and CSV.

This manager class has various methods that can process data that comes from different sources and goes to different destinations (files, input and output streams, etc.).

net.sf.jasperreports.engine.JasperRunManager

Sometimes it is useful to produce documents only in a popular format such as PDF or HTML, without having to store on disk the serialized, intermediate `net.sf.jasperreports.engine.JasperPrint` object produced by the report-filling process.

This can be achieved using this manager class, which immediately exports the document produced by the report-filling process into the desired output format.

The use of this manager class is shown and can be tested in the supplied `/demo/samples/webapp` sample, where PDF and HTML content is produced on the fly.

net.sf.jasperreports.view.JRViewer

This class is different from the rest of the classes listed previously in that it is more like a pluggable visual component than a utility class. It can be used in Swing-based applications to view the reports generated by the JasperReports library.

This visual component is not meant to satisfy everybody. It was included like a demo component to show how the core printing functionality can be used to display the reports in Swing-based applications.

The preferred way to adapt this component to a particular application is by subclassing it. The "Customizing Viewers" section of Chapter 19 gives more details about this.

net.sf.jasperreports.view.JasperViewer

This class also serves a didactical purpose. It uses the `net.sf.jasperreports.view.JRViewer` component to display reports. It represents a simple Java Swing application that can load and display reports. It is used in almost all of the supplied samples to display the generated documents.

net.sf.jasperreports.view.JasperDesignViewer

Usually, an application that uses the JasperReports library for reporting purposes will never use this class. This class can be used at design time to preview the report templates. It was included in the main library as a development tool in order to make up for the missing visual designer.

This class is also used in all the samples to preview the report designs, either in raw JRXML form or the compiled form.

net.sf.jasperreports.engine.util.JRLoader

Many JasperReports processes, like report compilation, report filling, and exporting, often work with serialized objects. Sometimes it is useful to manually load those serialized objects before submitting them to the desired JasperReport process.

The `net.sf.jasperreports.engine.util.JRLoader` class is a utility class that helps load serialized objects found in various locations such as files, URLs, and input streams.

The most interesting method exposed by this class is `loadObjectFromLocation(String)`. When calling this method to load an object from the supplied location, the program first tries to interpret the location as a valid URL. If this fails, then the program assumes that the supplied location is the name of a file on disk and tries to read from it. If no file is found at that location, it will try to locate a resource through the classpath that would correspond to the location. Only after this third try fails is an exception thrown.

net.sf.jasperreports.engine.util.JRSaver

This utility class can be used when serializable objects must be saved on disk or sent over the network through an output stream.

net.sf.jasperreports.engine.xml.JRXmlLoader

Parsing a JRXML file into a `JasperDesign` object can be done using one of the methods published by this class. Applications might need to do this in cases where report templates kept in their source form (JRXML) must be modified at runtime based on some user input and then compiled on the fly for filling with data.

net.sf.jasperreports.engine.xml.JRPrintXmlLoader

Generated documents can be stored in XML format if they are exported using the `net.sf.jasperreports.engine.export.JRXmlExporter`. After they're exported, you can parse them back into `net.sf.jasperreports.engine.JasperPrint` objects by using this `JRPrintXmlLoader`.

CHAPTER 7

Report Template Structure

Generally speaking, a report template contains all the information about the structure and the aspects of the documents that will be generated when the data is provided. This information determines the position and content of various text or graphic elements that will appear in the document, their appearance, the custom calculations, the data grouping and data manipulation that should be performed when the documents are generated, and so on.

Creating report templates was discussed in Chapter 3. This chapter will delve into the structure of a report template and demonstrate how each component and property can be used to achieve specific functionality.

JRXML

JRXML is the name we use when referring to XML files that represent the definition of a JasperReports template and that comply with the mentioned DTD structure.

When working with JRXML report templates, JasperReports uses its own internal DTD files to validate the XML content it receives for processing. If the XML validation passes, it means that the supplied report design corresponds to the JasperReports-required XML structure and syntax, and the engine is able to generate the compiled version of the report design.

Valid JRXML report templates always point to the JasperReports internal DTD files for validation. If the DTD reference is not specified, report compilation will fail abruptly. This should not be a big problem since the DTD reference is always the same and can simply be copied from previous report templates. To start with, you can copy it from the supplied samples.

DTD Reference

As already mentioned, the engine recognizes only the DTD references that point to its internal DTD files. You cannot make a copy of the DTD files found among the library source files and point to that copy in your JRXML report templates. To do that, you must alter the code of some of the library classes, including the `net.sf.jasperreports.engine.xml.JRXmlDigester` class.

If you encounter problems, such as the engine not finding its own internal DTD files due to some resource-loading problems, make sure you have eliminated every possible cause before deciding to use external DTD files. You will probably not encounter such a problem since the resource-loading mechanism of the library has improved with time.

There are only two valid DTD references for the JRXML report templates:

```
<!DOCTYPE jasperReport PUBLIC "-//JasperReports//DTD JasperReport //EN"
"http://jasperreports.sourceforge.net/dtds/jasperreport.dtd">
```

The root element of a JRXML report template is `<jasperReport>`. This is what a typical JasperReports JRXML report template file looks like:

```
<?xml version="1.0"?>
<!DOCTYPE jasperReport PUBLIC "-//JasperReports//DTD JasperReport //EN"
"http://jasperreports.sourceforge.net/dtds/jasperreport.dtd">

<jasperReport name="name_of_the_report" ... >
...
</jasperReport>
```

The first ellipsis (`...`) represents the report-design properties and settings, and the second ellipsis represents the various suppressed report-design elements, such as report parameters, fields, variables, groups, report sections, and so on. Examples of these follow in later chapters of this book.

JRXML Encoding

When creating JRXML report templates in different languages, pay special attention to the encoding attribute that can be used in the header of the XML file. By default, if no value is specified for this attribute, the XML parser uses UTF-8 as the encoding for the content of the XML file.

This is important because the report design often contains localized static texts, which are introduced when manually editing the JRXML file.

For most Western European languages, the `ISO-8859-1` encoding, also known as `LATIN1`, is sufficient. For example, it includes the special French characters *é*, *â*, *è*, and *ç*, and can be specified using the encoding attribute shown in the following example:

```
<?xml version="1.0" encoding="ISO-8859-1"?>
<!DOCTYPE jasperReport PUBLIC "-//JasperReports//DTD JasperReport //EN"
"http://jasperreports.sourceforge.net/dtds/jasperreport.dtd">

<jasperReport name="name_of_the_report" ... >
...
</jasperReport>
```

To find out the encoding type to specify when editing XML files in a particular language, check the XML documentation.

Report Template Properties

You have already seen that `<jasperReport>` is the root element of a JRXML report design. This section will show in detail the properties of a report-design object and the JRXML attributes that correspond to them.

Listing 7-1 gives the JRXML syntax for the report template properties.

Listing 7-1. *JRXML Syntax*

```
<!ELEMENT jasperReport (property*, import*, reportFont*, style*, subDataset*,
parameter*, queryString?, field*, sortField*, variable*, filterExpression?, group*,
background?, title?, pageHeader?, columnHeader?, detail?, columnFooter?,
pageFooter?, lastPageFooter?, summary?)>

<!ATTLIST jasperReport
    name CDATA #REQUIRED
    language CDATA "java"
    columnCount NMTOKEN "1"
    printOrder (Vertical | Horizontal) "Vertical"
    pageWidth NMTOKEN "595"
    pageHeight NMTOKEN "842"
    orientation (Portrait | Landscape) "Portrait"
    whenNoDataType (NoPages | BlankPage | AllSectionsNoDetail) "NoPages"
    columnWidth NMTOKEN "555"
    columnSpacing NMTOKEN "0"
    leftMargin NMTOKEN "20"
    rightMargin NMTOKEN "20"
    topMargin NMTOKEN "30"
    bottomMargin NMTOKEN "30"
    isTitleNewPage (true | false) "false"
    isSummaryNewPage (true | false) "false"
    isFloatColumnFooter (true | false) "false"
    scriptletClass CDATA #IMPLIED
    resourceBundle CDATA #IMPLIED
    whenResourceMissingType (Null | Empty | Key | Error) "Null"
    isIgnorePagination (true | false) "false"
    formatFactoryClass CDATA #IMPLIED
>
```

Report Name

Every report design needs a name. Its name is important because the library uses it when generating files, especially when the default behavior is preferred for compiling, filling, or exporting the report.

The name of the report is specified using the `name` attribute of the `<jasperReport>` element, and its inclusion is mandatory. Spaces are not allowed in the report name—it must be a single word.

Language

Report expressions are usually written using the Java language. However, you can use other languages as long as a report compiler is available to help evaluate these expressions at report-filling time.

The default value for the `language` property is `java`, meaning that the Java language is used for writing expressions, and that a report compiler capable of generating and compiling a Java class on the fly is used for producing the bytecode needed for expression evaluation at runtime.

This property is read by the report compilers to see whether they can compile the supplied report template or whether a different report compiler should be used, depending on the actual scripting language.

The distribution includes a sample inside the `/demo/samples/groovy` folder, which demonstrates how other scripting languages can be used in JasperReports templates.

Column Count

JasperReports lets users create reports with more than one column on each page. Multi-column report templates also have an associated column-filling order specified by the next attribute in this section, `printOrder`. Figure 3-1 in Chapter 3 shows an example of what multi-column report templates look like.

By default, the reporting engine creates reports with one column on each page.

Print Order

For reports having more that one column, it is important to specify the order in which the columns will be filled. You can do this using the `printOrder` attribute of the `<jasperReport>` element.

There are two possible situations:

- *Vertical filling*: Columns are filled from top to bottom and then left to right (`printOrder="Vertical"`).
- *Horizontal filling*: Columns are filled from left to right and then top to bottom (`printOrder="Horizontal"`).

The default print order is `printOrder="Vertical"`.

Page Size

There are two attributes at this level to specify the page size of the document that will be generated: `pageWidth` and `pageHeight`. Like all the other JasperReports attributes that represent element dimensions and position, these are specified in pixels. JasperReports uses the default Java resolution of 72 dots per inch (dpi). This means that `pageWidth="595"` will be about 8.26 inches, which is roughly the width of an A4 sheet of paper.

The default page size corresponds to an A4 sheet of paper:

```
pageWith="595" pageHeight="842"
```

Page Orientation

The orientation attribute determines whether the documents use the Portrait or the Landscape format. JasperReports requires you to adapt the page width and the page height when switching from Portrait documents to Landscape, and vice versa. For example, assume that you want to create an A4 report using the Portrait layout.

An A4 report has approximately this size:

```
pageWidth="595" pageHeight="842" orientation="Portrait"
```

If you decide to use the Landscape layout for your A4 document, you must be sure to modify the page width and page height accordingly, as follows:

```
pageWidth="842" pageHeight="595" orientation="Landscape"
```

This is because JasperReports has to know exactly the absolute width and height of the pages it will draw on, and does not necessarily consider the value supplied in the orientation attribute, at least not at report-filling time.

This orientation attribute is useful only at report-printing time to inform the printer about the page orientation, and in some special exporters. The default page orientation is "Portrait".

Page Margins

Once the page size is decided, you can specify what margins the reporting engine should preserve when generating the reports. Four attributes control this: topMargin, leftMargin, bottomMargin, and rightMargin (see Figure 3-1 in Chapter 3).

The default margin for the top and bottom of the page is 20 pixels. The default margin for the right and left margins is 30 pixels.

Column Size and Spacing

Reports may have more that one column, as shown in the preceding discussion of the columnCount attribute. However, the reporting engine has to know how large a column can be and how much space should be allowed between columns. Two attributes control this: columnWidth and columnSpacing.

Also, a validation check is performed when you compile report designs, which prevents the width of the overall columns and the space between them from exceeding the specified page width and page margins.

Since there is only one column by default, the default column spacing is 0 pixels and the default column width is 555 pixels (the default page width minus the default left and right margins).

Empty Data Source Behavior

The data source for a report might not contain any records. In this case, it is not clear what the output should be. Some may expect to see a blank document and others may want some of the report sections to be displayed anyway.

The whenNoDataType attribute lets you decide how the generated document should look when there is no data in the data source supplied to it.

The possible values of this attribute are as follows:

- *Empty document*: The generated document will have no pages in it. Viewers might throw an error when trying to load such documents (`whenNoDataType="NoPages"`).
- *Blank page*: The generated document will contain a single blank page (`whenNoDataType="BlankPage"`).
- *All sections displayed*: All the report sections except the detail section will appear in the generated document (`whenNoDataType="AllSectionsNoDetail"`).

The default value for this attribute is `whenNoDataType="NoPages"`.

Title and Summary Section Placement

To display the title or summary section on a separate page, set one or both of the following attributes to `true`: `isTitleNewPage` and `isSummaryNewPage`.

Both of these Boolean attributes are set to `false` by default.

■ **Note** Even if you choose to display the summary section in the remaining space of the last page, a new page will automatically start if the report has more than one column and the second column has already started on the last page.

Column Footer Placement

The `isFloatColumnFooter` Boolean property lets users customize the behavior of the column footer section. By default, this section is rendered at the bottom of the page, just above the page footer. In certain cases, it is useful to render it higher on the page, just below the last detail or group footer on that particular column. To do this, set the `isFloatColumnFooter` property to `true`.

Scriptlet Class

The `scriptletClass` attribute lets you specify the name of the scriptlet class designed for the current report. You will learn more about scriptlets in Chapter 15.

This attribute is used by the engine only if no value is supplied for the built-in `JRParameter.REPORT_SCRIPTLET` parameter. If neither the attribute nor the parameter is used, the reporting engine uses a `net.sf.jasperreports.engine.JRDefaultScriptlet` instance instead.

Resource Bundle

To generate reports in different languages from the same report template, associate a resource bundle with the template and make sure that the locale-specific resources inside report expressions are retrieved based on the `$R{}` syntax (explained in Chapter 8).

There are two ways to associate the `java.util.ResourceBundle` object with the report template.

The first is a static association made by setting the resourceBundle property of the report template object to the base name of the target resource bundle.

A dynamic association can be made by supplying a java.util.ResourceBundle object as the value for the REPORT_RESOURCE_BUNDLE parameter at report-filling time. Check Chapter 16 for more details.

Missing Resources Behavior

The whenResourceMissingType property allows users to choose the desired behavior of the engine when it deals with missing locale-specific resources in the supplied resource bundle. There are four different values that can be used to deal with missing resources:

- Null: The null value is used (whenResourceMissingType="Null").
- Empty: An empty string is used (whenResourceMissingType="Empty").
- Key: The key is used (whenResourceMissingType="Empty").
- Error: An exception is raised in case a locale-specific resource is not found in the supplied resource bundle for the given key and locale (whenResourceMissingType="Error").

Pagination

When the isIgnorePagination property is set to true, the report-filling engine will completely ignore page break–related settings inside the report template and generate the document on a single, very long page. The value of this property can be overridden at runtime using the optional, built-in IS_IGNORE_PAGINATION parameter.

Formatting Numbers, Dates, and Times

The formatFactoryClass attribute lets you specify the name of the factory class implementing the net.sf.jasperreports.engine.util.FormatFactory interface, which should be instantiated by the engine in order to produce java.text.DateFormat and java.text.NumberFormat objects to use for date and number formatting in the current report.

This attribute specifying the factory class name is used only if no value is supplied for the built-in JRParameter.REPORT_FORMAT_FACTORY parameter.

If neither of the attribute nor the parameter is used, the engine will eventually instantiate the net.sf.jasperreports.engine.util.DefaultFormatFactory implementation of the factory interface, which produces java.text.SimpleDateFormat and java.text.DecimalFormat objects for date and number formatting.

You need to use this attribute or the built-in JRParameter.REPORT_FORMAT_FACTORY parameter only if the report relies on custom date and number formatters.

Custom Properties

Sometimes it is useful to put some information into the report template itself. This information can be used by the parent application at runtime after loading the report template, or it can be used by the UI report-design tools to store designer-specific information, like whether to display the rules, the size of the snap grid, and so on.

The report templates can store application or user-defined properties in the form of named values that can be archived by using any number or <property> tags inside the report template.

Listing 7-2 gives the JRXML syntax for the report custom properties.

Listing 7-2. *JRXML Syntax*

```
<!ELEMENT property EMPTY>

<!ATTLIST property
    name CDATA #REQUIRED
    value CDATA #IMPLIED
>
```

It is recommended that property names rely on some namespace policy, just as Java application packages do, to ensure that no naming conflict arises when several applications store information in the same report template.

Here is how a named value can be put inside the report template:

```
<property name="com.mycompany.report.author" value="John Smith"/>
<property name="com.mycompany.report.description" value="Displays sales data"/>
```

At runtime, this application-defined data can be retrieved from the report template using the API, as follows:

```
JasperReport jasperReport =
    (JasperReport)JRLoader.loadObjectFromLocation(
        "C:/MyApp/src/reports/MyReport.jasper");

String author = jasperReport.getProperty("com.mycompany.report.author");
String desc = jasperReport.getProperty("com.mycompany.report.description");
```

Importing Packages

Using the Java language for writing the report expressions gives great flexibility to the library because report designers can leverage existing code inside JasperReports's parent Java applications.

When using Java, all the report expressions are put into a Java source file that is created on the fly at report-compilation time. This source file is compiled to bytecode by the report compiler and used for expression evaluation at report-filling time. Being a normal Java source file, it can have import statements at the top to simplify how classes are referenced inside the source code. When entire packages are imported, report expressions can reference application classes by name rather than full class name (including the package), resulting in shorter and simpler report expressions.

For importing entire packages or single classes, several `<import>` tags can be used inside the report template.

Listing 7-3 gives the JRXML syntax for importing packages.

Listing 7-3. *JRXML Syntax*

```
<!ELEMENT import EMPTY>

<!ATTLIST import
    value CDATA #REQUIRED
>
```

The following example shows how to import an entire package and a single class:

```
<import value="com.mycompany.myapp.mypackage.*"/>
<import value="com.mycompany.myapp.MyClass"/>
```

A report template can contain any number of import tags.

Styles

A report style is a collection of style settings declared at the report level. These settings can be reused throughout the entire report template when setting the style properties of report elements.

Listing 7-4 gives the JRXML syntax for the report style definitions.

Listing 7-4. *JRXML Syntax*

```
<!ELEMENT style (conditionalStyle*)>

<!ATTLIST style
    name CDATA #IMPLIED
    isDefault (true | false) "false"
    style CDATA #IMPLIED
    mode (Opaque | Transparent) #IMPLIED
    forecolor CDATA #IMPLIED
    backcolor CDATA #IMPLIED
    pen (None | Thin | 1Point | 2Point | 4Point | Dotted) #IMPLIED
    fill (Solid) #IMPLIED
    radius NMTOKEN #IMPLIED
    scaleImage (Clip | FillFrame | RetainShape) #IMPLIED
    hAlign (Left | Center | Right | Justified) #IMPLIED
    vAlign (Top | Middle | Bottom) #IMPLIED
    border (None | Thin | 1Point | 2Point | 4Point | Dotted) #IMPLIED
    borderColor CDATA #IMPLIED
    padding NMTOKEN #IMPLIED
    topBorder (None | Thin | 1Point | 2Point | 4Point | Dotted) #IMPLIED
```

```
    topBorderColor CDATA #IMPLIED
    topPadding NMTOKEN #IMPLIED
    leftBorder (None | Thin | 1Point | 2Point | 4Point | Dotted) #IMPLIED
    leftBorderColor CDATA #IMPLIED
    leftPadding NMTOKEN #IMPLIED
    bottomBorder (None | Thin | 1Point | 2Point | 4Point | Dotted) #IMPLIED
    bottomBorderColor CDATA #IMPLIED
    bottomPadding NMTOKEN #IMPLIED
    rightBorder (None | Thin | 1Point | 2Point | 4Point | Dotted) #IMPLIED
    rightBorderColor CDATA #IMPLIED
    rightPadding NMTOKEN #IMPLIED
    rotation (None | Left | Right | UpsideDown) #IMPLIED
    lineSpacing (Single | 1_1_2 | Double) #IMPLIED
    isStyledText (true | false) #IMPLIED
    fontName CDATA #IMPLIED
    fontSize NMTOKEN #IMPLIED
    isBold (true | false) #IMPLIED
    isItalic (true | false) #IMPLIED
    isUnderline (true | false) #IMPLIED
    isStrikeThrough (true | false) #IMPLIED
    pdfFontName CDATA #IMPLIED
    pdfEncoding CDATA #IMPLIED
    isPdfEmbedded (true | false) #IMPLIED
    pattern CDATA #IMPLIED
    isBlankWhenNull (true | false) #IMPLIED
>

<!ELEMENT conditionalStyle (conditionExpression?, style)>

<!ELEMENT conditionExpression (#PCDATA)>
```

Report Style Name

The name attribute of a <style> element is mandatory. It must be unique because it references the corresponding report style throughout the report.

Default Report Style

You can use isDefault="true" for one of your report style declarations to mark the default for elements that do not or cannot have another style specified.

Cascading Report Styles

Each report style definition can reference another style definition from which it will inherit some or all of its properties. The style attribute specifies the name of the parent report style.

Note All the other report style properties are explained in detail in the chapters that present the report elements to which they apply.

Conditional Styles

Sometimes users need to change a report element style at runtime based on certain conditions (e.g., to alternate adjacent row colors in a report detail section). To achieve this goal, you can set some style properties to be enabled only if a specified condition is `true`. This is done using conditional styles.

A conditional style has two elements: a Boolean condition expression and a style. The style is used only if the condition evaluates to `true`. The following code gives an example of using a conditional style:

```
<style name="alternateStyle" fontName="Arial" forecolor="red">
  <conditionalStyle>
    <conditionExpression>
      new Boolean($V{REPORT_COUNT}.intValue() % 2 == 0)
    </conditionExpression>
    <style forecolor="blue"/>
  </conditionalStyle>
</style>
```

In the preceding example, elements with this style will have red `forecolor`. But the presence of the conditional style modifies the behavior, and when rendered on an even row, the same elements will have blue `forecolor`.

An important aspect is the priority of styles. When applied, a conditional style will override the properties of its parent style. In the preceding example, an even detail row will inherit the `fontName` property from the parent style and overwrite the `forecolor` property.

A style can contain more than one conditional style. In this case, all conditionals that evaluate to `true` will be appended to the existing style (the second style will be appended to the first, and so on). Here is a more elaborate example:

```
<style name="alternateStyle" fontName="Arial" forecolor="red">
  <conditionalStyle>
    <conditionExpression>
      new Boolean($V{REPORT_COUNT}.intValue() % 2 == 0)
    </conditionExpression>
    <style forecolor="blue"/>
  </conditionalStyle>
  <conditionalStyle>
    <conditionExpression>
      new Boolean($F{AMOUNT}.intValue() > 10000)
    </conditionExpression>
    <style isBold="true"/>
  </conditionalStyle>
```

```
  <conditionalStyle>
    <conditionExpression>
      new Boolean($F{AMOUNT}.intValue() > 20000)
    </conditionExpression>
    <style isBold="false" isItalic="true"/>
  </conditionalStyle>
</style>
```

In this example, if the field amount is greater than 10000, the second conditional style is `true`, and the element displays in bold (it also has red color or blue color depending on whether it is on an even or odd row).

If the amount is greater than 20000, then the last two style conditions will be `true` and will be applied in order. They will override `isBold` and add `isItalic`.

For amounts over 10000, elements will be written in bold, and for amounts over 20000, elements will be written in italic (but not bold). Of course, all conditional styles will inherit the font from the parent style.

Referencing a Report Style

All report elements can reference a report style to inherit all or part of the style properties. A report style declaration groups all the style-related properties supported throughout the library, but an individual element inherits only those style properties that apply to it. The others will be ignored.

See Chapter 10 for details about applying styles to report elements.

CHAPTER 8

Reporting Data

In Chapter 3, we mentioned that there are three entities that must be supplied as input to the report-filling process: the report template, the parameter values, and the data source of the report.

Previous chapters have addressed the report templates. Now we are going to take a closer look at parameters and the report data source. These are the only sources of data that the reporting engine uses to fill the report. This data is organized according to the template defined in the report design to produce a ready-to-print, page-oriented document.

Expressions

Expressions are a powerful feature of JasperReports. They can be used to declare report variables that perform various calculations, group data on the report, specify report text field content, or further customize the appearance of report objects.

We mentioned in the "Expressions Scripting Language" section of Chapter 2 that by default, the Java language is used for writing report expressions, but other scripting languages can be used if a corresponding report compiler able to produce the information needed for expression evaluation at runtime is available. Currently, JasperReports ships with a report compiler that can compile report templates using the Groovy scripting language inside report expressions.

For simplicity's sake, we'll explain how report expressions work assuming that they have been written using the Java language only.

Since all JasperReports expressions are (or are assumed to be) real Java expressions, you can use inside them any class you like, as long as you refer to it using the complete class name (including the package), or are adding the proper imports to your report template, as explained in Chapter 7. You also have to make sure that the classes you are using in the report expressions are available in the classpath when you compile your report and when you fill it with data.

In a JRXML report template, there are several elements that define expressions, including `<variableExpression>`, `<initialValueExpression>`, `<groupExpression>`, `<printWhenExpression>`, `<imageExpression>`, and `<textFieldExpression>`.

Syntax

Report expressions would be useless if there were no way to reference in them the report parameters, report fields, or declared report variables. For this reason, a special JasperReports syntax on top of the scripting language allows you to introduce such references in the report expressions you create in the JRXML report template.

Report parameter references are introduced using the `$P{}` character sequence, as in the following example:

```
<textFieldExpression>
  $P{ReportTitle}
</textFieldExpression>
```

This example assumes that the report design declares a report parameter named `ReportTitle`, whose class is `java.lang.String`. The text field will display the value of this parameter when the report is filled.

To use a report field reference in an expression, you must put the name of the field between the `$F{` and `}` character sequences. For example, to display the concatenated values of two data source fields in a text field, define an expression like this one:

```
<textFieldExpression>
  $F{FirstName} + " " + $F{LastName}
</textFieldExpression>
```

The expression can be even more complex, as in the following example:

```
<textFieldExpression>
  $F{FirstName} + " " + $F{LastName} + " was hired on " +
  (new SimpleDateFormat("MM/dd/yyyy")).format($F{HireDate}) + "."
</textFieldExpression>
```

To reference a report variable in an expression, you must put the name of the variable between `$V{` and `}`, as in this example:

```
<textFieldExpression>
  "Total quantity : " + $V{QuantitySum} + " kg."
</textFieldExpression>
```

As you can see, the parameter, field, and variable references introduced by the special JasperReports syntax are in fact real Java objects. Knowing their class from the parameter, field or variable declaration made in the report template, you can even call methods on those object references in your expressions.

Here's one way to extract and display the first letter from a `java.lang.String` report field:

```
<textFieldExpression>
  $F{FirstName}.substring(0, 1)
</textFieldExpression>
```

When support for internationalization was added to JasperReports, a new token was introduced in the JasperReports syntax to allow access to the locale-specific resources inside the report's associated resource bundle. The `$R{}` character syntax extracts the locale-specific resource from the resource bundle based on the key that must be put between the brackets:

```
<textFieldExpression>
  $R{report.title}
</textFieldExpression>
```

The preceding text field displays the title of the report by extracting the `String` value from the resource bundle associated with the report template based on the runtime-supplied locale and the `report.title` key. More on internationalization can be found in Chapter 16.

In some rare cases (e.g., debugging), there is the need to escape an expression token like the ones described previously. The escape syntax for the tokens requires duplicating the `$` character. Escaping a `$P{paramName}` token is achieved by writing `$$P{paramName}` in the expression. When escaped, an expression token is preserved as-is in the resulting expression, and no attempt to parse the token is made.

Calculator

What is the calculator object? It is the entity inside JasperReports that evaluates expressions and increments variables or datasets at report-filling time. When a report template is compiled, the report compiler produces and stores in the compiled report template (`JasperReport` object) information that it will use at report-filling time to build an instance of the `net.sf.jasperreports.engine.fill.JRCalculator` class.

The Java-based report compilers generate a Java source file and compile it on the fly. This generated class is a subclass of the `JRCalculator`, and the bytecode produced by compiling it is stored inside the `JasperReport` object. At report-filling time, this bytecode is loaded and the resulting class is instantiated to obtain the calculator object needed for expression evaluation.

To better understand this calculator object, look at the provided `/demo/samples/beanshell` sample, which shows how the BeanShell scripting library can be used with JasperReports for expressions evaluation. During report compilation using the supplied `net.sf.jasperreports.compilers.JRBshCompiler`, a BeanShell script is generated and kept inside the resulting JasperReport object. At report-filling time, this script will be loaded by an instance of the `net.sf.jasperreports.compilers.JRBshCalculator` implementation and will serve for expression evaluation.

Only the report compiler creates the calculator instance because only the report compiler can make sense of the information it stored in the compiled report template at report-compilation time.

Built-In Functions

When JasperReports was internationalized, some of the data and message-formatting logic was placed inside the engine itself to avoid forcing users to rely on external utility classes.

Report expressions can perform method calls on various objects that are available during report filling, such as parameters, fields, or variable values, but can also call methods on a special object that is already available as the `this` reference. This is the calculator object presented in the previous section. It has public utility methods that are ready to use inside report expressions.

Currently, there are only a few utility methods of the calculator object available as built-in functions inside report expressions. These are the following:

- `msg`: This function offers a convenient way to format messages based on the current report locale, just as you would normally do when using a `java.text.MessageFormat` instance. Furthermore, several signatures for this function take up to three message parameters in order to make the formatting functionality easier to use.

- `str`: This function is the equivalent of the `$R{}` syntax. It gives access to locale-specific resources from the associated resource bundle.

Conditional Expressions

As the Java language documentation states, an *expression* is a series of variables, operators, and method calls (constructed according to the syntax of the language) that evaluate to a single value.

So even if you rely on the Java language for writing report expressions, you cannot use Java statements like `if else`, `for`, or `while`.

However, quite often an expression must return a value that is calculated based on a condition or even multiple conditions. To accomplish this, use the conditional operator `?:`. You can even nest this operator inside a Java expression to obtain the desired output based on multiple conditions.

The following text field displays `No data` if the value for the `quantity` field is `null`:

```
<textFieldExpression>
  $F{quantity} == null ? "No data" : String.valueOf($F{quantity})
</textFieldExpression>
```

Parameters

Parameters are object references that are passed into the report-filling operations. They are very useful for passing to the report engine data that it cannot normally find in its data source.

For example, you could pass to the report engine the name of the user who launched the report-filling operation if you want it to appear on the report, or you could dynamically change the title of your report.

Listing 8-1 gives the JRXML syntax for the report parameters.

Listing 8-1. *JRXML Syntax*

```
<!ELEMENT parameter (property*, parameterDescription?, defaultValueExpression?)>

<!ATTLIST parameter
    name NMTOKEN #REQUIRED
    class CDATA #REQUIRED
    isForPrompting (true | false) "true"
>
```

```
<!ELEMENT parameterDescription (#PCDATA)>

<!ELEMENT defaultValueExpression (#PCDATA)>
```

Declaring a parameter in a report template is very simple. Simply specify only its name and its class:

```
<parameter name="ReportTitle" class="java.lang.String"/>
<parameter name="MaxOrderID" class="java.lang.Integer"/>
<parameter name="SummaryImage" class="java.awt.Image"/>
```

The supplied values for the report parameters can be used in the various report expressions, in the report SQL query, or even in the report scriptlet class. The following special sections of this book address each report expression, the query, and the scriptlets.

The following subsections describe the components that make a report parameter definition complete.

Parameter Name

The name attribute of the <parameter> element is mandatory and allows referencing the parameter by its declared name. The naming conventions of JasperReports are similar to those of the Java language regarding variable declaration. That means that the parameter name should be a single word containing no special characters like a dot or a comma.

Parameter Class

The second mandatory attribute for a report parameter specifies the class name for the parameter values. The class attribute can have any value as long it represents a class name that is available in the classpath both at report-compilation time and report-filling time.

Prompting for Parameter Values

In some GUI applications, it is useful to establish the set of report parameters for which the application should request user input, before launching the report-filling process.

It is also useful to specify the text description that will prompt for the user input for each of those parameters.

This is why we have the Boolean isForPrompting attribute in the parameter declaration sequence and the inner <parameterDescription> element.

The following example shows the declaration of a text parameter, along with the description that could be used at runtime when requesting the user to input the parameter value, in a custom-made dialog window:

```
<parameter name="Comments" class="java.lang.String" isForPrompting="true">
  <parameterDescription>
    <![CDATA[
      Please type here the report comments, if any
    ]]>
  </parameterDescription>
</parameter>
```

Note the `<![CDATA[` and `]]>` character sequences that delimit the parameter description. Those are part of the XML-specific syntax that instructs the XML parser to not parse the text inside. This allows you to use special XML characters like the >, <, ", and others in your texts. You'll see this syntax used in other examples throughout this book and the samples.

Parameter Custom Properties

In addition to the parameter description and the prompting flag mentioned previously, some applications might need to attach more information or metadata to a report parameter definition. This is now why report parameters can have any number of custom-defined name/value property pairs, just like the report template itself could have at the top level (see the "Custom Properties" section of Chapter 7 for details).

Parameter Default Value

Parameter values are supplied to the report-filling process packed in a `java.util.Map` object with the parameter names as the keys. This way, you are not obliged to supply a value for each parameter every time.

If you do not supply a value for a parameter, its value is considered to be `null`, unless you specify a default value expression in the report template for this particular report parameter. This expression is only evaluated if you don't supply a value for the given parameter.

Here's a `java.util.Date` parameter whose value will be the current date if you do not supply a specific date value when filling the report:

```
<parameter name="MyDate" class="java.util.Date">
  <defaultValueExpression>
    new java.util.Date()
  </defaultValueExpression>
</parameter>
```

In the default value expression of a parameter, you can only use previously defined report parameters.

Built-In Report Parameters

Every report template contains some predefined report parameters, along with the ones that the report template creator decides to introduce. These built-in parameters are presented in the following subsections.

REPORT_PARAMETERS_MAP

This is a built-in parameter that will always point to the `java.util.Map` object that contains the user-defined parameters passed when calling the report-filling process.

This parameter is especially useful when you want to pass to the subreports the same set of report parameters that the master report has received.

REPORT_CONNECTION

This report parameter points to the `java.sql.Connection` object that was supplied to the engine for execution of the SQL report query through JDBC, if it is the case. It has a value different than `null` only if the report (or subreport) has received a `java.sql.Connection` when the report-filling process was launched and not a `net.sf.jasperreports.engine.JRDataSource` instance.

This parameter is also useful for passing the same JDBC connection object that was used by the master report to its subreports. You can see this in action in the supplied subreport sample.

REPORT_DATA_SOURCE

When filling a report, a data source object is either directly supplied by the parent application or created behind the scenes by the reporting engine when a JDBC connection is supplied. This built-in parameter allows you access to the report's data source in the report expressions or in the scriptlets.

REPORT_MAX_COUNT

You may want to limit the number of records from the report data source during the report-filling process. This built-in parameter accepts `java.lang.Integer` values representing the number of records from the data source that the engine will process during the report filling. When the internal record counter reaches the specified value, the engine will assume that it has reached the last record from the data source and will stop the iteration through the rest of the data source.

REPORT_SCRIPTLET

Even if the report does not use scriptlets, this built-in parameter will point to a `net.sf.jasperreports.engine.JRAbstractScriptlet` instance, which in this case is a `net.sf.jasperreports.engine.JRDefaultScriptlet` object. When using scriptlets, this reference to the scriptlet class instance that is created when filling the report allows specific methods to be called on it. This is so the data that the scriptlet object has prepared during the filling process can be used or manipulated. This is shown on the last page of the scriptlet sample report when a call is made to this scriptlet object. See Chapter 15 for more details about this parameter.

REPORT_LOCALE

Report templates can be reused to generate documents in different languages. The target language used during report filling is specified by the `java.util.Locale` object supplied as the value for the `REPORT_LOCALE` parameter. The engine uses `Locale.getDefault()` if no value is explicitly supplied for this built-in parameter at runtime.

More about this parameter can be found in Chapter 16.

REPORT_RESOURCE_BUNDLE

This parameter points to the `java.util.ResourceBundle` object that contains localized information associated with the report template. This object can be supplied directly by the caller application or created by the engine using the resource bundle base name specified in the `resourceBundle` property of the report template. The engine tries to read locale-specific information from this object based on the report-supplied locale and the key used inside the report expressions. More details about internationalization can be found in Chapter 16.

REPORT_TIME_ZONE

The `java.util.TimeZone` instance supplied as value for this built-in parameter is used during the report-filling process to format all date and time values. If no value is supplied for this parameter at runtime, the default time zone of the host machine is used.

REPORT_VIRTUALIZER

When very large reports are generated and memory becomes insufficient, the engine can rely on the report virtualization mechanism to optimize memory consumption during report filling. Report virtualization is activated by supplying an instance of the `net.sf.jasperreports.engine.JRVirtualizer` interface as the value for the `REPORT_VIRTUALIZER` built-in parameter. By doing this, the engine will store temporary data in a serialized form in order to minimize the amount of memory needed during report filling. Report virtualization is explained in the *6* Large files support chapter.

IS_IGNORE_PAGINATION

By default, JasperReports produces page-oriented documents that are ready for printing. Sometimes, especially in Web applications, pagination is irrelevant. One way to avoid breaking documents into multiple pages and to obtain a more flow-oriented document layout is to set this built-in parameter to `Boolean.TRUE` at runtime. By doing this, the engine will ignore all the report settings that are related to page breaking and will produce a document that contains a single very large page.

When used, this fill-time parameter overrides the value of the `isIgnorePagination` property of the report template.

REPORT_CLASS_LOADER

Resources such as images, fonts, and subreports can be referenced using their relative classpath location. By default, JasperReports uses the current thread's context class loader to locate the resource. If that fails, it then falls back to the class loader that loads the library's classes themselves. To extend the resource-lookup mechanism and give greater flexibility to the library, you can pass a custom-made class loader implementation as the value for the `REPORT_CLASS_LOADER` fill-time parameter. This would allow applications to load resources from repository locations that are not normally part of the overall application classpath.

The equivalent export-time parameter is the `CLASS_LOADER` exporter parameter. This is used by exporter implementations to look up lazy images or font files based on their classpath-relative location.

REPORT_URL_HANDLER_FACTORY

When images, fonts, and subreports templates are referenced using URLs, the program recognizes only some common protocols by default. File system–based and HTTP-based URLs that start with the `file:` and `http:` prefixes, respectively, work without need for any special configuration.

If custom-made protocols are required to locate and retrieve the resources, there is a need for a mechanism that associates an URL handler to a specific protocol. Java provides two such standard mechanisms (see the Javadoc for `java.net.URL.URL(String protocol, String host, int port, String file)`). However, neither of the two solutions is possible in certain scenarios (for instance, when an web application deployed in Apache Tomcat needs to use custom URL handlers present in the application's classpath). To work around this limitation, the JasperReports library has created its own alternative mechanism to associate URL handlers for custom URLs used as image, font, or subreport locations.

JasperReports provides several ways to register a `java.net.URLStreamHandlerFactory` instance, either globally or locally:

- Globally, by calling `JRResourcesUtil.setGlobalURLHandlerFactory()`
- Locally, in the following ways:
  - When filling a report, by setting the `URLStreamHandlerFactory` instance as the value of the built-in `REPORT_URL_HANDLER_FACTORY` parameter (the name of the parameter is accessible via the `JRParameter.REPORT_URL_HANDLER_FACTORY` constant)
  - When exporting a report, by using the `JRExporterParameter.URL_HANDLER_FACTORY` export parameter
  - By calling `JRResourcesUtil.setThreadURLHandlerFactory()` directly

When a local/context or global URL handler factory is registered with JasperReports, the engine uses it (the local one takes precedence when both are registered) to obtain an URL handler while creating `java.net.URL` instances from `java.lang.String` locations. When the location of a resource is specified as a `java.lang.String` value, the engine will check whether the location begins with a protocol token followed by a colon (`:`) and whether the registered URL handler factory returns a valid URL handler for the specific protocol. If so, the URL handler will be used to create the `java.net.URL` instance and to open the URL and read data from it.

This mechanism would mainly apply to the following cases:

- Report images can have custom URLs specified as a `java.lang.String` location, for instance `<imageExpression>"my_protocol://image_host/logo.jpg"</imageExpression>`. (Note that the image source should not be a `java.net.URL` object.)
- Subreports can specify custom URLs as location.
- PDF fonts names can be defined as custom URLs.

Client code using the JasperReports APIs can also benefit from the mechanism by using methods of the `JRResourcesUtil` or `JRLoader` utility classes.

Therefore, when one or more custom URL protocols have to be used as locations for various report resources, you only need to write an implementation of `java.net.URLStreamHandlerFactory` and make sure that the `createURLStreamHandler(String protocol)` method returns non-null protocol handlers for each custom protocol.

REPORT_FORMAT_FACTORY

The value for this parameter is an instance of the `net.sf.jasperreports.engine.util.FormatFactory` interface, which is either provided directly by the calling program or created internally by the reporting engine, using the `formatFactoryClass` attribute of the report template. If this parameter is provided with a value by the report-filling process caller, it takes precedence over the attribute in the report template.

Data Sources

When filling the report, the JasperReports engine iterates through the records of the supplied data source object and generates every section according to the template defined in the report design.

Normally, the engine expects to receive a `net.sf.jasperreports.engine.JRDataSource` object as the data source of the report that it has to fill. But as we shall see, another feature lets users supply a JDCB connection object instead of the usual data source object when the report data is found in a relational database.

The `net.sf.jasperreports.engine.JRDataSource` interface is very simple. You implement only two methods:

```
public boolean next() throws JRException;

public Object getFieldValue(JRField jrField) throws JRException;
```

The `next()` method is called on the data source object by the reporting engine when iterating through the data at report-filling time. The second method provides the value for each report field in the current data source record.

It is very important to know that the only way to retrieve data from the data source is by using the report fields. A data source object is more like a table with columns and rows containing data in the table cells. The rows of this table are the records through which the reporting engine iterates when filling the report and each column should be mapped to a report field, so that we can make use of the data source content in the report expressions.

There are several default implementations of the `net.sf.jasperreports.engine.JRDataSource` interface, and we shall take a closer look to each of them.

JDBC Data Source

The `net.sf.jasperreports.engine.JRResultSetDataSource` is a very useful implementation of the `net.sf.jasperreports.engine.JRDataSource` interface because it wraps a `java.sql.ResultSet` object. Since most reports are generated using data in relational databases, this is probably the most commonly used implementation for the data source interface.

Interestingly, you might end up using this implementation even if you do not instantiate this class yourself when filling your reports. This is what happens: if you specify the SQL query in your report template, the reporting engine executes the specified SQL query and wraps the returned `java.sql.ResultSet` object in a `net.sf.jasperreports.engine.JRResultSetDataSource` instance. The only thing the engine needs to execute the query is a `java.sql.Connection` object. You supply this connection object instead of supplying the usual data source object. You can see this in such samples as `jasper`, `scriptlet`, `subreport`, and `query`, found under the `/demo/samples` directory of the distributed package.

Of course, you could execute the SQL query in the parent application, outside JasperReports, if you want (or have) to. In this case, you could manually wrap the `java.sql.ResultSet` obtained using an instance of this data source class before calling the report-filling process.

The most important thing to know when using this type of data source is that you must declare a report field for each column in the result set. The name of the report field must be the same as the name of the column it maps, as well as the data type.

If this is not possible for some reason, the data source also allows users to retrieve data from a particular column in the `java.sql.ResultSet` by index. The report field that maps the specified column can be named `COLUMN_x`, where `x` is the one-based index of the result set column.

For maximum portability, as stated in the JDBC documentation, the values from a `java.sql.ResultSet` object should be retrieved from left to right and only once. To ensure that they work this way, consider declaring the report fields in the same order as they appear in the SQL query.

BLOB and CLOB Support

When the SQL query retrieves data from table columns that have large binary or large char data types and are mapped to `java.sql.Blob` and `java.sql.Clob` values through JDBC, the current data source implementation tries to simplify the data by using intelligent field mapping.

For instance, in most cases, BLOB columns are used to store images in the database that the application might need to use inside a report. If the report field that maps a given BLOB column from the `java.sql.ResultSet` is of type `java.awt.Image`, the data source will try to read from the `java.sql.Blob` instance and load an image object using a `java.awt.MediaTracker`.

Or, if very large chunks of text are stored in large character columns inside the database, then the data source will try to read the text from the database and load it in `java.lang.String` objects, in case the corresponding report field was declared as being of type `String`.

The supported mappings are as follows:

- BLOB: `java.sql.Blob`, `java.io.InputStream`, and `java.awt.Image`
- CLOB: `java.sql.Clob`, `java.io.InputStream`, `java.io.Reader`, and `java.lang.String`

JavaBeans Data Sources

The library is shipped with two data source implementations that can wrap collections or arrays of JavaBean objects. Both implementations rely on Java reflection to retrieve report field data from the JavaBean objects wrapped inside the data sources. These data sources can be used to generate reports using data already available in-memory in the form of EJBs, Hibernate, JDO objects, or even POJOs.

The net.sf.jasperreports.engine.data.JRBeanArrayDataSource is for wrapping an array of JavaBean objects to use for filling a report with data, and the net.sf.jasperreports.engine.data.JRBeanCollectionDataSource is for wrapping a collection of JavaBeans. Each object inside the array or the collection will be seen as one record in this type of data source.

The mapping between a particular JavaBean property and the corresponding report field is made by naming conventions. The name of the report field must be the same as the name of the JavaBean property as specified by the JavaBeans specifications.

For instance, to retrieve the value of a report field named productDescription, the program will try to call through reflection a method called getProductDescription() on the current JavaBean object.

Note that the current implementations rely on the Jakarta Commons BeanUtils library to retrieve JavaBean property values, so check their documentation to see how nested JavaBean properties can be used with report fields.

Let's say that the current JavaBean object inside the data source is of type Product and contains nested supplier information accessible by calling the getSupplier() method, which returns a Supplier object. In this case, you could have a report field that maps to the supplier's address if it is called supplier.address.

Note that in the past, report fields did not accept dots, spaces, or other special characters in their names. Therefore, to access nested JavaBean properties, the data source relied on the field's description, if present, to identify the property, because dots might appear inside the field's description. For backward-compatibility reasons, the current implementations still look into the field's description first, by default. If there is no description, then the report field name is used for locating the JavaBean property. If this default behavior is not desirable, especially if the field description is already used for other purposes, you can use special data source constructors that receive a flag called isUseFieldDescription to suppress this behavior.

Map-Based Data Sources

JasperReports is shipped with two data source implementations that can wrap arrays or collections of java.util.Map objects.

The net.sf.jasperreports.engine.data.JRMapArrayDataSource wraps an array of Map objects, and net.sf.jasperreports.engine.data.JRMapCollectionDataSource can be used to wrap a java.util.Collection of Map objects.

These implementations are useful if the parent application already stores the reporting data available in-memory as Map objects. Each Map object in the wrapped array or collection is considered a virtual record in the data source, and the value of each report field is extracted from the map using the report field name as the key.

TableModel Data Source

In some Swing-based desktop client applications, the reporting data might already be available in the form of a javax.swing.table.TableModel implementation used for rendering javax.swing.JTable components on various forms. JasperReports can generate reports using this kind of data if a given javax.swing.table.TableModel object is wrapped in a net.sf.jasperreports.engine.data.JRTableModelDataSource instance before being passed as the data source for the report-filling process.

There are two ways to use this type of data source. Normally, to retrieve data from it, you must declare a report field for each column in the `javax.swing.table.TableModel` object bearing the same name as the column it maps. Sometimes it is not possible or desirable to use the column name, however, because the report field name and columns could still be bound to report fields using their zero-based index instead of their names.

For instance, if you know that a particular column is the third column in the table model object (`index=2`), then you could name the corresponding field "`COLUMN_2`" and use the column data without problems.

An example is provided in the `/demo/samples/datasource` sample.

XML Data Sources

XML documents can be used as report data sources by means of a data source implementation. JasperReports features a built-in XML data source implementation (`net.sf.jasperreports.engine.data.JRXmlDataSource`) that is based on DOM and uses XPath expressions to select data from the XML document.

An XML data source instantiation involves the following inputs:

- An XML document. The parsed document, its location, or its source is provided as an argument to the data source constructor.
- An XPath expression to select the node set that corresponds to the data source record list. The expression is passed to the data source as a constructor argument. The default XPath expression selects the document node itself; in this case the data source would produce a single record. The XPath expression is executed when the data source is instantiated; each item in the resulting node set will generate a record/row in the data source.
- For every field in the report/data set, an XPath expression to select the field value for each record. The field's XPath expression is provided by the field description (`<fieldDescription>` element in JRXML). The field's XPath expression is executed for each record using as a context node the current node from the main node set.

An XML data source can be used create sub–data sources to be used for subreports or subdatasets. There are two methods of creating a sub–data source from a parent XML data source:

- A sub–data source can be created for a new document that uses the current node as a root node. An XPath expression can additionally be specified to select the list of nodes for the sub–data source. The `subDataSource()` and `subDataSource(String selectExpression)` methods should be used to create sub–data sources in this scenario.
- The same document can be reused for a new sub–data source, which would specify a different XPath expression for the main node set. This can be accomplished via `dataSource()` and `dataSource(String selectExpression)` methods calls.

Note The built-in XML data source is a generic implementation that is very flexible due to the power of XPath and hence convenient in many cases. However, especially when dealing with large XML documents, this implementation might not perform optimally because DOM would require large amounts of heap space for the in-memory document, and XPath expression evaluations would cause slower data processing speeds. In such cases, custom data source implementations that use SAX or other stream parser mechanisms to process specific XML documents would significantly increase the performance.

To illustrate the preceding concepts, consider the following XML document:

```
<CompanyData>
  <Info>
    <Reference>123</Reference>
  </Info>
  <Customer ID="ALFKI">
    <CompanyName>Alfreds Futterkiste</CompanyName>
    <Address>Obere Str. 57</Address>
    <Phone type="Fixed">075-5554321</Phone>
    <Phone type="Mobile">030-0074321</Phone>
    <Order>
      <OrderID>10248</OrderID>
      <OrderDate>1996-07-04</OrderDate>
    </Order>
    <Order>
      <OrderID>10249</OrderID>
      <OrderDate>1996-07-05</OrderDate>
    </Order>
  </Customer>
  <Customer ID="ANATR">
    <CompanyName>Ana Trujillo Emparedados y helados</CompanyName>
    <Address>Avda. de la Constitución 2222</Address>
    <Phone type="Fixed">(5) 555-4729</Phone>
    <Order>
      <OrderID>10242</OrderID>
      <OrderDate>1996-07-01</OrderDate>
    </Order>
  </Customer>
</CompanyData>
```

To create a data source that iterates the `Customer` nodes, you could use the following:

```
new JRXmlDataSource(document, "/CompanyData/Customer")
```

Possible field mappings would be as follows:

- `@ID`: Map the `ID` attribute of the current `Customer` node.
- `CompanyName`: Map the value of the `CompanyName` child node of the current node.

- `Phone[@type = "Fixed"]`: Map the fixed phone number of the current customer.
- `/CompanyData/Info/Reference`: Absolute XPath expressions are also possible; the field would yield the same value for each record.

To create a sub–data source that iterates on the `Order` nodes under the current `Customer` node, the following expression could be used as a subreport data source:

```
((JRXmlDataSource) $P{REPORT_DATA_SOURCE}).subDataSource("/Customer/Order")
```

To create a sub–data source that only includes the `Info` node, you could use the following:

```
((JRXmlDataSource) $P{REPORT_DATA_SOURCE}).dataSource("/CompanyData/Info")
```

Localization Support

The XML data source provides localization support for both number and date/time values rendered as text in the wrapped XML document.

In order to parse these text values into `java.lang.Number` or `java.util.Date` values according to the declared report field type in the report template, the program needs to know which pattern and locale to use. For date/time report fields, if the text value inside the XML representing time is rendered in a specific time zone, then this time zone needs to be provided to the data source so that it is taken into account when parsing.

There are four setter methods in the `JRXmlDataSource` class for specifying:

- *Number pattern*: To use for parsing all text values corresponding to report fields of type `java.lang.Number` or any subclass of it (`setNumberPattern(java.lang.String)` method)
- *Date pattern*: To use for parsing all date/time values corresponding to report fields of type `java.util.Date` or any subclass of it (`setDatePattern(java.lang.String)` method)
- *Locale*: To use for getting localized number and date parsers (`setLocale(java.util.Locale)` method)
- *Time zone*: To use for properly translating time values when they are not expressed in GMT (`setTimeZone(java.util.TimeZone)` method)

Patterns should be non-localized and in accordance with the `java.text.DecimalFormat` and `java.text.SimpleDateFormat` pattern syntax. If specific patterns are not supplied, the defaults for these two format classes apply.

You can see how this data source implementation works by checking the `/demo/samples/xmldatasource` sample provided with the project source files.

CSV Data Sources

Sometimes data that users need to fill the report with is found in plain text files, in a certain format, such as the popular CSV (comma-separated value).

JasperReports provides an implementation for such a data source, by wrapping the CSV data from a text file into a `net.sf.jasperreports.engine.data.JRCsvDataSource`.

The CSV data source usually needs to read a file from disk, or at least from an input stream. Thus, the `JRCsvDataSource` can be initialized in three ways, depending on where it gets the data:

- *A file*: `new JRCsvDataSource(File)`
- *An input stream*: `new JRCsvDataSource(InputStream)`
- *A reader*: `new JRCsvDataSource(Reader)`

The CSV format has certain formatting rules. Data rows are separated by a record delimiter (text sequence) and fields inside each row are separated by a field delimiter (character). Fields containing delimiter characters can be placed inside quotes. If fields contain quotes themselves, these are duplicated (e.g., `"John ""Doe"""` will be displayed as `John "Doe"`).

The default values in JasperReports (and also the most common for CSV files) are a comma for field delimiter and a newline (`\n`) for record delimiter. Users can override these default values by calling `setFieldDelimiter(char)` and `setRecordDelimiter(String)`. For example, on some systems, users may need to replace the default `\n` delimiter with `\r\n`.

Since CSV does not specify column names, the default convention is to name report fields `COLUMN_x` and map each column with the field found at index `x` in each row (these indices start with 0). To avoid this situation, users have two possible solutions:

- Using the `setUseFirstRowAsHeader(true)` method to force the program to read the column name from the first line of the CSV file.
- Providing an array of column names using the `setColumnNames(String[])` method.

Note that in both cases, the number of provided column names must be at least equal with the number of actual fields in any record, otherwise an exception will be thrown. Also, for any column name in the data source, an equivalent report field must exist.

Handling data types for fields in CSV data sources is special since the CSV file format does not provide such information. This matter is solved by trying to match each field in the data source to its corresponding report field type. For number and date/time fields, converting text values to `java.lang.Number` and `java.util.Date` values respectively requires parsing using format objects. This is controlled by specifying the date and number format objects to be used with the `JRCsvDataSource` instance by calling its `setDateFormat(DateFormat)` and `setNumberFormat(NumberFormat)` methods before passing it to the report-filling process.

The CSV data source implementation also has a `JRCsvDataSourceProvider` class, useful for design tools creators. See the "Data Source Provider" section later in this chapter for more details.

Empty Data Sources

The `net.sf.jasperreports.engine.JREmptyDataSource` class is a very simple data source implementation that simulates a data source with a given number of virtual records inside. It is called "empty data source" because even though it has one or more records inside, all the report fields are null for all the virtual records of the data source.

Such a simple data source implementation is used by the UI tools to offer basic report preview functionality, or in special report templates, or for testing and debugging purposes.

Rewindable Data Sources

The `net.sf.jasperreports.engine.JRRewindableDataSource` is an extension of the basic `net.sf.jasperreports.engine.JRDataSource` interface, to which it adds the possibility of moving the record pointer back before the first virtual record. It adds only one method, called `moveFirst()`, to the interface.

Rewindable data sources are useful when working with subreports. If a subreport is placed inside a band that is not allowed to split due to the `isSplitAllowed="false"` setting and there is not enough space on the current page for the subreport to be rendered, then the engine has to give up rendering the current band, introduce a page break, and restart the band and the subreport on the next page. But since the subreport has already consumed some of the supplied data source records when trying to render the band on the previous page, it needs to move the record pointer of the data source back before the first data source for the subreport to restart properly.

All built-in data source implementations are rewindable except for the `net.sf.jasperreports.engine.JRResultSetDataSource`, which does not support moving the record pointer back. This is a problem only if this data source is used to manually wrap a `java.sql.ResultSet` before passing it to the subreport. It is not a problem if the SQL query resides in the subreport template because the engine will reexecute it when restarting the subreport on the next page.

Data Source Provider

To simplify integration with the GUI tools for creating and previewing report templates, the JasperReports library has published an interface that allows those tools to create and dispose of data source objects. This is the standard way to plug custom data sources into a design tool.

This is very useful when the developer wants to preview the reports with the design tool and use the actual data that the target application will supply at runtime. In order to achieve this, simply create a custom implementation of the `net.sf.jasperreports.engine.JRDataSourceProvider` interface and make it available to the design tool to create the required data sources to use during report preview.

The data source provider interface has only a few methods that allow creating and disposing of data source objects and also methods for listing the available report fields inside the data source if possible. Knowing which fields will be found in the created data sources helps you to create report field wizards inside the design tools to simplify report creation.

The library also comes with an abstract implementation of the `JRDataSourceProvider` interface that can be used as the base class for creating data source provider implementations that produce JavaBean-based data sources.

The `net.sf.jasperreports.engine.data.JRAbstractBeanDataSourceProvider` uses Java reflection to provide available report fields names for a given JavaBean class.

For more details about data source providers, check the Javadoc API documentation.

Report Queries

To fill a report, provide the reporting engine with the report data, or at least instruct it how to get this data.

JasperReports normally expects to receive a `net.sf.jasperreports.engine.JRDataSource` object as the report data source, but it has also been enhanced to work with JDBC so that it can retrieve data from relational databases if required.

SQL Queries

The library allows the report template to specify the SQL query for report data if this data is located in relational databases.

The SQL query specified in the report template is taken into account and executed only if a `java.sql.Connection` object is supplied instead of the normal `net.sf.jasperreports.engine.JRDataSource` object when filling the report.

This query can be introduced in the JRXML report template using the `<queryString>` element. If present, this element comes after the report parameter declarations and before the report fields. It's complete syntax is given in Listing 8-2.

Listing 8-2. *JRXML Syntax*

```
<!ELEMENT queryString (#PCDATA)>
<!ATTLIST queryString
    language CDATA "sql"
>
```

Here is a simple SQL query that retrieves data from a table called `Orders` placed in a relational database:

```
<queryString><![CDATA[SELECT * FROM Orders]]></queryString>
```

Report parameters in the query string are important to further refine the data retrieved from the database. These parameters can act as dynamic filters in the query that supplies data for the report. Parameters are introduced using a special syntax, similar to the one used in report expressions.

There are three possible ways to use parameters in the query, described in the following subsections.

$P{paramName} Syntax

The parameters are used like normal `java.sql.PreparedStatement` parameters, using the following syntax:

```
<queryString>
  <![CDATA[
   SELECT * FROM Orders WHERE OrderID <= $P{MaxOrderID} ORDER BY ShipCountry
  ]]>
</queryString>
```

$P!{paramName} Syntax

Sometimes it is useful to use parameters to dynamically modify portions of the SQL query or to pass the entire SQL query as a parameter to the report-filling routines. In such cases, the syntax differs a little, as shown in the following example. Notice the ! character:

```
<queryString>
  <![CDATA[
    SELECT * FROM $P!{MyTable} ORDER BY $P!{OrderByClause}
  ]]>
</queryString>
```

What is different in this second example? Parameters are used for the missing table name in the FROM clause and the missing column names in the ORDER BY clause. Note that you cannot use normal IN parameters to dynamically change portions of your query that you execute using a java.sql.PreparedStatement object.

The special syntax that introduces the parameter values in this example ensures that the value supplied for those parameters replace the parameter references in the query, before it is sent to the database server using a java.sql.PreparedStatement object.

In fact, the reporting engine first deals with the $P!{} parameter references by using their values to obtain the final form of the SQL query, and only after that transforms the rest of the $P{} normal parameter references into usual IN parameters used when working with prepared JDBC statements.

For more details about what type of parameters to use in your report queries, you must be familiar with JDBC technology, especially the java.sql.PreparedStatement interface and its parameters.

This second type of parameter reference used in the SQL query allows you to pass the entire SQL query at runtime if you like:

```
<queryString>$P!{MySQLQuery}</queryString>
```

■ **Note** It is possible to put other parameter references into a parameter value. That is, when supplying the entire SQL query as a report parameter, that query can itself contain some other parameter references, and the program will expand them recursively.

$X{functionName, param1, param2,...} Syntax

There are also cases when a part of the query needs to be dynamically built starting from a report parameter value, with the query part containing both query text and bind parameters. This is the case, for instance, with IN and NOT IN query clauses that need to use a collection report parameter as a list of values.

Such complex query clauses are introduced into the query using the $X{} syntax. The general form of a $X{} clause is $X{functionName, param1, param2,...}.

JasperReports has built-in support for two clause functions: `IN` and `NOTIN`. Both functions expect two parameters:

- The SQL column or expression to be used as the left side in the `IN`/`NOT IN` clause.
- The name of the report parameter that will supply the values list. The value of this parameter can either be a `java.util.Collection` instance or an object or primitive Java array.

For instance, if a report receives as a parameter a list of countries and needs to filter orders based on this list, you would write a query of the following form:

```
<parameter name="CountryList" class="java.util.List"/>

<queryString><![CDATA[
SELECT * FROM Orders WHERE $X{IN, ShipCountry, CountryList}
]]></queryString>
```

Before the query is executed, `$X{IN, <column>, <param>}` and `$X{NOTIN, <column>, <param>}` expand to the following:

- `<column> IN/NOT IN (?, ?, ..)` when the parameter value is neither null nor empty. Each component in the collection/array generates a bind parameter; the type of the bind parameters is decided based on the runtime value of the collection/array component.
- A `true` clause (`0 = 0`) when the parameter value is null or empty.

New clause functions (in addition to the built-in `IN` and `NOTIN`) can be added by implementing `net.sf.jasperreports.engine.query.JRClauseFunction` and by extending the query executer to register the new functions.

Some of the provided samples, such as `jasper`, `subreport`, `scriptlet`, and `query`, use internal SQL queries to retrieve data. The most interesting sample illustrating this is in the `query` sample found in the `/demo/samples/query` directory of the project's distribution.

Stored Procedures

In the majority of cases, the SQL query text placed inside a report template is a `SELECT` statement. JasperReports uses a `java.sql.PreparedStatement` behind the scenes to execute that SQL query through JDBC and retrieve a `java.sql.ResultSet` object to use for report filling. However, the SQL query string might also contain stored procedure calls.

Certain conditions must be met to put stored procedure calls in the SQL query string of a report template:

- The stored procedure must return a `java.sql.ResultSet` when called through JDBC.
- The stored procedure cannot have `OUT` parameters.

These two conditions imply that the stored procedure can be called using a `java.sql.PreparedStatement` and does not need to be called through a `java.sql.CallableStatement` in order to work with JasperReports.

Query Executer API

Starting with JasperReports version 1.2.0, report data can be produced by specifying queries in languages other than SQL. Each query language is associated a query executer factory implementation. JasperReports has built-in query executer implementations for SQL, Hibernate 3, and XPath queries.

The query language is specified in JRXML using the `language` attribute of the `<queryString>` tag. Using the API, the query language is set by `JRDesignQuery.setLanguage(String)`. The default language is SQL, thus ensuring backward compatibility for report queries that do not specify a query language.

To register a query executer factory for a query language, you have to define a JasperReports property named `net.sf.jasperreports.query.executer.factory.<language>` (see Chapter 18 for details). The same mechanism can be used to override the built-in query executers for a query language, for instance to use a custom query executer for SQL queries.

The API for query executers involves an executer factory interface, a query executer interface, implementations of these interfaces, and `JRDataSource` implementations.

`JRQueryExecuterFactory` is a factory interface used to query executers for a specific language and to provide information regarding the connection parameters required by the query executer to run the query. It has the following methods:

- `JRQueryExecuter createQueryExecuter(JRDataset dataset, Map parameters)`: This method creates a query executer. The dataset includes the query string and the fields that will be requested from the data source created by the query executer. The parameters map contains parameter types and runtime values to be used for query parameters. This method usually sends the dataset and parameters map to the created query executer.

- `Object[] getBuiltinParameters()`: This method returns parameters that will be automatically registered with a report/dataset based on the query language. These parameters will be used by query executers as the context/connection on which to execute the query. For instance, the Hibernate query executer factory specifies a `HIBERNATE_SESSION` parameter of type `org.hibernate.Session` whose value will be used by the query executer to run the query.

- `boolean supportsQueryParameterType(String className)`: This method is used on report validation to determine whether a query parameter type (for a parameter specified in the query using `$P{..}`) is supported by the query executer implementation.

A `JRQueryExecuter` is responsible for running a query, creating a data source out of the result, and closing the result. It includes these methods:

- `JRDataSource createDatasource()`: This method processes and runs the query and creates a data source out of the query result. Usually, the required data (query string and parameter values) is made available to the query executer by the factory on creation.

- `void close()`: This method closes the query execution result and any other resource associated with it. This method is called after all data produced by the query executer has been fetched.

- `boolean cancelQuery()`: This method is called when the user decides to cancel a report fill process. The implementation should check whether the query is currently being executed and ask the underlying mechanism to abort the execution. The method should return `true` if the query was being executed and the execution was canceled. If execution abortion is not supported, the method will always return `false`.

Query executer implementation can benefit from using `JRAbstractQueryExecuter` as a base. The abstract base provides query parameter processing functionality and other utility methods.

In most of the cases, a query executer needs a new `JRDataSource` implementation to wrap its specific query results. Still, in some of the cases, query executers can use existing `JRDataSource` implementations.

SQL Query Executer

The SQL query executer is a JDBC-based executer for SQL queries. It replaces the mechanism used before the 1.2.0 release for executing report queries, preserving all its functionality.

The SQL query executer factory does not register any parameter as the `REPORT_CONNECTION` parameter is kept in all reports for backward compatibility. The SQL query executer uses this parameter to retrieve a `java.sql.Connection` object.

The query executer creates a `JRResultSetDataSource` data source to wrap the JDBC result set.

Aborting the currently running query is supported using `java.sql.PreparedStatement.cancel()`. The fetch size of the JDBC statement used by the query executer behind the scenes can be set using the `net.sf.jasperreports.jdbc.fetch.size` configuration property at report level or globally.

XPath Query Executer

The XPath query executer permits reports using XML data sources to specify the XPath that produces the list of nodes/records as the report query.

The query executer factory registers a parameter named `XML_DATA_DOCUMENT` of type `org.w3c.dom.Document`. The query executer will run the XPath query against this document and produce a `JRXmlDataSource` data source.

Parameters are supported in the XPath query. All parameters will be replaced in the query string by their `java.lang.String` values.

This query executer recognizes four additional parameters that serve for localization purposes when creating the `JRXmlDataSource` instance:

```
JRXPathQueryExecuterFactory.XML_LOCALE
JRXPathQueryExecuterFactory.XML_NUMBER_PATTERN
JRXPathQueryExecuterFactory.XML_DATE_PATTERN
JRXPathQueryExecuterFactory.XML_TIME_ZONE
```

More details about how the built-in XPath data source works can be found in the "XML Data Sources" section, earlier in this chapter, and you can see this query executer being used in the `/demo/samples/xmldatasource` sample provided with the project source files.

Hibernate Query Executer

Hibernate 3 support is present in JasperReports in the form of a query executer. This allows users to specify in a report an HQL query that should be used to retrieve report data.

For reports having an HQL query, the executer factory will automatically define a parameter named `HIBERNATE_SESSION` of type `org.hibernate.Session`. Its value will be used by the query executer to create the query.

Query Parameters

Like SQL queries, HQL queries can embed two types of parameters:

- *Query parameters* are embedded using the `$P{..}` syntax. These parameters are used as named parameters of the Hibernate query. The correspondence between Java parameter types and Hibernate types is resolved according to Table 8-1.

Table 8-1. *Parameter Type Mapping*

Parameter Type (Java)	Hibernate Type
`java.lang.Boolean`	`boolean`
`java.lang.Byte`	`byte`
`java.lang.Double`	`double`
`java.lang.Float`	`float`
`java.lang.Integer`	`integer`
`java.lang.Long`	`long`
`java.lang.Short`	`short`
`java.math.BigDecimal`	`big_decimal`
`java.math.BigInteger`	`big_integer`
`java.lang.Character`	`character`
`java.lang.String`	`string`
`java.util.Date`	`date`
`java.sql.Timestamp`	`timestamp`
`java.sql.Time`	`time`
`java.util.Collections` implementation	Multiple-value parameter; the type is guessed by Hibernate
Mapped entity class	Mapped persistent entity
Other	Guessed by Hibernate

- *Statement substitution parameters* are embedded using the `$P!{..}` syntax. The `java.lang.String` value of the parameter is substituted as-is in the query string before creating the Hibernate query. This type of parameter can be used to dynamically specify query clauses/parts.

Query Execution

The result of a Hibernate query can be obtained in several ways. The Hibernate query executer chooses the way the query result will be produced based on a property named `net.sf.jasperreports.hql.query.run.type`.

This property can be specified both globally as a JasperReports property (see Chapter 18) and as a property of the report/dataset (using the `<property>` element in JRXML or the `setProperty(String, String)` method). The report/dataset property value overrides the global value.

The run type can be one of the following:

- `list`: The result is fetched using `org.hibernate.Query.list()`. The result rows can be fetched all at once or in fixed-sized chunks. To enable paginated result row retrieval, the `net.sf.jasperreports.hql.query.list.page.size` configuration property should have a positive value.
- `scroll`: The result is fetched using `org.hibernate.Query.scroll()`.
- `iterate`: The result is fetched using `org.hibernate.Query.iterate()`.

The fetch size of the query can be set using the `net.sf.jasperreports.jdbc.fetch.size` configuration property at report level or globally.

However, when dealing with large amounts of data, using pagination is the most common way to present the document content. In this case, it is necessary to clear Hibernate's first-level cache after each page fetching, otherwise Hibernate will eventually cause an `OutOfMemory` error. If the Hibernate's session cache is regularly cleared, the memory trap can be avoided. Because flushing data and clearing the cache is a time-consuming process, you should use it only if really huge datasets are involved.

This is why the `net.sf.jasperreports.hql.clear.cache` property was introduced. Normally, it defaults to `false`. If set to `true`, the periodic Hibernate session cache cleanup is performed after each page fetching.

Field Mapping

A report/dataset field is mapped to a value from the Hibernate query result either by its description or its name. By default, the program uses the report field name, but the report field description property can be used instead if the `net.sf.jasperreports.hql.field.mapping.descriptions` configuration property is set to `true` either in the report template or globally.

The mappings are similar to the ones used by JavaBeans data sources (see the "JavaBeans Data Sources" section, earlier in this chapter), except that select aliases are used when queries return tuples instead of single objects.

The field mappings are resolved according to this scheme:

- If the query returns one object per row
    - If the object's type is a Hibernate entity or component type, the field mappings are resolved as property names of the entity/component. If a select alias is present, it can be used to map a field to the whole entity/component object. Otherwise, the object type is considered scalar and only one field can be mapped to its value.

- If the query returns a tuple (object array) per row, then a field mapping can be one of
    - A select alias—the field will be mapped to the value corresponding to the alias.
    - A property name prefixed by a select alias and a dot (`.`). The field will be mapped to the value of the property for the object corresponding to the alias. The type corresponding to the select alias has to be an entity or component type.

Field mappings do not yet support queries like `select new list(..)` or `select new map(..)`.

MDX Query Executer

Reporting on OLAP data is supported in JasperReports via an MDX query executer and a data source that use the Mondrian APIs (this is why often we refer to this query executer also as the Mondrian query executer). Users can create reports with MDX queries and map report fields onto the OLAP result; the engine will execute the query via Mondrian and pass the result to a data source implementation, which will be used to fill the report.

The Mondrian query executer is registered by default for queries having `MDX` or `mdx` as the language specified in the report template. You can use JasperReports configuration properties to register additional or alternative query language to query executer mappings (see the "Query Executer API" section earlier in this chapter).

Connection Parameter

The Mondrian query executer requires a single connection parameter named `MONDRIAN_CONNECTION` of type `mondrian.olap.Connection`.

When filling reports with MDX queries, the caller is required to supply a valid Mondrian connection to be used for executing the query. The connection can be obtained as follows:

```
mondrian.olap.Connection connection = ...;
parameters.put(
    JRMondrianQueryExecuterFactory.PARAMETER_MONDRIAN_CONNECTION,
    connection
    );
JasperPrint print = JasperFillManager.fillReport(report, parameters);
```

Query Parameters

MDX queries can contain placeholders for parameters of any type. When the query gets executed, each parameter placeholder will be replaced in the query string by its `toString()` value. Therefore, for MDX queries, `$P{...}` parameters are equivalent to `$P!{...}` query fragments.

Data Source

The Mondrian query executer passes the query result to a Mondrian data source, which will be used to iterate the result and map values from the result to the report fields.

The field mapping deals with mapping values from the OLAP result to the report fields. As an OLAP result has a multidimensional and hierarchical structure while a JasperReports data source has a tabular structure, mapping values to fields is not a trivial task.

A special syntax is used to specify what value should be mapped to a field. The field description is used to hold the mapping specification.

Using the mapping syntax, one can map two types of values from the OLAP result:

- Member values are names or properties of members of the result axes.
- Data/measure values are cell values from the result.

The Mondrian data source performs a traversal of the OLAP result by iterating the members of the result axes. On every step, each field is checked for whether its mapping matches the current position in the OLAP result. If so, the value is extracted from the result and set to the field.

A member mapping matches members on an axis specified either by name or index. Each element on an axis is a tuple. To match a single member in a tuple, an index or dimension name is used. If a level is specified either by depth or level name, then the specified level member is matched.

The member level can be used to map members that are parents of the current member in the dimension hierarchy. The fields, which are mapped to higher-level members, can then be used for grouping. For example, if the result cube has members of the `Store` dimension on the `Rows` axis, you can map `Rows[Store][Store Country]` to a country field and `Rows[Store][Store City]` to a city field, and use the country field to create a report group.

A member mapping yields the following value:

- If a property is specified, then the property value is retrieved from the member.
- Otherwise
  - If a level is specified, then the value is the name of the member (`mondrian.olap.Member.getName()`).
  - Otherwise, the value is the member itself (`mondrian.olap.Member` instance).

Following are some member mapping examples:

- `Rows[Store][Store State]`: Yields the `Store State` name of the `Store` dimension member on the `Rows` axis of the result.
- `Rows[Store][Store Name](Store Manager)`: Yields the `Store Manager` property of the `Store Name` level of the `Store` dimension member on the `Rows` axis.

A data mapping matches data cells corresponding to a member-level filter and fixed axis positions.

A member-level filter consists of several member-level specifications. The data mapping matches the current axis members only if for each filter entry the level of the corresponding axis member is the same as the filter level. If a member level for an axis/dimension is not present in the filter, the data mapping will match any member for the axis/dimension.

The member filter can be used to map data values aggregated at higher levels and use these values as totals instead of variables calculated by the JasperReports engine. For example, you can map a field to `Data(Rows[Store][Store Country])` to get the aggregated country total and another field to `Data(Rows[Store][Store City])` to get the city total.

Fixed positions on an axis can be specified for a data mapping. This means that the entries on that axis will not be iterated, but the fixed value will be used when retrieving the data cell for the data mapping. The positions correspond to the axes, and if there is no fixed position for an axis, ? should be used. For instance, `[?, 1, ?]` corresponds to the second entry on the `Rows` axis and the current (iterated) positions on the `Columns` and `Pages` axes.

Fixed positions can be specified either by numerical indexes or by MDX tuple names. The syntax is similar to the MDX syntax, except that all the member names need to be enclosed in brackets. If a tuple is composed of only one member, then the tuple name would be something like

```
[Store].[All Stores].[USA].[CA]
```

while for tuples composed of multiple members, the name would be something of the form

```
([Store].[All Stores].[USA].[CA],[Customers].[All Customers].[USA].[CA])
```

The names are matched against `mondrian.olap.Member.getUniqueName()`.

A data mapping yields the cell value if the data label is `Data`, and yields the cell's formatted value if the label is `FormattedData`.

Following are some data mapping examples:

- `Data`: Yields the cell value corresponding to the current axis positions; all the result axes will be iterated in this case.
- `Data([Measures].[Unit Sales],?)`: Yields the cell value corresponding to the `[Measures].[Unit Sales]` member on the `Columns` axis and the current position on the `Rows` axis; only the `Rows` axis will be iterated in this case.
- `FormattedData(Rows[Store][Store State])([Measures].[Customer Count],?)`: Yields the formatted cell value at the `Store State` level on the `Rows` axis (and corresponding to the `[Measures].[Customer Count]` member on the `Columns` axis).
- `Data(Columns[Time][Month],Rows[Store][Store Country])`: Yields the cell value for the `Month` level on the `Columns` axis and the `Store Country` level on the `Rows` axis; both the `Columns` and the `Rows` axis will be iterated.

The Mondrian data source performs a Cartesian iteration on the entries of axes that do not have fixed positions. If axis positions are not specified, then all the axes are iterated. For example, if the data mappings specify positions that look like `[?, ?, x]`, then the `Columns` and `Rows` axis entries will be iterated by first going through the `Rows` entries, and then going through the `Columns` entries for each of them.

The most common case is to iterate on only one axis. In this case, the conversion from the OLAP result to a JasperReports data source is more natural.

At an iteration step, a data source row is produced only if the maximum level of member mappings for each axis/dimension is reached by the current axis members. If the maximum level is not reached for an axis/dimension, then the matching mapping values are collected and the axis iterations continue without producing a data source row. The reason behind this logic is that the higher levels of OLAP dimensions conceptually correspond to JasperReports groups, not data source rows. Values found at the higher levels can be mapped to report fields using level specifications and member-level filters, and can be used in the report group headers or footers.

For example, suppose the data source iterates on the following entries on the `Rows` axis:

```
[Store].[All Stores].[USA]
[Store].[All Stores].[USA].[CA]
[Store].[All Stores].[USA].[CA].[Los Angeles]
[Store].[All Stores].[USA].[CA].[Sacramento]
[Store].[All Stores].[USA].[CA].[San Francisco]
```

Presuming that the maximum level of the member mappings is `[Store].[Store City]`, the first two entries of the axis would not produce a data source row, as the maximum level is not reached. Member or data values can be mapped for the country or state levels and used in group headers/footers or in the detail band.

Mapping Syntax Reference

Table 8-2 can be used as a reference for the field mapping syntax.

Table 8-2. *Field Mapping Syntax*

<table>
<tr><th>Syntax Element</th><th>Syntax Rule</th><th>Description</th></tr>
<tr><td>Mapping</td><td>Member_mapping | Cell_mapping</td><td>A field mapping is either a member mapping or cell mapping.</td></tr>
<tr><td>Member_mapping</td><td>Member [Property]</td><td>A member mapping consists of a member specification and an optional property.</td></tr>
<tr><td>Member</td><td>Axis Axis_position [Level]</td><td>A member specification consists of an axis, an axis position, and an optional level specification.</td></tr>
<tr><td>Axis</td><td>Axis_no | Axis_name</td><td>An axis is either specified by index or name.</td></tr>
<tr><td>Axis_no</td><td>"Axis(" <number> ")"</td><td>An axis is specified by number.</td></tr>
<tr><td>Axis_name</td><td>"Columns" | "Rows" | "Pages" | "Chapters" | "Sections"</td><td>An axis is specified by name.</td></tr>
<tr><td>Axis_position</td><td>"[" (<number> | <name>) "]"</td><td>An axis position is specified by either an index of the axis tuple or a dimension name.</td></tr>
<tr><td>Level</td><td>"[" (<number> | <name>) "]"</td><td>A level is specified either by a depth or by a level name.</td></tr>
<tr><td>Property</td><td>"(" <name> ")"</td><td>A property is specified by name.</td></tr>
<tr><td>Cell_mapping</td><td>Data [Member_filter] [Axis_indexes]</td><td>A cell mapping consists of a data specification, an optional member filter, and optional axis indexes.</td></tr>
<tr><td>Data</td><td>"Data" | "FormattedData"</td><td>A data specification can point to either the actual cell value or the cell's formatted value.</td></tr>
<tr><td>Member_filter</td><td>"(" Member ("," Member)* ")"</td><td>A member filter consists of one or more member specifications, separated by commas.</td></tr>
</table>

<table>
<tr><th>Syntax Element</th><th>Syntax Rule</th><th>Description</th></tr>
<tr><td>Axis_ indexes</td><td>"(" Axis_index ("," Axis_index)* ")"</td><td>Axis indexes are separated by comma. Note that the number of indexes must be the same as the number of query axes.</td></tr>
<tr><td>Axis_index</td><td>"?" | <number> | Axis_tuple | Axis_member</td><td>An axis index is either the question mark character(?, meaning all axes), a number, an axis tuple, or an axis member.</td></tr>
<tr><td>Axis_tuple</td><td>"(" Axis_member ("," Axis_member)* ")"</td><td>An axis tuple consists of a list of axis members, separated by commas.</td></tr>
<tr><td>Axis_member</td><td>"[" <name> "]" (".[" + <name> + "]")*</td><td>An axis member is an MDX member having all the names enclosed in brackets.</td></tr>
</table>

You can see a working example of the MDX query executer in the supplied /demo/samples/mondrian sample, which is part of the project distribution source files.

XMLA Query Executer

MDX queries can also be executed on remote OLAP data sources via the XML for Analysis interface. This functionality is implemented in JasperReports as a query executer.

Just like the Mondrian query executer presented in the previous section, the XMLA query executer is also mapped by default to the MDX and mdx query languages, but the Mondrian query executer takes precedence.

The dispatch between the two query executers that are mapped on the same query language is done by a special query executer implementation. It is actually the JRMdxQueryExecuterFactory class that is registered by default with the MDX and mdx query languages, and it delegates the creation of the query instances at runtime to either the JRMondrianQueryExecuterFactory or the JRXmlaQueryExecuterFactory, depending on the specific parameter values that are passed in at report-filling time.

It first checks for the JRMondrianQueryExecuterFactory.PARAMETER_MONDRIAN_CONNECTION parameter, and if found, the Mondrian query executer takes over. If this parameter is not found, it then checks for the JRXmlaQueryExecuterFactory.PARAMETER_XMLA_URL to see if the XMLA query executer can be used.

Connection Parameters

The XMLA query executer defines three connection parameters, as shown in Table 8-3.

Table 8-3. *XMLA Connection Parameters*

Name	Type	Description
XMLA_URL	java.lang.String	The XMLA/SOAP service URL
XMLA_DATASOURCE	java.lang.String	The information required to connect to the OLAP data source
XMLA_CATALOG	java.lang.String	The name of the OLAP catalog to use

The parameter names can be referred to in Java code using constants from the `JRXmlaQueryExecuterFactory` class.

Data Source

The XMLA query executer creates a data source equivalent to the one created by the Mondrian query executer explained in the previous chapter, with a few minor exceptions. This means that the result cube traversal and field mapping logic described in the previous "MDX Query Executer" section of this chapter applies for the XMLA query executer as well.

The XMLA query executer lacks some of the functionality of the Mondrian query executer, due to inherent limitations of the XML for Analysis standard. The missing features are the following:

- *Mapping report fields to custom member properties*: The Mondrian data source allows field mappings like `Rows[Store][Store Name](Store Manager)`, which yields the `Store Manager` property of the `Store Name` level of the `Store` dimension. This mapping doesn't require an explicit mention of the property in the MDX query; the user only needs to select the member and can access all its properties.

  But this does not work with XMLA; therefore, a query that could be used to retrieve custom member properties when using a Mondrian data source will not be able to do so when executed through XMLA.

  A workaround would be to use calculated members, like in the following query:

  ```
  with member [Measures].[Store Manager]
  as [Store].[Store Name].CurrentMember.Properties("Store Manager")
  select [Measures].[Store Manager] on columns ...
  ```

- *Mapping report fields to* `mondrian.olap.Member` *instances*: If a report field member mapping doesn't specify a dimension level (e.g., `Rows[Store]`), then the Mondrian data source yields the `mondrian.olap.Member` instance as field value. The report designer would use this object to retrieve additional member information that is not accessible via other mapping conventions.

  For XMLA, it is not possible to produce a complete `mondrian.olap.Member` object, hence this feature is not supported.

- *Parent member matching*: Using the Mondrian query executer, if a result axis contains, for instance, only members on the `Store Name` level of the `Store` dimension, you can still map fields to members on the `Store State` level (which is a parent of the `Store Name` level). This is implemented using the `mondrian.olap.Member.getParent()` method.

  This does not work via XMLA since the parent member information is not present in the response. The workaround is to make sure that required parent members get selected on the result axis.

EJB QL/JPA Query Executer

The EJB QL report query executer adds support for reporting on EJB 3.0 persistent entities data. For an EJB QL query in a report, the query executer will use the EJB 3.0 Java Persistence API to execute the query against an entity manager provided at runtime, and use the query result as a data source for the report.

The built-in EJB QL query executer is registered by default for queries having `EJBQL` or `ejbql` as their language. This mapping can be changed by using JasperReports properties (see the "Query Executer API" section, earlier in this chapter).

Query Execution

The EJB QL query executer contributes built-in parameters to the report:

- The entity manager to be used for executing the query
- An optional query hints map

When the report template contains an EJB QL query, you must provide a JPA entity manager at runtime; the query executer will run the query using the supplied entity manager. The entity manager is of type `javax.persistence.EntityManager` and should be provided via the `JPA_ENTITY_MANAGER` built-in parameter:

```
Map parameters = new HashMap();
javax.persistence.EntityManager entityManager = createEntityManager();
parameters.put(
    JRJpaQueryExecuterFactory.PARAMETER_JPA_ENTITY_MANAGER,
    entityManager
    );
JasperFillManager.fillReport(jasperReport, parameters);
```

The means of getting hold of an entity manager depends on the particular EJB/JPA environment and implementation.

An additional parameter named `JPA_QUERY_HINTS_MAP` allows you to specify query hints for running the query. The parameter value should be a map containing hint values mapped to hint names. The hints are set using the `javax.persistence.Query.setHint(String hintName, Object value)` method.

Hints can also be specified statically by using report properties. The query executer treats any report property starting with `net.sf.jasperreports.ejbql.query.hint.<hintName>` as a hint by interpreting the property suffix as the hint name and the property value as the hint value. Thus, if the following property is present in the report:

```
<property name="net.sf.jasperreports.ejbql.query.hint.cacheType" value="Shared"/>
```

then the `cacheType` hint having `Shared` as value will be set when running the query. Note that only hints that accept `String` values can be set using this mechanism.

A separate report property can be used to paginate the query result. This property can be used for controlling the amount of Java heap space used by the query executer while filling the report. The property can be set in the following manner:

```
<property name="net.sf.jasperreports.ejbql.query.page.size" value="500"/>
```

The results of the query will be fetched in chunks containing 500 rows.

The pagination is achieved via the `javax.persistence.Query.setMaxResults()` and `setFirstResult()` methods. Obviously, using pagination could result in performance loss. Therefore enabling it is primarily recommended when the query results are very large.

EJB QL report queries can contain parameters of any type. At runtime, the value of the parameter is directly set by using `javax.persistence.Query.setParameter(String name, Object value)`, with no other processing.

Data Source

The result of the query execution is sent to a data source implementation, which iterates over it and extracts report field values. Fields are mapped to specific values in the query result by specifying the mapping as field description or field name.

The JPA data source can handle two types of query results:

- Queries returning a single entity/bean per row
- Queries returning object tuples as rows

When the query returns a single entity/bean per row, as in

```
SELECT m FROM Movie m
```

or

```
SELECT NEW MovieDescription(m.title, m.gender) FROM Movie m
```

then the field mappings are interpreted as bean property names.

The same conventions as for JavaBeans data sources are used (see "JavaBeans Data Sources" section earlier in this chapter).

When the query returns multiple objects per row, as in

```
SELECT m.title, m.gender FROM Movie m
```

then the fields are mapped using one of the following forms:

- `COLUMN_<index>`: Maps the field to a value specified by its position in the resulting tuple. The positions start from 1.
- `COLUMN_<index>.<property>`: Maps the field to a property of a value specified by its position in the resulting tuple.

For instance, the following mappings could be used for a query returning multiple objects per row: `COLUMN_1`, `COLUMN_2`, `COLUMN_1.title`, and `COLUMN_2.movie.title`.

The EJB QL query executer and the corresponding JPA data source are used in the `/demo/samples/ejbql` sample supplied as part of the JasperReports distribution package.

Fields

The report fields represent the only way to map data from the data source into the report template and to use this data in report expressions to obtain the desired output. Listing 8-3 gives the JRXML syntax for report field declarations.

When declaring report fields, make sure that the data source you supply at report-filling time can provide values for all those fields.

For example, if you use the `net.sf.jasperreports.engine.JRResultSetDataSource` implementation when the report's SQL query is used, make sure that there is a column for each field in the result set obtained after the execution of the query. The corresponding column must bear the same name and have the same data type as the field that maps it.

Listing 8-3. *JRXML Syntax*

```
<!ELEMENT field (property*, fieldDescription?)>

<!ATTLIST field
    name CDATA #REQUIRED
    class CDATA "java.lang.String"
>

<!ELEMENT fieldDescription (#PCDATA)>
```

Following is a small example that shows the fields to declare to map the columns of a database table, called `Employees`, that has the structure shown in Table 8-4.

Table 8-4. *Employees Table Structure*

Column Name	Data Type	Length
EmployeeID	int	4
LastName	varchar	50
FirstName	varchar	50
HireDate	datetime	8

The report fields should declare the field as follows:

```
<field name="EmployeeID" class="java.lang.Integer"/>
<field name="LastName" class="java.lang.String"/>
<field name="FirstName" class="java.lang.String"/>
<field name="HireDate" class="java.util.Date"/>
```

If you declare a field without a corresponding column in the result set, an exception will be thrown at runtime. The columns in the result set produced by the execution of the SQL query that do not have corresponding fields in the report template will not affect the report-filling operations, but they also won't be accessible for display on the report.

The following subsections describe the components of a report field definition.

Field Name

The name attribute of the <field> element is mandatory. It lets you reference the field in report expressions by name.

Field Class

The second attribute for a report field specifies the class name for the field values. Its default value is java.lang.String, but it can be changed to any class available at runtime. Regardless of the type of a report field, the engine makes the appropriate cast in report expressions in which the $F{} token is used, making manual casts unnecessary.

Field Description

This additional text chunk can prove very useful when implementing a custom data source, for example. You could store in it a key, or whatever information you might need in order to retrieve the field's value from the custom data source at runtime.

By using the optional <fieldDesciption> element instead of the field name, you can easily overcome restrictions of field-naming conventions when retrieving the field values from the data source.

```
<field name="PersonName" class="java.lang.String" isForPrompting="true">
  <fieldDesciption>PERSON NAME</fieldDesciption>
</field>
```

The field description is less important than in previous versions of the library because now even the field's name accepts dots, spaces, and other special characters.

Custom Field Properties

Just like the report template and report parameters, report fields can have custom-defined properties, too. This comes in addition to the field description, which can be considered a built-in report field property. Custom properties are useful in some cases where more information or metadata needs to be associated with the report field definition. This additional information can be leveraged by query executer or data source implementations.

Sort Fields

JasperReports supports in-memory field-based data source sorting. This functionality can be used, for instance, when data sorting is required and the data source implementation does not support it (as in the case of the CSV data source).

The sorting is activated by the presence of one or more <sortField> elements in the report template. When at least one sort field is specified for the report, the original report data source (either passed directly or provided by a query executer) is passed to a JRSortableDataSource instance that fetches all the records from it, performs an in-memory sort according to the specified fields, and replaces the original data source in the report-filling process.

The JRXML syntax for <sortField> elements is given in Listing 8-4.

Listing 8-4. *JRXML Syntax*

```
<!ELEMENT sortField EMPTY>

<!ATTLIST sortField
    name CDATA #REQUIRED
    order (Ascending | Descending) "Ascending"
>
```

The sort field name should coincide with a report field name. Fields used for sorting should have types that implement `java.util.Comparable`. Sorting will be performed using the natural order for all fields except those of type `java.lang.String`, for which a collator corresponding to the report fill locale is used.

When several sort fields are specified, the sorting will be performed using the fields as sort keys in the order in which they appear in the report template.

Check the supplied `/demo/samples/csvdatasource` sample to see how in-memory data source sorting could be used.

Variables

Report variables are special objects built on top of a report expression. They can simplify the report template by isolating in one place an expression that is heavily used throughout the report template, and they can perform various calculations based on the corresponding expression.

Listing 8-5 gives the JRXML syntax for report variables.

Listing 8-5. *JRXML Syntax*

```
<!ELEMENT variable (variableExpression?, initialValueExpression?)>

<!ATTLIST variable
    name CDATA #REQUIRED
    class CDATA "java.lang.String"
    resetType (None | Report | Page | Column | Group) "Report"
    resetGroup CDATA #IMPLIED
    incrementType (None | Report | Page | Column | Group) "None"
    incrementGroup CDATA #IMPLIED
    calculation (Nothing | Count | DistinctCount | Sum | Average | Lowest
        | Highest | StandardDeviation | Variance | System | First) "Nothing"
    incrementerFactoryClass CDATA #IMPLIED
>

<!ELEMENT variableExpression (#PCDATA)>

<!ELEMENT initialValueExpression (#PCDATA)>
```

In its expression, a variable can reference other report variables, fields, or parameters. With every iteration through the data source, variables are evaluated/incremented in the same order as they are declared. Therefore, the order of variables as they appear in the report template is very important.

Variable Name

Just as for parameters and fields, the `name` attribute of the `<variable>` element is mandatory and allows referencing the variable by its declared name in report expressions.

Variable Class

The class attribute contains the name of the class to which the variable values belong. The default is `java.lang.String`, but you can declare report variables of any class as long as the class is available in the classpath, both at report-compilation time and report-filling time.

Reset Type

The value of a report variable can change with every iteration, but it can be brought back to the value returned by its initial value expression at specified times during the report-filling process. This behavior is controlled using the `resetType` attribute, which indicates when the variable should be reinitialized during the report-filling process.

There are five reset types for a variable:

- *No reset*: The variable will never be initialized using its initial value expression and will only contain values obtained by evaluating the variable's expression (`resetType="None"`).
- *Report-level reset*: The variable is initialized only once, at the beginning of the report-filling process, with the value returned by the variable's initial value expression (`resetType="Report"`).
- *Page-level reset*: The variable is reinitialized at the beginning of each new page (`resetType="Page"`).
- *Column-level reset*: The variable is reinitialized at the beginning of each new column (`resetType="Column"`).
- *Group-level reset*: The variable is reinitialized every time the group specified by the `resetGroup` attributes breaks (`resetType="Group"`).

The default value for this attribute is `resetType="Report"`.

Reset Group

If present, the `resetGroup` attribute contains the name of a report group and works only in conjunction with the `resetType` attribute, whose value must be `resetType="Group"`.

Increment Type

This property lets you choose the exact moment to increment the variable. By default, variables are incremented with each record in the data source, but in reports with multiple levels of data grouping, some variables might calculate higher-level totals and would need to be incremented only occasionally, not with every iteration through the data source.

This attribute uses the same values as the `resetType` attribute, as follows:

- *Row-level increment*: The variable is incremented with every record during the iteration through the data source (`incrementType="None"`).
- *Report-level increment*: The variable never gets incremented during the report-filling process (`incrementType="Report"`).
- *Page-level increment*: The variable is incremented with each new page (`incrementType="Page"`).
- *Column-level increment*: The variable is incremented with each new column (`incrementType="Column"`).
- *Group-level increment*: The variable is incremented every time the group specified by the `incrementGroup` attributes breaks (`incrementType="Group"`).

Increment Group

If present, the `incrementGroup` attribute contains the name of a report group. It works only in conjunction with the `incrementType` attribute, whose value must be `incrementType="Group"`.

Calculations

As mentioned, variables can perform built-in types of calculations on their corresponding expression values. The following subsections describe all the possible values for the calculation attribute of the `<variable>` element.

Calculation Nothing

This is the default calculation type that a variable performs. It means that the variable's value is recalculated with every iteration in the data source and that the value returned is obtained by simply evaluating the variable's expression.

Calculation Count

A count variable includes in the count the non-null values returned after evaluating the variable's main expression, with every iteration in the data source. Count variables must always be of a numeric type. However, they can have nonnumeric expressions as their main expression since the engine does not care about the expression type, but only counts for the non-null values returned, regardless of their type.

Only the variable's initial value expression should be numeric and compatible with the variable's type, since this value will be directly assigned to the count variable when initialized.

Calculation DistinctCount

This type of calculation works just like the Count calculation, the only difference being that it ignores repeating values and counts only for distinct non-null values.

Calculation Sum

The reporting engine can sum up the values returned by the variable's main expression if you choose this type of calculation; but make sure the variable has a numeric type. You cannot calculate the sum of a java.lang.String or java.util.Date type of report variable unless a customized variable incrementer is used, as explained in the "Incrementers" section later in this chapter.

Calculation Average

The reporting engine can also calculate the average for the series of values obtained by evaluating the variable's expression for each record in the data source. This type of calculation can be performed only for numeric variables (see the following "Incrementers" section, later in this chapter for details).

Calculation Lowest and Highest

Choose this type of calculation when you want to obtain the lowest or highest value in the series of values obtained by evaluating the variable's expression for each data source record.

Calculation StandardDeviation and Variance

In some special reports, you might want to perform more advanced types of calculations on numeric expressions. JasperReports has built-in algorithms to obtain the standard deviation and the variance for the series of values returned by evaluation of a report variable's expression.

Calculation System

This type of calculation can be chosen only when you don't want the engine to calculate any value for your variable. That means you are calculating the value for that variable yourself, almost certainly using the scriptlets functionality of JasperReports.

For this type of calculation, the only thing the engine does is to conserve the value you have calculated yourself, from one iteration in the data source to the next.

Calculation First

When using the calculation type First, the variable will keep the value obtained after the first incrementation and will not change it until the reset event occurs.

Here is a simple report variable declaration that calculates the sum for a numeric report field called Quantity:

```
<variable name="QuantitySum" class="java.lang.Double" calculation="Sum">
  <variableExpression>$F{Quantity}</variableExpression>
</variable>
```

If you want the sum of this field for each page, here's the complete variable declaration:

```
<variable name="QuantitySum"
    class="java.lang.Double" resetType="Page" calculation="Sum">
  <variableExpression>$F{Quantity}</variableExpression>
  <initialValueExpression>new Double(0)</initialValueExpression>
</variable>
```

In this example, our page sum variable will be initialized with zero at the beginning of each new page.

Incrementers

All calculations in the JasperReports engine are performed incrementally. This is obvious for variables that calculate counts, sums, or the highest and lowest value of a series, but is also true for more complex calculations like average or standard deviation. There are formulas that allow updating the average value of a series when a new element is added, so the average is updated with each iteration through the data source.

JasperReports provides a built-in set of calculations that depend on the type of the data involved. You can also create custom calculation capabilities using simple interfaces.

If a variable needs to perform a certain type of calculation on some special data, implement the `net.sf.jasperreports.engine.fill.JRIncrementer` interface and associate that implementation with a report variable that shows the JasperReports engine how to handle that custom calculation.

To associate custom types of calculations with a given report variable, set the `incrementerFactoryClass` attribute to the name of a class that implements the `net.sf.jasperreports.engine.fill.JRIncrementerFactory` interface. The factory class will be used by the engine to instantiate incrementer objects at runtime depending on the `calculation` attribute set for the variable.

Such customized calculations could be useful for making JasperReports sum up `java.lang.String` values or for teaching it how to calculate the average value of some custom-made numeric data (third-party optimized implementations of big decimal numbers, for instance).

Built-In Report Variables

The following built-in system variables are also provided in expressions.

PAGE_NUMBER

This variable's value is its current page number. At the end of the report-filling process, it will contain the total number of pages in the document. It can be used to display both the current page number and the total number of pages using a special feature of JasperReports text field elements, the `evaluationTime` attribute. You can see this happening in most of the samples. Check the `/demo/samples/jasper` sample for an example.

COLUMN_NUMBER

This variable contains the current column number. For example, on a report with three columns, the possible values are 1, 2, and 3. The variable restarts from 1 and runs up to the defined number of columns for each page in the generated document.

REPORT_COUNT

After finishing the iteration through the data source, this report variable contains the total number of records processed.

PAGE_COUNT

This variable contains the number of records that were processed when generating the current page.

COLUMN_COUNT

This variable contains the number of records that were processed when generating the current column.

GroupName_COUNT

When declaring a report group, the engine automatically creates a count variable that calculates the number of records that make up the current group (that is, the number of records processed between group ruptures).

The name of this variable is derived from the name of the group it corresponds to, suffixed with the `_COUNT` sequence. It can be used like any other report variable, in any report expression, even in the current group expression, as shown in the `BreakGroup` group of the `/demo/samples/jasper` sample).

Data Filters

Sometimes it is useful to have a way to filter out records from the data source. When SQL queries are used, the filtering is usually done through the `WHERE` clause of the query.

But when reporting data comes from a data source that is not already filtered, or when preprocessing the data would require significant overhead, JasperReports offers an easy way to eliminate unwanted records based on a `Boolean` expression.

Listing 8-6 gives the JRXML syntax for the data filter.

Listing 8-6. *JRXML Syntax*

```
<!ELEMENT filterExpression (#PCDATA)>
```

The `<filterExpression>` (if present) is evaluated immediately after moving the record pointer to the next record in the data source. The evaluation is performed using field and variable values corresponding to the new record. If the result of the evaluation is `Boolean.TRUE`, then the record gets processed by the report-filling engine. If the result is `null` or `Boolean.FALSE`, then the current record will be skipped and the data source pointer will be moved to the following record.

CHAPTER 9

Report Sections

JasperReports works with templates that are structured into multiple sections, like any traditional reporting tool. At report-filling time, the engine iterates through the virtual records of the supplied report data source and renders each report section when appropriate, depending on each section's defined behavior.

For instance, the detail section is rendered for each record in the data source. When page breaks occur, the page header and page footer sections are rendered as needed.

Sections are portions of the report template that have a specified height and width and can contain report elements like lines, rectangles, images, and text fields. These sections are filled repeatedly at report-generating time and make up the final document.

Band Content

When declaring the content and layout of a report section, in an JRXML report design, use the generic element `<band>`. Listing 9-1 shows JRXML syntax for report bands.

Listing 9-1. *JRXML Syntax*

```
<!ELEMENT band (printWhenExpression?, (break | line | rectangle | ellipse | image
| staticText | textField | subreport | pieChart | pie3DChart | barChart
| bar3DChart | xyBarChart | stackedBarChart | stackedBar3DChart| lineChart
| xyLineChart | areaChart | xyAreaChart | scatterChart | bubbleChart
| timeSeriesChart | highLowChart | candlestickChart | meterChart
| thermometerChart | multiAxisChart | stackedAreaChart | elementGroup | crosstab
| frame)*)>

<!ATTLIST band
    height NMTOKEN "0"
    isSplitAllowed (true | false) "true"
>
```

Report sections, sometimes referred to as report bands, represent a feature and functionality common to almost all reporting tools.

Band Height

The height attribute in a report band declaration specifies the height in pixels for that particular band and is very important in the overall report design.

The elements contained by a certain report band should always fit the band's dimensions; this will prevent potentially bad results when generating the reports. The engine issues a warning if it finds elements outside the band borders when compiling report designs.

Preventing Band Split

In some cases it is desirable to keep whole content of a given band in one piece and to prevent page breaks that split the band when it stretches beyond its initial specified height. To do this, use the isSplitAllowed flag, which is true by default.

Skipping Bands

All the report sections allow you to define a report expression that will be evaluated at runtime to decide if that section should be generated or skipped when producing the document.

This expression is introduced by the <printWhenExpression> tag, which is available in any <band> element of the JRXML report design and should always return a java.lang.Boolean object or null.

Main Sections

When building a report template, you must define the content and the layout of its sections. The entire structure of the report template is based on the following sections: <title>, <pageHeader>, <columnHeader>, <groupHeader>, <detail>, <groupFooter>, <columnFooter>, <pageFooter>, <lastPageFooter>, <summary>, and <background>. All report sections are optional, but of course all useful templates have at least one such section.

Listing 9-2 gives the JRXML syntax for including the main report sections.

Listing 9-2. *JRXML Syntax*

```
<!ELEMENT background (band?)>

<!ELEMENT title (band?)>

<!ELEMENT pageHeader (band?)>

<!ELEMENT columnHeader (band?)>

<!ELEMENT detail (band?)>

<!ELEMENT columnFooter (band?)>
```

```
<!ELEMENT pageFooter (band?)>

<!ELEMENT lastPageFooter (band?)>

<!ELEMENT summary (band?)>
```

So let's take a closer look at each report section and see how it behaves.

Title

This is the first section of the report. It is generated only once during the report-filling process and represents the beginning of the resulting document.

The title section precedes even the page header section. To print the page header before the title section, put the elements on the page header at the beginning of the title section as well. You can suppress the actual page header on the first page using the `<printWhenExpression>`, based on the `PAGE_NUMBER` report variable.

As described in the "Report Template Properties" section of Chapter 7, the title section can be followed by a page break if the `isTitleNewPage` attribute is set to `true`.

Page Header

This section appears at the top of each page in the generated document.

Column Header

This section appears at the top of each column in the generated document.

Detail

For each record in the data source, the engine tries to generate this section.

Column Footer

This section appears at the bottom of each column in the generated document. It never stretches downward to acquire the content of its containing text fields. Its rendering position is controlled by the `isFloatColumnFooter` flag declared at report template level.

Page Footer

This section appears at the bottom of each page in the generated document. Just like the column footer section, the page footer never stretches downwards to acquire the content of its containing text fields and always retains the declared fixed height.

Summary

This section is generated only once per report and appears at the end of the generated document, but is not necessarily the last section generated. This is because in some cases the column footer and/or page footer of the last page follows it.

As mentioned in the "Report Template Properties" section of Chapter 7, you can have the summary section start a new page of its own by setting the `isSummaryNewPage` attribute to `true`. Even if this attribute remains `false`, the summary section always starts a new page if it does not fit on the remaining space of the last page, or if the report has more than one column and it has already started a second column on the last page.

Last Page Footer

If present, this section replaces the normal page footer section, but only on the last occurrence of the page footer, which might not be the last page if the summary is present and it overflows on multiple pages or it is rendered alone on its own last page. So it behaves more like *the last* page footer than the footer of the *last page*.

Background

This is a special section that is rendered on all pages and its content placed underneath all other report sections. Normal report sections are rendered one after the other, but the background section does not interfere with the other report sections and can be used to achieve watermark effects or to create the same background for all pages.

If the main report sections described here don't meet your needs, you might consider introducing supplementary sections like group headers and group footers.

The following section shows how to group data on the report.

Data Grouping

Groups represent a flexible way to organize data on a report. A report group is represented by sequence of consecutive records in the data source that have something in common, like the value of a certain report field.

A report group has three components:

- Group expression
- Group header section
- Group footer section

The value of the associated group expression is what makes group records stick together. This value is what they have in common. When the value of the group expression changes during the iteration through the data source at report-filling time, a group rupture occurs and the corresponding `<groupFooter>` and `<groupHeader>` sections are inserted in the resulting document.

You can have as many groups as you want on a report. The order of groups declared in a report template is important because groups contain each other. One group contains the following group, and so on. When a larger group encounters a rupture, all subsequent groups are reinitialized.

■Note Data grouping works as expected only when the records in the data source are already ordered according to the group expressions used in the report.

For example, if you want to group some products by the country and city of the manufacturer, the engine expects to find the records in the data source already ordered by country and city.

If they aren't, you can expect to find records belonging to a specific country or city in different parts of the resulting document, because JasperReports does not sort the data before using it.

Listing 9-3 gives the JRXML syntax for a report group.

Listing 9-3. *JRXML Syntax*

```
<!ELEMENT group (groupExpression?, groupHeader?, groupFooter?)>

<!ATTLIST group
    name CDATA #REQUIRED
    isStartNewColumn (true | false) "false"
    isStartNewPage (true | false) "false"
    isResetPageNumber (true | false) "false"
    isReprintHeaderOnEachPage (true | false) "false"
    minHeightToStartNewPage NMTOKEN "0"
>

<!ELEMENT groupExpression (#PCDATA)>

<!ELEMENT groupHeader (band?)>

<!ELEMENT groupFooter (band?)>
```

Group Name

The name unequivocally identifies the group and can be used in other JRXML attributes when you want to refer a particular report group. The name of a group is mandatory and obeys the same naming convention that we mentioned for the report parameters, fields, and report variables.

Starting a New Page or Column When a Group Breaks

Sometimes it is useful to introduce a page or column break when a new group starts, usually because that particular group is more important and should start on a page or column of its own.

To instruct the engine to start a new page or column for a certain group instead of printing it on the remaining space at the bottom of the page or column, you must set either the `isStartNewPage` or `isStartNewColumn` attribute to `true`.

These two attributes represent one of the most common ways to control page and column breaks in a report. The other one is by using the special break element, which is explained in the "Page Breaks and Column Breaks" section of Chapter 10. In all other situations, the reporting engine introduces page breaks automatically if content overflows onto a new page or column during the report-filling process.

In some report templates, you may want to introduce page breaks on purpose when a report section is larger than one page. Using the break element would not help, as the report template, having a band larger than the page size, would not get past the report validation process. To do this, you would need to introduce special dummy groups, as explained in the FAQs section of the freely available documentation published on the JasperReports web site (`http://jasperforge.org/sf/projects/jasperreports`).

However, if you don't want to consistently introduce page or column breaks for a particular group, but prefer to do that only if the remaining space at the bottom of the page or column is too small, use the `minHeightToStartNewPage` attribute. This attribute specifies the minimum remaining vertical space that prevents the group from starting a new page of its own. It is measured in pixels.

Resetting Page Number

If required, report groups have the power to reset the built-in report variable that contains the current page number (variable `PAGE_NUMBER`). To do this, set the `isResetPageNumber` attribute to `true`.

Group Header

This section marks the start of a new group in the resulting document. It is inserted in the document every time the value of the group expression changes during the iteration through the data source.

Group Footer

Every time a report group changes, the engine adds the corresponding group footer section before starting the new group or when the report ends.

Check the provided samples like `jasper`, `datasource` or `query`, placed inside the `/demo/samples` directory of the project to see how report groups can be used.

CHAPTER 10

■ ■ ■

Report Elements

The reports you generate will be empty if you do not put some report elements in the report template. *Report elements* are displayable objects like static texts, text fields, images, lines, and rectangles that you put in your report template sections. Report elements come in two flavors:

- *Text elements*: Static texts and text fields that display dynamic content
- *Graphic elements*: Lines, rectangles, ellipses, images, and charts

The following sections provide details on these two element categories. For now, we are going to present in detail the element properties that both categories share.

Report Element Properties

When you add a report element to one of your report sections, you must specify the relative position of this element in that particular section and its size, along with other general report element properties like color, transparency, stretch behavior, and so forth.

The properties that are common to all types of report elements are grouped in the `<reportElement>` tag, which appears in the declaration of all report elements.

Listing 10-1 gives the JRXML syntax for the report element.

Listing 10-1. *JRXML Syntax*

```
<!ELEMENT reportElement (printWhenExpression?)>

<!ATTLIST reportElement
    key CDATA #IMPLIED
    style CDATA #IMPLIED
    positionType (Float | FixRelativeToTop | FixRelativeToBottom) "FixRelativeToTop"
    stretchType (NoStretch
        | RelativeToTallestObject | RelativeToBandHeight) "NoStretch"
    isPrintRepeatedValues (true | false) "true"
    mode (Opaque | Transparent) #IMPLIED
    x NMTOKEN #REQUIRED
    y NMTOKEN #REQUIRED
```

```
    width NMTOKEN #REQUIRED
    height NMTOKEN #REQUIRED
    isRemoveLineWhenBlank (true | false) "false"
    isPrintInFirstWholeBand (true | false) "false"
    isPrintWhenDetailOverflows (true | false) "false"
    printWhenGroupChanges CDATA #IMPLIED
    forecolor CDATA #IMPLIED
    backcolor CDATA #IMPLIED
>

<!ELEMENT printWhenExpression (#PCDATA)>
```

Element Key

Unlike variables and parameters, report elements are not required to have a name, because normally you do not need to obtain any individual element inside a report template. However, in some cases it is useful to be able to locate an element to alter one of its properties before using the report template.

This could be the case in an application for which the color of some elements in the report template needs to change based on user input. To locate the report elements that need to have their colors altered, the caller program could use the `getElementByKey(String)` method available at band level. A key value must be associated with the report element and it must be unique within the overall band for the lookup to work.

The `key` attribute is used as an example in the provided `/demo/samples/alterdesign` sample.

Style

Any type of report element can reference a report style definition using the `style` attribute. By doing so, all the style properties declared by the style definition that are applicable to the current element will be inherited. Style properties specified at the report element level can be used to override the inherited values.

Absolute Position

The `x` and `y` attributes of any report element are mandatory and represent the x and y coordinates, measured in pixels, that mark the absolute position of the top-left corner of the specified element within its parent report section.

Relative Position

Some report elements, such as text fields, have special properties that allow them to stretch downward to acquire all the information they have to display. Their height is calculated at runtime and may affect the neighboring elements in the same report section, especially those placed immediately below them.

The `positionType` attribute specifies the behavior that the report element will have if the layout of the report section in which it is been placed is stretched.

There are three possible values for the `positionType` attribute:

- *Floating position*: The element floats in its parent section if it is pushed downward by other elements found above it. It tries to conserve the distance between it and the neighboring elements placed immediately above it (`positionType="Float"`).
- *Fixed position relative to the top of the parent band*: The current report element simply ignores what happens to the other section elements and tries to conserve the y offset measured from the top of its parent report section (`positionType="FixRelativeToTop"`).
- *Fixed position relative to the bottom of the parent band*: If the height of the parent report section is affected by elements that stretch, the current element tries to conserve the original distance between its bottom margin and the bottom of the band (`positionType="FixRelativeToBottom"`).

A report element called `e2` will float when another report element `e1` stretches only if these three conditions are met:

```
e2 has positionType="Float"
e1.y + e1.height <= e2.y
e1.width + e2.width > max(e1.x + e1.width, e2.x + e2.width) - min(e1.x, e2.x)
```

The second and third conditions together imply that the element `e2` must be placed below the `e1`. By default, all elements have a fixed position relative to the top of the band. To see how element stretching and element floating work together, check the provided `/demo/samples/stretch` sample.

Element Size

The `width` and `height` attributes are mandatory and represent the size of the report element measured in pixels. Other element stretching settings may instruct the reporting engine to ignore the specified element height. Even in this case, the attributes remain mandatory since even when the height is calculated dynamically, the element will not be smaller than the originally specified height.

Element Color

Two attributes represent colors: `forecolor` and `backcolor`. The *fore color* is for the text of the text elements and the border of the graphic elements. The *background color* fills the background of the specified report element, if it is not transparent.

You can also use the decimal or hexadecimal representation for the desired color. The preferred way to specify colors in JRXML is using the hexadecimal representation, because it lets you control the level for each base color of the RGB system. For example, you can display a text field in red by setting its `forecolor` attribute as follows:

```
forecolor="#FF0000"
```

The equivalent using the decimal representation would be the following:

```
forecolor="16711680"
```

The default fore color is `black` and the default background color is `white`.

Element Transparency

Report elements can either be transparent or opaque, depending on the value you specify for the `mode` attribute. The default value for this attribute depends on the type of the report element. Graphic elements like rectangles and lines are opaque by default, while images are transparent. Both static texts and text fields are transparent by default, and so are the subreport elements.

Skipping Element Display

The engine can decide at runtime if it really should display a report element if you use `<printWhenExpression>`, which is available for all types of report elements.

If present, this report expression should return a `java.lang.Boolean` object or `null`. It is evaluated every time the section containing the current element is generated, in order to see whether this particular element should appear in the report or not. If the expression returns `null`, it is equivalent to returning `java.lang.Boolean.FALSE`. If the expression is missing, then the report element will get printed every time—that is, if other settings do not intervene, as you shall see shortly.

Reprinting Elements on Section Overflows

When generating a report section, the engine might be forced to start a new page or column because the remaining space at the bottom of the current page or column is not sufficient for all the section elements to fit in, probably because some elements have stretched. In such cases, you might want to reprint some of the already displayed elements on the new page or column to recreate the context in which the page/column break occurred.

To achieve this, set `isPrintWhenDetailOverflows="true"` for all report elements you want to reappear on the next page or column.

Suppressing Repeating Values Display

First, let's see what exactly a "repeating value" is. It very much depends on the type of the report element we are talking about. For text field elements, this is very intuitive. In Table 10-1, which contains names taken from an ordinary phone book, you can see that for some consecutive lines, the value of the `Family Name` column repeats itself (dummy phone numbers are used).

Table 10-1. *Sample Data with Repeating Values*

Family Name	First Name	Phone
Johnson	Adam	256.12.35
Johnson	Christine	589.54.52
Johnson	Peter	546.85.95
Johnson	Richard	125.49.56
Smith	John	469.85.45
Smith	Laura	459.86.54
Smith	Denise	884.51.25

You might want to suppress the repeating `Family Name` values and print something like that shown in Table 10-2.

Table 10-2. *Sample Data with Suppressed Repeating Values*

Family Name	First Name	Phone
Johnson	Adam	256.12.35
	Christine	589.54.52
	Peter	546.85.95
	Richard	125.49.56
Smith	John	469.85.45
	Laura	459.86.54
	Denise	884.51.25

To do that, set the following for the text field that displays the family name:

```
isPrintRepeatedValues="false"
```

The static text elements behave in the same way. As you would expect, their value always repeats and in fact never changes until the end of the report. This is why we call them static texts. So, if you set `isPrintRepeatedValues="false"` for one of your `<staticText>` elements, it is displayed only once, the first time, at the beginning of the report, and never again.

Now, what about graphic elements? An image is considered to be repeating itself if its bytes are exactly the same from one occurrence to the next. This happens only if you choose to cache your images using the `isUsingCache` attribute available in the `<image>` element and if the corresponding `<imageExpression>` returns the same value from one iteration to the next (the same file name, the same URL, etc.).

Lines and rectangles always repeat themselves because they are static elements, just like the static texts shown previously. So, when you suppress repeating values for a line or a rectangle, it is displayed only once, at the beginning of the report, and then ignored until the end of the report.

Note The `isPrintRepeatedValues` attribute works only if the corresponding `<printWhenExpression>` is missing. If it is not missing, it will always dictate whether the element should be printed, regardless of the repeating values.

If you decide to not display the repeating values for some of your report elements, you can modify this behavior by indicating the exceptional occasions in which you might want to have a particular value redisplayed during the report-generation process.

When the repeating value spans multiple pages or columns, you can redisplay this repeating value at least once for every page or column. If you set `isPrintInFirstWholeBand="true"`, then the report element will reappear in the first band of a new page or column that is not an overflow from a previous page or column. Also, if the repeating value you have suppressed spans multiple groups, you can make it reappear at the beginning of a certain report group if you specify the name of that particular group in the `printWhenGroupChanges` attribute.

Removing Blank Space

When a report element is not displayed for some reason (e.g., `<printWhenExpression>` evaluates to `Boolean.FALSE`, or a repeated value is suppressed), the area where the report element stood at design time will be left empty. This blank space also appears if a text field displays only blank characters or an empty text value. You can eliminate this unwanted blank space on the vertical axis only if certain conditions are met.

For example, say you have three successive text fields, one on top of the other, like this:

```
TextField1
TextField2
TextField3
```

If the second field has an empty string as its value or contains a repeated value that you chose to suppress, the output would look like this:

```
TextField1

TextField3
```

In order to eliminate the gap between the first text field and the third, set `isRemoveLineWhenBlank= "true"` for the second text field. The following then displays:

```
TextField1
TextField3
```

However, certain conditions must be met in order for this functionality to work. The blank space will not be removed if your second text field shares some vertical space with other report elements that are printed, even if this second text field does not print.

For example, you might have some vertical lines on the sides of your report section, like this:

```
|   TextField1   |
|                |
|   TextField3   |
```

or you might have a rectangle that draws a box around your text fields:

```
------------------
|   TextField1   |
|                |
|   TextField3   |
------------------
```

or even other text elements that are placed on the same horizontal line with your second text field:

```
Label1   TextField1
Label2
Label3   TextField3
```

In all these situations, the blank space between the first and the third text field cannot be removed because it is being used by other visible report elements.

■ **Note** The blank vertical space between elements can be removed using the `isRemoveWhenBlank` attribute only if it is not used by other elements, as explained previously.

Stretch Behavior

The `stretchType` attribute of a report element can be used to customize the stretch behavior of the element when, on the same report section, there are text fields that stretch themselves because their text content is too large for the original text field height. When stretchable text fields are present on a report section, the height of the report section itself is affected by the stretch.

A report element can respond to the modification of the report section layout in three ways:

- *Won't stretch*: The report element preserves its original specified height (`strechType="NoStretch"`).
- *Stretching relative to the parent band height*: The report element adapts its height to match the new height of the report section it is placed on, which has been affected by stretch (`stretchType="RelativeToBandHeight"`).
- *Stretching relative to the tallest element in group*: You have the possibility of grouping the elements of a report section in multiple nested groups, if you like. The only reason to group your report elements is to customize their stretch behavior. Details about how to group elements are supplied in the "Element Groups" section, later in this chapter. Report elements can be made to automatically adapt their height to fit the amount of stretch suffered by the tallest element in the group that they are part of (`stretchType="RelativeToTallestObject"`).

Text Elements

There are two kinds of text elements in JasperReports: static texts and text fields. As their names suggest, the first are text elements with fixed, static content, they do not change during the report-filling process, and they are used especially for introducing labels into the final document. Text fields, however, have an associated expression that is evaluated at runtime to produce the text content that will be displayed. Both types of text elements share some properties, and those are introduced using a `<textElement>` element. We are now going to show them in detail.

Listing 10-2 gives the JRXML syntax for text element properties.

Listing 10-2. *JRXML Syntax*

```
<!ELEMENT textElement (font?)>

<!ATTLIST textElement
    textAlignment (Left | Center | Right | Justified) #IMPLIED
    verticalAlignment (Top | Middle | Bottom) #IMPLIED
    rotation (None | Left | Right | UpsideDown) #IMPLIED
    lineSpacing (Single | 1_1_2 | Double) #IMPLIED
    isStyledText (true | false) #IMPLIED
>
```

Horizontal Alignment

To specify how the content of a text element should be aligned on the horizontal, use the `textAlignment` attribute and choose one of the four possible values `Left`, `Center`, `Right`, or `Justified`. The default horizontal alignment for text is `Left`.

Vertical Alignment

You can align text inside the element bounds on the vertical axis by using the `verticalAlignment` attribute and choosing one of the three possible values `Top`, `Middle`, or `Bottom`. By default, text elements are aligned at the top.

Rotating Text

The `rotation` attribute, available for text elements, allows changing the text direction by rotating it 90 degrees to the right or to the left, or by rotating it 180 degrees to be rendered upside down.

Line Spacing

The amount of space between consecutive lines of text can be set using the `lineSpacing` attribute:

- *Single*: The paragraph text advances normally using an offset equal to the text line height (`lineSpacing="Single"`).
- *1.5 Lines*: The offset between two consecutive text lines is 1.5 lines (`lineSpacing="1_1_2"`).
- *Double*: The space between text lines is double the height of a single text line (`lineSpacing="Double"`).

The font settings for the text elements are also part of the `<textElement>` tag. Font settings are explained in a later section.

Styled Text

The `isStyledText` attribute is a flag that indicates whether the text content of the element is pure text or has embedded styling information like colors, fonts, and so on. More about styled text functionality can be found in the "Styled Text" section later in this chapter.

Fonts and Unicode Support

Each text element present on your report can have its own font settings. Those settings can be specified using the `<font>` tag available in the `<textElement>` tag.

Since a report template usually uses only a few types of fonts shared by different text elements, there's no point forcing JRXML report template creators to specify the same font settings repeatedly for each text element. Instead, reference a report-level font declaration and adjust only some of the font settings, on the spot, if a particular text element requires it.

Report Fonts

A report font is a collection of font settings, declared at the report level, that can be reused throughout the entire report template when setting the font properties of text elements.

Note Report fonts are now deprecated and report style definitions should be used instead. Please refer to the "Styles" section of Chapter 7 for more details on styles.

Listing 10-3 gives the JRXML syntax for report fonts.

Listing 10-3. *JRXML Syntax*

```
<!ELEMENT reportFont EMPTY>

<!ATTLIST reportFont
    name CDATA #REQUIRED
    isDefault (true | false) "false"
    fontName CDATA #IMPLIED
    size NMTOKEN #IMPLIED
    isBold (true | false) #IMPLIED
    isItalic (true | false) #IMPLIED
    isUnderline (true | false) #IMPLIED
    isStrikeThrough (true | false) #IMPLIED
    pdfFontName CDATA #IMPLIED
    pdfEncoding CDATA #IMPLIED
    isPdfEmbedded (true | false) #IMPLIED
>
```

Report Font Name

The name attribute of a <reportFont> element is mandatory and must be unique, because it will be used when referencing the corresponding report font throughout the report.

Default Report Font

You can use isDefault="true" for one of your report font declarations. It marks the default base font that the reporting engine uses when dealing with text elements that do not reference a particular report font. This default font is also used by the text elements that do not have any font settings at all.

All the other report font properties are the same as those for a normal <font> element, as shown in Listing 10-4.

Listing 10-4. *JRXML Syntax*

```
<!ELEMENT font EMPTY>

<!ATTLIST font
    reportFont CDATA #IMPLIED
    fontName CDATA #IMPLIED
    size NMTOKEN #IMPLIED
    isBold (true | false) #IMPLIED
    isItalic (true | false) #IMPLIED
    isUnderline (true | false) #IMPLIED
    isStrikeThrough (true | false) #IMPLIED
    pdfFontName CDATA #IMPLIED
    pdfEncoding CDATA #IMPLIED
    isPdfEmbedded (true | false) #IMPLIED
>
```

Referencing a Report Font

When introducing the font settings for a text element of your report, you can use a report font declaration as a base for the font settings you want to obtain. The attributes of the <font> element, if present, are used only to override the same-named attributes that are present in the report font declaration referenced using the reportFont attribute.

For example, if the report contains a font like the following:

```
<reportFont
    name="Arial_Normal"
    isDefault="true"
    fontName="Arial"
    size="8"
    pdfFontName="Helvetica"
    pdfEncoding="Cp1252"
    isPdfEmbedded="false"/>
```

and you want to create a text field that has the same font settings as those in this report font, only larger, simply reference this report font using the reportFont attribute and specify the desired font size like this:

```
<textElement>
    <font reportFont="Arial_Normal" size="14"/>
</textElement>
```

When the reportFont attribute is missing, the default report font is used as the base font.

Font Name

In Java, there are two types of fonts: physical fonts and logical fonts. Physical fonts are the actual font libraries consisting of, for example, TrueType or PostScript Type 1 fonts. The physical fonts may be Arial, Time, Helvetica, Courier, or any number of other fonts, including international fonts.

Logical fonts are the five font types that have been recognized by the Java platform since version 1.0: Serif, Sans-Serif, Monospaced, Dialog, and DialogInput. These logical fonts are not actual font libraries that are installed anywhere on your system. They are merely font type names recognized by the Java runtime, which must be mapped to some physical font that is installed on your system.

In the fontName attribute of the <font> element or the <reportFont> element, you must specify the name of a physical font or the name of a logical font. You only need to make sure the font you specify really exists and is available on your system.

For more details about fonts in Java, check the Java tutorial or the JDK documentation.

Font Size

The font size is measured in points and can be specified using the size attribute.

Font Styles and Decorations

There are four Boolean attributes available in the <font> and <reportFont> elements that control the font style and/or decoration. They are isBold, isItalic, isUnderline, and isStrikeThrough. Their meanings are obvious.

PDF Font Name

When exporting reports to PDF format, the JasperReports library uses the iText library.

As the name (Portable Document Format) implies, PDF files can be viewed on various platforms and will always look the same. This is partially because in this format there is a special way of dealing with fonts.

If you want to design your reports so that they will eventually be exported to PDF, make sure you choose the appropriate PDF font settings that correspond to the Java font settings of your text elements.

The iText library knows how to deal with built-in fonts and TTF files. It recognizes the following built-in font names:

Courier

Courier-Bold

Courier-BoldOblique

Courier-Oblique

Helvetica

Helvetica-Bold

Helvetica-BoldOblique

Helvetica-Oblique

Symbol

Times-Roman

Times-Bold

Times-BoldItalic

Times-Italic

ZapfDingbats

Every time you work with fonts, the iText library requires you to specify as the font name one of the following:

- A built-in font name from the preceding list
- The name of a TTF file that it can locate on disk
- The real name of the font, provided that the TTF file containing the font has been previously registered with iText or that an alias was defined when the font was registered

The font name introduced by the previously explained `fontName` attribute is of no use when exporting to PDF. The special font attributes exist so that you can specify the font settings that the iText library expects from you.

Configuration properties (see Chapter 18) are used to register fonts with iText so that the real font name or a given alias can be used to specify the PDF font name. Font files, font collection files, and font directories can be registered with iText.

To register a font file or font collection, create a property having a key that starts with `net.sf.jasperreports.export.pdf.font` and the file location as the property value. The file location can be the name of a file to be loaded from the file system, the name of a resource present on the classpath, or a URL. You can register a font directory on the file system with iText by creating a property having a key starting with `net.sf.jasperreports.export.pdf.fontdir`. When registering a directory, all the font files in that directory are loaded, and the real font name will be accepted when working with iText fonts.

The `pdfFontName` attribute can contain one of the following values:

- The name of a built-in PDF font from the preceding list
- The name of a TTF file that can be located on disk at runtime when exporting to PDF
- The real name of a registered font
- The suffix of the key (the part after `net.sf.jasperreports.export.pdf.font`) for a font registered with iText as a font file

---

Note The report template creator must choose the right value for the `pdfFontName` attribute that corresponds exactly to the physical or logical Java font specified using the `fontName` attribute. If those two fonts (one used by the Java viewers and printers and the other used in the PDF format) do not represent the same font or do not at least look alike, you might get unexpected results when exporting to PDF format.

Additional PDF fonts can be installed on your system if you choose one of Acrobat Reader's font packs. For example, by installing the Asian font pack from Adobe on your system, you could use font names like those in Table 10-3 for the `pdfFontName` attribute.

Table 10-3. *Acrobat Reader's Asian Fonts Pack*

Language	PDF Font Name
Simplified Chinese	`STSong-Light`
Traditional Chinese	`MHei-Medium` `MSung-Light`
Japanese	`HeiseiKakuGo-W5` `HeiseiMin-W3`
Korean	`HYGoThic-Medium` `HYSMyeongJo-Medium`

For more details about how to work with fonts when generating PDF documents, check the iText library documentation.

PDF Encoding

When creating reports in different languages for export to PDF, make sure that you choose the appropriate character encoding type. For example, an encoding type widely used in Europe is `Cp1252`, also known as `LATIN1`. Examples of some other possible encoding types are shown in Table 10-4.

Table 10-4. *Encoding Short List*

Character Set	Encoding
Latin 2: Eastern Europe	Cp1250
Cyrillic	Cp1251
Greek	Cp1253
Turkish	Cp1254
Windows Baltic	Cp1257
Simplified Chinese	UniGB-UCS2-H UniGB-UCS2-V
Traditional Chinese	UniCNS-UCS2-H UniCNS-UCS2-V
Japanese	UniJIS-UCS2-H UniJIS-UCS2-V UniJIS-UCS2-HW-H UniJIS-UCS2-HW-V
Korean	UniKS-UCS2-H UniKS-UCS2-V

You can find more details about how to work with fonts and character encoding when generating PDF documents in the iText library documentation.

Embedded PDF Fonts

To use a TTF file when exporting your reports to PDF format and make sure everybody will be able to view it without problems, make sure that at least one of the following conditions are met:

- The TTF font is installed on the user's system.
- The font is embedded in the PDF document itself.

It's not easy to comply with the first condition; therefore, it is advisable to meet the second condition. You can do that by setting the `isPdfEmbedded` attribute to `true`.

For further details about how to embed fonts in PDF documents, see the iText documentation. A very useful example is available in the `/demo/samples/unicode` sample provided with the project.

Static Texts

Static texts are text elements with fixed content, which does not change during the report-filling process. They are used mostly to introduce static text labels into the generated documents.

Listing 10-5 gives the JRXML syntax for static text elements.

Listing 10-5. *JRXML Syntax*

```
<!ELEMENT staticText (reportElement, box?, textElement?, text?)>

<!ELEMENT text (#PCDATA)>
```

As you can see from the preceding syntax, besides the general element properties and the text-specific properties that we've already explained, a static text definition has only the <text> tag, which introduces the fixed text content of the static text element.

Text Fields

Unlike static text elements, which do not change their text content, text fields have an associated expression that is evaluated with every iteration in the data source to obtain the text content to be displayed.

Listing 10-6 gives the JRXML syntax for text fields.

Listing 10-6. *JRXML Syntax*

```
<!ELEMENT textField (reportElement, box?, textElement?, textFieldExpression?,
anchorNameExpression?, hyperlinkReferenceExpression?, hyperlinkAnchorExpression?,
hyperlinkPageExpression?, hyperlinkTooltipExpression?, hyperlinkParameter*)>

<!ATTLIST textField
    isStretchWithOverflow (true | false) "false"
    evaluationTime (Now | Report | Page | Column | Group | Band | Auto) "Now"
    evaluationGroup CDATA #IMPLIED
    pattern CDATA #IMPLIED
    isBlankWhenNull (true | false) #IMPLIED
    hyperlinkType CDATA "None"
    hyperlinkTarget (Self | Blank) "Self"
    bookmarkLevel NMTOKEN "0"
>

<!ELEMENT textFieldExpression (#PCDATA)>

<!ATTLIST textFieldExpression
    class (java.lang.Boolean | java.lang.Byte | java.util.Date | java.sql.Timestamp
| java.sql.Time | java.lang.Double | java.lang.Float | java.lang.Integer
| java.lang.Long | java.lang.Short | java.math.BigDecimal | java.lang.Number
| java.lang.String) "java.lang.String"
>
```

Variable-Height Text Fields

Because text fields have dynamic content, most of the time you can't anticipate the exact amount of space to provide for them. If the space you reserve for your text fields is not sufficient, the text content is truncated so that it fits into the available area.

This scenario is not always acceptable, so you can let the reporting engine calculate the amount of space required to display the entire content of the text field at runtime, and automatically adjust the size of the report element.

To do this, set `isStretchWithOverflow` to `true` for the particular text field elements you are interested in. By doing this, you'll ensure that if the specified height for the text field is not sufficient, it will automatically be increased (never decreased) in order to be able to display the entire text content.

When text fields are affected by this stretch mechanism, the entire report section to which they belong is also stretched.

Evaluating Text Fields

Normally, all report expressions are evaluated immediately, using the current values of all the parameters, fields, and variables at that particular moment. It is like making a photo of all data for every iteration in the data source during the report-filling process.

This means that at any particular time, you won't have access to values that are going to be calculated later in the report-filling process. This makes perfect sense, since all the variables are calculated step by step and reach their final value only when the iteration arrives at the end of the data source range they cover.

For example, a report variable that calculates the sum of a field for each page will not contain the expected sum until the end of the page is reached. That's because the sum is calculated step by step as the data source records are iterated through. At any particular time, the sum will only be partial, since not all the records of the specified range will have been processed.

As a consequence, you cannot display a sum on the page header, since this value will be known only when the end of the page is reached. At the beginning of the page, when generating the page header, the sum variable would contain zero, or its initial value. To address this problem, JasperReports provides a feature (the `evaluationTime` attribute) that lets you decide the exact moment you want the text field expression to be evaluated, avoiding the default behavior in which the expression is evaluated immediately when the current report section is generated.

The `evaluationTime` attribute can have one of the following values:

- *Immediate evaluation*: The text field expression is evaluated when the current band is filled (`evaluationTime="Now"`).
- *End-of-report evaluation*: The text field expression is evaluated when the end of the report is reached (`evaluationTime="Report"`).
- *End-of-page evaluation*: The text field expression is evaluated when the end of the current page is reached (`evaluationTime="Page"`).
- *End-of-column evaluation*: The text field expression is evaluated when the end of the current column is reached (`evaluationTime="Column"`).
- *End-of-group evaluation*: The text field expression is evaluated when the group specified by the `evaluationGroup` attribute changes (`evaluationTime="Group"`).
- *Auto evaluation*: Each variable participating in the text field expression is evaluated at a time corresponding to its reset type. Fields are evaluated `Now`. This evaluation type should be used for text field expressions that combine values evaluated at different times, like the percentage out of a total (`evaluationTime="Auto"`).

The default value for this attribute is Now, as already mentioned. In the example presented previously, you could easily specify evaluationTime="Page" for the text field placed in the page header section, so that it displays the value of the sum variable only when reaching the end of the current page.

Note Text fields with delayed evaluation do not stretch to acquire all the expression's content. This is because the text element height is calculated when the report section is generated, and even if the engine comes back later with the text content of the text field, the element height will not adapt, because this would ruin the already created layout.

Also, avoid using evaluation type Auto when other types suffice, as it can lead to performance loss.

Suppressing the Display of Null Values

If the text field expression returns null, your text field will display the null text in the generated document. A simple way to avoid this is to set the isBlankWhenNull attribute to true. By doing this, the text field will cease to display null and will instead display an empty string. This way nothing will appear on your document if the text field value is null.

Formatting Output

Of course, when dealing with numeric or date/time values, you can use the Java API to format the output of the text field expressions. But there is a more convenient way to do it: by using the pattern attribute available in the <textField> element.

The engine instantiates the java.text.DecimalFormat class if the text field expression returns subclasses of the java.lang.Number class, or instantiates the java.text.SimpleDataFormat if the text field expression returns java.util.Date, java.sql.Timestamp or java.sql.Time objects.

For numeric fields, the value you should supply to this attribute is the same as if you formatted the value using java.text.DecimalFormat.

For date/time fields, the value of this attribute has to be one of the following:

- A style for the date part of the value and one for the time part, separated by a comma, or one style for both the date part and the time part. A style is one of Short, Medium, Long, Full, Default (corresponding to java.text.DateFormat styles), or Hide. The formatter is constructed by calling one of the getDateTimeInstance(), getDateInstance(), or getTimeInstance() methods of java.text.DateFormat (depending on one of the date/time parts being hidden) and supplying the date/time styles and report locale.
- A pattern that can be supplied to java.text.SimpleDateFormat. Note that in this case the internationalization support is limited.

For more detail about the syntax of this pattern attribute, check the Java API documentation for the java.text.DecimalFormat and java.text.SimpleDateFormat classes.

Text Field Expression

We have already talked about the text field expression. It is introduced by the `<textFieldExpression>` element and can return values from only the limited range of classes listed following:

```
java.lang.Boolean
java.lang.Byte
java.util.Date
java.sql.Timestamp
java.sql.Time
java.lang.Double
java.lang.Float
java.lang.Integer
java.lang.Long
java.lang.Short
java.math.BigDecimal
java.lang.Number
java.lang.String
```

If the text field expression class is not specified using the class attribute, it is assumed to be `java.lang.String` by default.

Styled Text

Normally, all the text content in a text element has the style specified by the text element attributes (text fore color, text background color, font name, font size, etc.). But in some cases, users will want to highlight a few words inside a text element, usually by changing the text fore color, changing the font style using an underline, or by making it bold or italic. In such cases, the text content of that particular text element will no longer be pure text. It will be specially structured XML content that includes style information in the text itself.

All text elements have a special flag called `isStyledText`. If set to `true`, this flag indicates to the rendering engine that the content of the text element mixes style information with text to produce richer visual output.

To change the style for a portion of text inside a text element, embed that portion inside a `<style>` tag or other simple HTML tag from the following list: `<b>`, `<u>`, `<i>`, `<font>`, `<sup>`, `<sub>`, `<li>`, or `<br>`. As already mentioned, for styled text elements, the content is considered XML, and the engine tries to parse it to extract the style information at runtime. If the parsing fails for any reason, including malformed XML tags, then the engine will simply render that content as pure text, not styled text.

The XML structure of styled text is very simple and consists only of embedded `<style>` tags and simple HTML tags. Those tags can be nested on an unlimited number of levels to override certain style settings for the embedded text.

The `<style>` tag has various attributes for altering the color, font, or other style properties of the text. From the standard HTML `<font>` tag, only the `fontFace`, `color`, and `size` attributes are recognized by the JasperReports engine.

Following is the equivalent DTD structure for the XML content of a styled text element:

```
<!ELEMENT style (style*, b*, u*, i*, font*, sup*, sub*, li*, br*)*>

<!ATTLIST style
    fontName CDATA #IMPLIED
    size NMTOKEN #IMPLIED
    isBold (true | false) #IMPLIED
    isItalic (true | false) #IMPLIED
    isUnderline (true | false) #IMPLIED
    isStrikeThrough (true | false) #IMPLIED
    pdfFontName CDATA #IMPLIED
    pdfEncoding CDATA #IMPLIED
    isPdfEmbedded (true | false) #IMPLIED
    forecolor CDATA #IMPLIED
    backcolor CDATA #IMPLIED
>
<!ATTLIST font
    fontFace CDATA #IMPLIED
    color CDATA #IMPLIED
    size NMTOKEN #IMPLIED
>
```

All style attributes inside a `<style>` or `<font>` tag are optional because each individual style property is inherited from the overall text element or from the parent `<style>` tag when nested `<style>` tags are used. Special XML characters like &, <, >, ", and ' must be XML-encoded when placed inside a text field.

To see how the style text feature works in JasperReports, check the `/demo/samples/styledtext` sample provided with the project source files.

Graphic Elements

Graphic elements are the second major category of report elements. This category includes lines, rectangles, and images. They all have some properties in common, which are grouped under the attributes of the `<graphicElement>` tag.

Listing 10-7 gives the JRXML syntax for graphic elements.

Listing 10-7. *JRXML Syntax*

```
<!ELEMENT graphicElement EMPTY>

<!ATTLIST graphicElement
   stretchType (NoStretch | RelativeToTallestObject | RelativeToBandHeight) #IMPLIED
   pen (None | Thin | 1Point | 2Point | 4Point | Dotted) #IMPLIED
   fill (Solid) #IMPLIED
>
```

Stretch Behavior

In early versions of JasperReports, only graphic elements could adapt their height depending on the height of other related elements through element grouping. But now all elements have this capability, and the `stretchType` attribute has been moved to the `<reportElement>` tag. It is still present inside the `<graphicElement>` tag for JRXML backward-compatibility reasons. Details about this attribute were given at the beginning of this chapter.

Border Style

In the past, only graphic elements could have a border. Since the introduction of the "box" concept, text elements can also have border-independent settings on all four sides of the element's rectangle area. Details about box elements are given in the "Box Elements" section, later in this chapter.

To specify the type of the border around a graphic element, use the `pen` attribute. This attribute is also used for specifying the type of lines drawn using `<line>` elements or for specifying the type of the contour for `<ellipse>` elements. The color of the border comes from the `forecolor` attribute presented when describing the `<reportElement>` tag, explained earlier in this chapter.

The possible types for a graphic element border are as follows:

- *No border*: The graphic element will not display any border around it (`pen="None"`).
- *Thin border*: The border around the graphic element will be half a point thick (`pen="Thin"`).
- *One-point-thick border*: The element will have a normal, one-point-thick border (`pen="1Point"`).
- *Two-point-thick border*: The element will have a thicker border (`pen="2Point"`).
- *Four-point-thick border*: The element will have a very thick border (`pen="4Point"`).
- *Dotted border*: The border will be one point thick and made of dots (`pen="Dotted"`).

The default border around a graphic element depends on its type. Lines and rectangles have a one-point-thick border by default. Images, by default, do not display any border.

Background Fill Style

The `fill` attribute specifies the style of the background of the graphic elements. The only style currently supported is the solid fill style, which is also the default (`fill="Solid"`).

Lines

When displaying a line element, JasperReports draws one of the two diagonals of the rectangle represented by the `x`, `y`, `width`, and `height` attributes specified for this element.

Listing 10-8 gives the JRXML syntax for line elements.

Listing 10-8. *JRXML Syntax*

```
<!ELEMENT line (reportElement, graphicElement?)>

<!ATTLIST line
    direction (TopDown | BottomUp) "TopDown"
>
```

Line Direction

The `direction` attribute determines which one of the two diagonals of the rectangle should be drawn:

- `direction="TopDown"` draws a diagonal line from the top-left corner of the rectangle to the bottom-right corner.
- `direction="BottomUp"` draws a diagonal line from the bottom-left corner to the upper-right corner.

The default direction for a line is top-down.

You can draw vertical lines by specifying `width="1"` and horizontal lines by setting `height="1"`. For vertical lines, the direction is not important.

Rectangles

Rectangle elements are the simplest report elements. They share almost all their settings with most other report elements.

Listing 10-9 gives the JRXML syntax for rectangle elements.

Listing 10-9. *JRXML Syntax*

```
<!ELEMENT rectangle (reportElement, graphicElement?)>

<!ATTLIST rectangle
    radius NMTOKEN #IMPLIED
>
```

Round Rectangles

The `radius` attribute specifies the radius for the arcs used to draw the corners of the rectangle. The default value is `0`, meaning that the rectangle has normal, square corners.

Ellipses

Ellipses are the most basic graphic elements. As such, there are no supplementary settings to declare an ellipse element besides those already mentioned in the sections for the `<reportElement>` and `<graphicElement>` tags.

Listing 10-10 gives the JRXML syntax for ellipses.

Listing 10-10. *JRXML Syntax*

```
<!ELEMENT ellipse (reportElement, graphicElement?)>
```

■Note For more detailed examples of lines, rectangles, and ellipses, check the `/demo/samples/shapes` sample.

Images

The most complex graphics on a report are the images. Just as for text field elements, their content is dynamically evaluated at runtime, using a report expression.

Listing 10-11 gives the JRXML syntax for images.

Listing 10-11. *JRXML Syntax*

```
<!ELEMENT image (reportElement, box?, graphicElement?, imageExpression?,
anchorNameExpression?, hyperlinkReferenceExpression?, hyperlinkAnchorExpression?,
hyperlinkPageExpression?, hyperlinkTooltipExpression?, hyperlinkParameter*)>

<!ATTLIST image
    scaleImage (Clip | FillFrame | RetainShape) #IMPLIED
    hAlign (Left | Center | Right) #IMPLIED
    vAlign (Top | Middle | Bottom) #IMPLIED
    isUsingCache (true | false) #IMPLIED
    isLazy (true | false) "false"
    onErrorType (Error | Blank | Icon) "Error"
    evaluationTime (Now | Report | Page | Column | Group | Band | Auto) "Now"
    evaluationGroup CDATA #IMPLIED
    hyperlinkType CDATA "None"
    hyperlinkTarget (Self | Blank) "Self"
    bookmarkLevel NMTOKEN "0"
>

<!ELEMENT imageExpression (#PCDATA)>

<!ATTLIST imageExpression
    class (java.lang.String | java.io.File | java.net.URL | java.io.InputStream
| java.awt.Image | net.sf.jasperreports.engine.JRRenderable) "java.lang.String"
>
```

Scaling Images

Since images are loaded at runtime, there is no way to know their exact size when creating the report template. The dimensions of the image element specified at design time may differ from that of the actual image loaded at runtime. Therefore, you must define how the image should behave to adapt to the original image element dimensions specified in the report template. The `scaleImage` attribute allows you to do that by choosing one of its three possible values (see Figure 10-1):

- *Clipping the image*: If the actual image is larger than the image element size, it will be cut off so that it keeps its original resolution, and only the region that fits the specified size will be displayed (`scaleImage="Clip"`).
- *Forcing the image size*: If the dimensions of the actual image do not fit those specified for the image element that displays it, the image is forced to obey them and stretch itself so that it fits in the designated output area. It will be deformed if necessary (`scaleImage="FillFrame"`).
- *Keeping the image proportions*: If the actual image does not fit into the image element, it can be adapted to those dimensions while keeping its original undeformed proportions (`scaleImage="RetainShape"`).

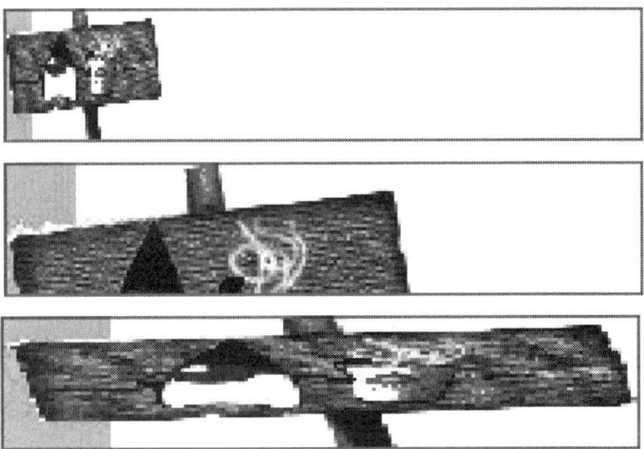

Figure 10-1. *Example of the three possible scaleImage attribute values: RetainShape (top), Clip (middle), and FillFrame (bottom)*

Image Alignment

If the scale type for the image is `Clip` or `RetainShape` and the actual image is smaller than its defined size in the report template or does not have the same proportions, the image might not occupy all the space allocated to it in the report template. In such cases, you can align the image inside its predefined report space using the `hAlign` and `vAlign` attributes, which specify the alignment of the image on the horizontal axis (`Left`, `Center`, `Right`) and the vertical axis (`Top`, `Middle`, `Bottom`). By default, images are aligned at the top and to the left inside their specified bounds.

Caching Images

All image elements have dynamic content. There are no special elements to introduce static images on the reports as there are for static text elements. However, most of the time, the images on a report are in fact static and do not necessarily come from the data source or from parameters. Usually, they are loaded from files on disk and represent logos and other static resources.

To display the same image multiple times on a report (e.g., a logo appearing on the page header), you do not need to load the image file each time. Instead, you can cache the image for better performance. When you set the `isUsingCache` attribute to `true`, the reporting engine will try to recognize previously loaded images using their specified source. For example, it will recognize an image if the image source is a file name that it has already loaded, or if it is the same URL.

This caching functionality is available for image elements whose expressions return objects of any type as the image source. The `isUsingCache` flag is set to `true` by default for images having `java.lang.String` expressions and to `false` for all other types. The key used for the cache is the value of the image source expression; key comparisons are performed using the standard equals method. As a corollary, for images having a `java.io.InputStream` source with caching enabled, the input stream is read only once, and subsequently the image will be taken from the cache.

The `isUsingCache` flag should not be set in cases when an image has a dynamic source (e.g., the image is loaded from a binary database field for each row) because the images would accumulate in the cache and the report filling would rapidly fail due to an out-of-memory error. Obviously, the flag should also not be set when a single source is used to produce different images (e.g., a URL that would return a different image each time it's accessed).

Lazy Loading Images

The `isLazy` Boolean attribute specifies whether the image should be loaded and processed during report filling or during exporting. This can be useful in cases in which the image is loaded from a URL and is not available at report-filling time, but will be available at report-export or display time. For instance, there might be a logo image that has to be loaded from a public web server to which the machine that fills the reports does not have access. However, if the reports will be rendered in HTML, the image can be loaded by the browser from the specified URL at report-display time. In such cases, the `isLazy` flag should be set to `true` (it is `false` by default) and the image expression should be of type `java.util.String`, even if the specified image location is actually a URL, a file, or a classpath resource. When lazy loading an image at fill time, the engine will no longer try to load the image from the specified `String` location but only store that location inside the generated document. The exporter class is responsible for using that `String` value to access the image at report-export time.

The `/demo/samples/images` sample contains an image element that points to the JasperReports logo, which is lazy loaded from the project's web site.

Missing Images Behavior

For various reasons, an image may be unavailable when the engine tries to load it either at report-filling or export time, especially if the image is loaded from some public URL. For this reason, you may want to customize the way the engine handles missing images during report generation. The `onErrorType` attribute available for images allows that. It can take the following values:

- *Error*: An exception is thrown if the engine cannot load the image (onErrorType="Error").
- *Blank*: Any image-loading exception is ignored and nothing will appear in the generated document (onErrorType="Blank").
- *Icon*: If the image does not load successfully, then the engine will put a small icon in the document to indicate that the actual image is missing (onErrorType="Icon").

Evaluating Images

As with text fields, you can postpone evaluating the image expression, which by default is performed immediately. This will allow you to display somewhere in the document images that will be built or chosen later in the report-filling process, due to complex algorithms, for example.

The same attributes that we talked about in the "Text Fields" section, evaluationTime and evaluationGroup, are available in the <image> element. The evaluationTime attribute can take the following values:

- *Immediate evaluation*: The image expression is evaluated when the current band is filled (evaluationTime="Now").
- *End-of-report evaluation*: The image expression is evaluated when the end of the report is reached (evaluationTime="Report").
- *End-of-page evaluation*: The image expression is evaluated when the end of the current page is reached (evaluationTime="Page").
- *End-of-column evaluation*: The image expression is evaluated when the end of the current column is reached (evaluationTime="Column").
- *End-of-group evaluation*: The image expression is evaluated when the group specified by the evaluationGroup attribute changes (evaluationTime="Group").
- *Auto evaluation*: Each variable participating in the image expression is evaluated at a time corresponding to its reset type. Fields are evaluated Now (evaluationTime="Auto").

The default value for this attribute is Now.

Image Expression

The value returned by the image expression is the source for the image to be displayed. The image expression is introduced by the <imageExpression> element and can return values from only the limited range of classes listed following:

```
java.lang.String
java.io.File
java.net.URL
java.io.InputStream
java.awt.Image
net.sf.jasperreports.engine.JRRenderable
```

■ **Note** When the image expression returns a `java.lang.String` value, the engine tries to see whether the value represents a URL from which to load the image. If it is not a valid URL representation, it tries to locate a file on disk and load the image from it, assuming that the value represents a file name. If no file is found, it finally assumes that the string value represents the location of a classpath resource and tries to load the image from there. An exception is thrown only if all these attempts fail.

If the image expression class is not specified using the class attribute, it is assumed to be `java.lang.String`, by default.

The `/demo/samples/images` sample provided with the project contains several examples of image elements.

Image Renderer

The content of an image element can come either directly from an image file like a JPG, GIF, PNG, or can be a Scalable Vector Graphics (SVG) file that is rendered using some business logic or a special graphics API like a charting or a barcode library. Either way, JasperReports treats images in a very transparent way because it relies on a special interface called `net.sf.jasperreports.engine.JRRenderable` to offer a common way to render images.

The `JRRenderer` interface has a method called `render(Graphics2D grx, Rectangle2D r)`, which gets called by the engine each time it needs to draw the image on a given device or graphic context. This approach provides the best quality for the SVG images when they must be drawn on unknown devices or zoomed into without losing sharpness.

Other methods specified in this interface can be used to obtain the native size of the actual image that the renderer wraps or the binary data for an image that must be stored in a separate file during export.

The library comes with a default implementation for the `JRRenderable` interface that wraps images that come from files or binary image data in JPG, GIF, or PNG format. The `net.sf.jasperreports.engine.JRImageRenderer` class is actually a container for this binary image data, which it uses to load a `java.awt.Image` object from it, which it then draws on the supplied `java.awt.Graphics2D` context when the engine requires it.

Image renderers are serializable because inside the generated document for each image is a renderer object kept as reference, which is serialized along with the whole `JasperPrint` object.

When a `JRImageRenderer` instance is serialized, so is the binary image data it contains. However, if the image element must be lazy loaded (see the `isLazy` attribute), then the engine will not load the binary image data at report-filling time. Rather, it stores inside the renderer only the `java.lang.String` location of the image. The actual image data is loaded only when needed for rendering at report-export or view time.

To simplify the implementation of SVG image renderers, JasperReports ships with an abstract rendered `net.sf.jasperreports.engine.JRAbstractSvgRenderer`. This implementation contains the code to produce binary image data from the SVG graphic in JPG format. This is needed when the image must be stored in separate files on disk or delivered in binary format to a consumer (like a web browser).

Charts and Graphics

The JasperReports library does not produce charts and graphics itself. This is not one of its goals. However, it can easily integrate charts, barcodes, and graphics produced by other more specialized Java libraries.

The great majority of available Java libraries that produce charts and graphics can output to image files or in-memory Java image objects. This is why it shouldn't be hard to put a chart or a graphic generated by one of those libraries into a JasperReports document using a normal image element, as described in the previous "Images" section of this chapter.

You can see this working in the `jfreechart`, `jcharts`, and `barbecue` samples, which are found in the `/demo/samples` directory of the project. The last one shows how barcodes can be rendered using the Barbecue library.

To simplify the integration of charts inside reports, a specialized `<chart>` element was added to JasperReports. Built-in support for charts is explained in Chapter 13.

Box Elements

Text elements, images, and charts are considered "box elements" because you can surround them by a border that's customizable on each side. When defining the border around such a box element, the user can control the width, style, and color of each of the four sides of the element, as well as the padding (the amount of blank space to reserve between the border of the element and its actual content).

Listing 10-12 gives the JRXML syntax for box elements.

Listing 10-12. *JRXML Syntax*

```
<!ELEMENT box EMPTY>

<!ATTLIST box
    border (None | Thin | 1Point | 2Point | 4Point | Dotted) #IMPLIED
    borderColor CDATA #IMPLIED
    padding NMTOKEN #IMPLIED
    topBorder (None | Thin | 1Point | 2Point | 4Point | Dotted) #IMPLIED
    topBorderColor CDATA #IMPLIED
    topPadding NMTOKEN #IMPLIED
    leftBorder (None | Thin | 1Point | 2Point | 4Point | Dotted) #IMPLIED
    leftBorderColor CDATA #IMPLIED
    leftPadding NMTOKEN #IMPLIED
    bottomBorder (None | Thin | 1Point | 2Point | 4Point | Dotted) #IMPLIED
    bottomBorderColor CDATA #IMPLIED
    bottomPadding NMTOKEN #IMPLIED
    rightBorder (None | Thin | 1Point | 2Point | 4Point | Dotted) #IMPLIED
    rightBorderColor CDATA #IMPLIED
    rightPadding NMTOKEN #IMPLIED
>
```

Border Style

If the border has the same style on all four sides of the element, then the `border` attribute should be used. This can be set to one of six possible values, which are the same as the ones used for the `pen` attribute available for graphic elements:

- *No border*: The graphic element will not display a border (`border="None"`).
- *Thin border*: The border around the graphic element will be half a point thick (`border="Thin"`).
- *One-point-thick border*: The element will have a normal, one-point-thick border (`pen="1Point"`).
- *Two-point-thick border*: The element will have a thicker border (`pen="2Point"`).
- *Four-point-thick border*: The element will have a very thick border (`pen="4Point"`).
- *Dotted border*: The border will be one point thick and made of dots (`border ="Dotted"`).

The attributes for specifying the border style for each side of the box are `topBorder`, `leftBorder`, `bottomBorder`, and `rightBorder`. These can be used for overriding the border style specified by the border attribute mentioned previously.

Border Color

If the border color is the same for all four sides of the box, the `borderColor` attribute can be used. If the border color must be overridden for a specific box side, then one or more of the following attributes can be set: `topBorderColor`, `leftBorderColor`, `bottomBorderColor` and `rightBorderColor`.

Box Padding

The amount of space to be left blank as margins within the bounds of a box element can be controlled using either the `padding` attribute (providing the same amount of padding on all four sides) or the individual attributes for each side: `topPadding`, `leftPadding`, `bottomPadding`, and `rightPadding`.

Hyperlinks, Anchors, and Bookmarks

JasperReports allows you to create drill-down reports, which introduce tables of contents in your documents or redirect viewers to external documents using special report elements called *hyperlinks*.

When the user clicks a hyperlink, he or she is redirected to a local destination within the current document or to an external resource. Hyperlinks are not the only actors in this viewer-redirecting scenario. You also need a way to specify the possible hyperlink destinations in a document. These local destinations are called *anchors*.

There are no special report elements that introduce hyperlinks or anchors in a report template, but rather special settings that make a usual report element a hyperlink and/or an anchor.

In JasperReports, only text field, image, and chart elements can be hyperlinks or anchors. This is because all these types of elements offer special settings that allow you to specify the hyperlink reference to which the hyperlink will point to or the name of the local anchor. Note that a particular text field or image can be both anchor and hyperlink at the same time.

Listing 10-13 gives the JRXML syntax for hyperlinks, anchors, and bookmarks.

Listing 10-13. *JRXML Syntax*

```
<!ELEMENT anchorNameExpression (#PCDATA)>

<!ELEMENT hyperlinkReferenceExpression (#PCDATA)>

<!ELEMENT hyperlinkAnchorExpression (#PCDATA)>

<!ELEMENT hyperlinkPageExpression (#PCDATA)>

<!ELEMENT hyperlinkTooltipExpression (#PCDATA)>

<!ELEMENT hyperlinkParameter (hyperlinkParameterExpression)>
<!ATTLIST hyperlinkParameter
    name CDATA #REQUIRED
>

<!ELEMENT hyperlinkParameterExpression (#PCDATA)>
<!ATTLIST hyperlinkParameterExpression
    class CDATA "java.lang.String"
>
```

Standard Hyperlinks

There are five standard types of hyperlinks supported by JasperReports by default. These are described in the following subsections.

Hyperlink Type

In Listings 10-6 and 10-11, in which the JRXML syntax for text field elements and image elements were respectively given, an attribute called `hyperlinkType` was mentioned. This attribute can hold any text value, but by default, the engine recognizes the following standard hyperlink types:

- *No hyperlink*: By default, neither the text fields nor the images represent hyperlinks, even if the special hyperlink expressions are present (`hyperlinkType="None"`).
- *External reference*: The current hyperlink points to an external resource specified by the corresponding `<hyperlinkReferenceExpression>` element, usually a URL (`hyperlinkType="Reference"`).
- *Local anchor*: The current hyperlink points to a local anchor specified by the corresponding `<hyperlinkAnchorExpression>` element (`hyperlinkType="LocalAnchor"`).

- *Local page*: The current hyperlink points to a one-based page index within the current document specified by the corresponding `<hyperlinkPageExpression>` element (`hyperlinkType="LocalPage"`).
- *Remote anchor*: The current hyperlink points to an anchor specified by the `<hyperlinkAnchorExpression>` element within an external document indicated by the corresponding `<hyperlinkReferenceExpression>` element (`hyperlinkType="RemoteAnchor"`).
- *Remote page*: The current hyperlink points to a one-based page index specified by the `<hyperlinkPageExpression>` element, within an external document indicated by the corresponding `<hyperlinkReferenceExpression>` element (`hyperlinkType="RemotePage"`).

Any `hyperlinkType` value not in the preceding list is considered a custom hyperlink type. More details about those are given in the "Custom Hyperlinks" section, which follows.

Hyperlink Expressions

Depending on the standard hyperlink type specified, one or two of the following expressions are evaluated and used to build the reference to which the hyperlink element will point:

```
<hyperlinkReferenceExpression>
<hyperlinkAnchorExpression>
<hyperlinkPageExpression>
```

Note that the first two should always return `java.lang.String` and the third should return `java.lang.Integer` values.

A special sample is provided in the `/demo/samples/hyperlink` directory of the projects, which shows how to use this type of report element.

Hyperlink Target

All hyperlink elements, like text fields, images, and charts, also expose an attribute called `hyperlinkTarget`. Its purpose is to help customize the behavior of the specified link when it is clicked in the viewer.

Currently, there are only two possible values for this attribute:

- *Self*: The document to which the hyperlink points will be opened in the current viewer window (`hyperlinkTarget="Self"`).
- *Blank*: The document to which the hyperlink points will be opened in a new viewer window (`hyperlinkTarget="Blank"`).

If not specified, the hyperlink target is `Self` by default.

Hyperlink Tooltips

The hyperlink element can have a tooltip, which is controlled by the `<hyperlinkTooltipExpression>` tag. The type of the expression should be `java.lang.String`. The tooltip expression will be evaluated along with the hyperlink and the result will be saved in the generated document.

The built-in JasperReports viewer and the HTML exporter will honor the hyperlink tooltip and display it while the user views the report.

Custom Hyperlinks

In addition to the standard hyperlink types, users can define hyperlinks having custom types. A custom-typed hyperlink can have arbitrary parameters and is meant to be processed by a hyperlink handler registered while exporting the report.

When a hyperlink is declared as having a type other than the built-in types, the hyperlink is considered of custom type and the user is expected to provide handlers to process the hyperlink when the report is exported.

Arbitrary hyperlink parameters can be added to a custom hyperlink using the `<hyperlinkParameter>` tag. These parameters are made available to the custom hyperlink handler so that it can generate a final hyperlink depending on the parameter values.

Hyperlink parameter expressions are evaluated along with the hyperlink, and the results are kept in the generated hyperlink object as parameter values.

When exporting the report to other formats such as HTML or PDF, the user can set a factory of hyperlink handlers using the `HYPERLINK_PRODUCER_FACTORY` export parameter. A factory is an implementation of `net.sf.jasperreports.engine.export.JRHyperlinkProducerFactory`, which is responsible for creating a hyperlink handler for a custom hyperlink type. This hyperlink handler created by the factory is a `net.sf.jasperreports.engine.export.JRHyperlinkProducer` instance, and it is used for generating a hyperlink reference in the export document by assembling hyperlink parameters and other information supplied at export time.

To handle custom hyperlinks in the built-in Swing viewer, you need to register a hyperlink listener by calling `addHyperlinkListener(listener)` on the `net.sf.jasperreports.view.JRViewer` component. The listener is an implementation of the `net.sf.jasperreports.view.JRHyperlinkListener` interface. When a report hyperlink gets clicked, the listener queries the hyperlink type and performs the desired actions.

Anchors

If present in a text field or image element declaration, the `<anchorNameExpression>` tag transforms that particular text field or image into a local anchor of the resulting document, to which hyperlinks can point. The anchor will bear the name returned after evaluation of the anchor name expression, which should always return `java.lang.String` values.

Bookmarks

Some of the document formats, such as PDF, have built-in support for tables of contents and bookmarks. To allow you to make use of this, JasperReports lets you transform anchors into document bookmarks. To be used as bookmarks, anchors should have an indentation level set. To do this, set a positive integer value for the `bookmarkLevel` attribute available for all hyperlink elements in JasperReports.

For more details about how to use hyperlink anchors as document bookmarks, see the supplied `/demo/samples/datasource` sample, which contains a table of contents when exported to PDF format.

Element Groups

Report elements placed in any report section can be arranged in multiple nested groups. The only reason for grouping your elements is to customize the stretch behavior of the report elements, as explained at the beginning of this chapter.

One possible value of the stretchType attribute, available for all report elements, is RelativeToTallestObject. If you choose this option, the engine tries to identify the object from the same group as the current graphic element that has suffered the biggest amount of stretch. It will then adapt the height of the current report element to the height of this tallest element of the group.

However, for this to work, you must group your elements. To do this, use the <elementGroup> and </elementGroup> tags to mark the elements that are part of the same group.

Listing 10-14 gives the JRXML syntax for element groups.

Listing 10-14. *JRXML Syntax*

```
<!ELEMENT elementGroup (break | line | rectangle | ellipse | image | staticText
| textField | subreport | pieChart | pie3DChart | barChart | bar3DChart | xyBarChart
| stackedBarChart | stackedBar3DChart | lineChart | xyLineChart | areaChart
| xyAreaChart | scatterChart | bubbleChart | timeSeriesChart | highLowChart
| candlestickChart | meterChart | thermometerChart | multiAxisChart
| stackedAreaChart | elementGroup | crosstab | frame)*>
```

Element groups can contain other nested element groups, and there is no limit on the number of the nested element groups.

Report sections are element groups themselves, so all report elements placed directly in a containing band are part of the same default element group, which is the band itself. As such, for these report elements, stretchType="RelativeToTallestObject" and stretchType= "RelativeToBandHeight" have the same effect.

Check the /demo/samples/stretch sample to see how element grouping works.

Frames

A frame is a report element that behaves like an element container. It is like a rectangle that can contain other report elements. Frames can be nested into one another to any depth.

Listing 10-15 gives the JRXML syntax for frames.

Listing 10-15. *JRXML Syntax*

```
<!ELEMENT frame (reportElement, box?, (break | line | rectangle | ellipse | image
| staticText | textField | subreport | pieChart | pie3DChart | barChart | bar3DChart
| xyBarChart | stackedBarChart | stackedBar3DChart| lineChart | xyLineChart
| areaChart | xyAreaChart | scatterChart | bubbleChart | timeSeriesChart
| highLowChart | candlestickChart | meterChart | thermometerChart
| multiAxisChart | stackedAreaChart | elementGroup | crosstab | frame)*)>
```

Frames have a background and a border, and they stretch to accommodate their content. They are usually helpful when a common background and/or common border must be put around a group of elements. The coordinates (x and y properties) and the positionType and stretchType properties of an element placed inside a frame are all relative to the frame, instead of the parent band.

Page Breaks and Column Breaks

A special break element was added to the list of elements that can be placed inside a band. This is used for introducing a page break or column break at a specified position within the band.

Listing 10-16 gives the JRXML syntax for page and column breaks.

Listing 10-16. *JRXML Syntax*

```
<!ELEMENT break (reportElement)>

<!ATTLIST break
    type (Page | Column) "Page"
>
```

In many ways, this break element behaves like any other normal element placed in a band. For instance, it can be conditionally displayed using <printWhenExpression>, and it can float within the band if positionType="Float" is used. Other common element properties like colors and styles do not make any sense for this kind of element, because it behaves like an invisible horizontal line that crosses the whole parent band and indicates the y position where a page break or column break should occur when the band content is rendered during the report-filling process.

Whether a page break or a column break should be introduced is specified using the type attribute available for this element. By default, page breaks are created.

CHAPTER 11

Subreports

Subreports are an important feature of a report-generating tool. They enable you to create more complex reports and simplify the design work. Subreports are very useful when creating master-detail reports or when the structure of a single report is not sufficient to describe the complexity of the desired output document.

Subreport Overview

A subreport is in fact a normal report that has been incorporated into another report. You can overlap subreports or make a subreport that contains other subreports, up to any level of nesting. Subreports are compiled and filled just like normal reports. Any report template can be used as a subreport when incorporated into another report template, without anything inside it having to change.

Listing 11-1 gives the details on using the `<subreport>` element when introducing subreports into master reports.

Listing 11-1. *JRXML Syntax*

```
<!ELEMENT subreport (reportElement, parametersMapExpression?, subreportParameter*,
(connectionExpression | dataSourceExpression)?, returnValue*, subreportExpression?)>
<!ATTLIST subreport
    isUsingCache (true | false) #IMPLIED
>
<!ELEMENT parametersMapExpression (#PCDATA)>
<!ELEMENT subreportParameter (subreportParameterExpression?)>
<!ATTLIST subreportParameter
    name CDATA #REQUIRED
>
<!ELEMENT subreportParameterExpression (#PCDATA)>

<!ELEMENT returnValue EMPTY>
<!ATTLIST returnValue
    subreportVariable CDATA #IMPLIED
    toVariable CDATA #IMPLIED
```

```
    calculation (Nothing | Count | DistinctCount | Sum | Average | Lowest | Highest
        | StandardDeviation | Variance) "Nothing"
    incrementerFactoryClass CDATA #IMPLIED
>

<!ELEMENT connectionExpression (#PCDATA)>
<!ELEMENT dataSourceExpression (#PCDATA)>
<!ELEMENT subreportExpression (#PCDATA)>
<!ATTLIST subreportExpression
    class (java.lang.String | java.io.File | java.net.URL | java.io.InputStream
| net.sf.jasperreports.engine.JasperReport | dori.jasper.engine.JasperReport)
"java.lang.String"
>
```

Subreport Expression

Just like normal report templates, subreport templates are in fact `net.sf.jasperreports.engine.JasperReport` objects, which are obtained after compiling a `net.sf.jasperreports.engine.design.JasperDesign` object, as described in the "Compiling Report Templates" section of Chapter 2.

We have shown that text field elements have an expression that is evaluated to obtain the text content to display. Image elements have an expression representing the source of the image to display. In the same way, subreport elements have an expression that is evaluated at runtime to obtain the source of the `net.sf.jasperreports.engine.JasperReport` object to load.

The so-called subreport expression is introduced by the `<subreportExpression>` element and can return values from the following classes:

```
java.lang.String
java.io.File
java.net.URL
java.io.InputStream
net.sf.jasperreports.engine.JasperReport
```

■ **Note** When the subreport expression returns a `java.lang.String` value, the engine tries to see whether the value represents a URL from which to load the subreport template object. If the value is not a valid URL representation, then the engine will try to locate a file on disk and load the subreport template from it, assuming that the value represents a file name. If no file is found, it will finally assume that the string value represents the location of a classpath resource and will try to load the subreport template from there. Only if all those fail will an exception be thrown.

If the subreport expression class is not specified using the class attribute, it is assumed to be `java.lang.String` by default.

Caching Subreports

A subreport element can load different subreport templates with every evaluation, giving you great flexibility in shaping your documents.

However, most of the time, the subreport elements on a report are in fact static and their sources do not necessarily change with each new evaluation of the subreport expression. Usually, the subreport templates are loaded from fixed locations: files on disk or static URLs. If the same subreport template is filled multiple times on a report, there is no point in loading the subreport template object from the source file every time you fill it with data. To avoid this, you can instruct the reporting engine to cache the subreport template object. This way, you make sure that the subreport template is loaded from disk or from its particular location only once, after which it will be reused only when it must be filled.

If you set the `isUsingCache` attribute to `true`, the reporting engine will try to recognize previously loaded subreport template objects, using their specified source. For example, it will recognize a subreport object if its source is a file name that it has already loaded, or if it is the same URL.

This caching functionality is available only for subreport elements that have expressions returning `java.lang.String` objects as the subreport template source, representing file names, URLs, or classpath resources. That's because the engine uses the subreport source string as the key to recognize that it is the same subreport template that it has cached.

Subreport Parameters

Since subreports are normal reports themselves, they are compiled and filled just like other reports. This means that they also require a data source from which to get the data when they are filled. They can also rely on parameters for additional information to use when being filled.

There are two ways to supply parameter values to a subreport.

You can supply a map containing the parameter values, as when filling a normal report with data, using one of the `fillReportXXX()` methods exposed by the `JasperFillManager` class (see Chapter 3).

To do this, use the `<parametersMapExpression>` element, which introduces the expression that will be evaluated to obtain the specified parameters map. This expression should always return a `java.util.Map` object in which the keys are the parameter names.

In addition to (or instead of) supplying the parameter values in a map, you can supply the parameter values individually, one by one, using a `<subreportParameter>` element for each relevant parameter. To do this, specify the name of the corresponding parameter using the mandatory `name` attribute and provide an expression that will be evaluated at runtime to obtain the value for that particular parameter, the value that will be supplied to the subreport-filling routines.

Note that you can use both ways to provide subreport parameter values simultaneously. When this happens, the parameter values specified individually, using the `<subreportParameter>` element, override the parameter values present in the parameters map that correspond to the same subreport parameter. If the map does not contain corresponding parameter values already, the individually specified parameter values are added to the map.

■ **Caution** When you supply the subreport parameter values, be aware that the reporting engine will affect the `java.util.Map` object it receives, adding the built-in report parameter values that correspond to the subreport. This map is also affected by the individually specified subreport parameter values, as already explained.

To avoid altering the original `java.util.Map` object that you send, wrap it in a different map before supplying it to the subreport-filling process, as follows:

```
new HashMap(myOriginalMap)
```

This way, your original map object remains unaffected and modifications are made to the wrapping map object.

This is especially useful when you want to supply to your subreport the same set of parameters that the master report has received and you are using the built-in `REPORT_PARAMETERS_MAP` report parameter of the master report. However, you don't want to affect the value of this built-in parameter, so wrap it as follows:

```
<parametersMapExpression>
    new HashMap($P{REPORT_PARAMETERS_MAP})
</parametersMapExpression>
```

Subreport Data Source

Subreports require a data source in order to generate their content, just like normal reports.

In Chapter 3, we demonstrated that when filling a report, you must supply either a data source object or a connection object, depending on the report type.

Subreports behave in the same way and expect to receive the same kind of input when they are being filled. You can supply to your subreport either a data source using the `<dataSourceExpression>` element or a JDBC connection for the engine to execute the subreport's internal SQL query using the `<connectionExpression>` element. These two XML elements cannot both be present at the same time in a `<subreport>` element declaration. This is because you cannot supply both a data source and a connection for your subreport. You must decide on one of them and stick to it.

The report engine expects that the data source expression will return a `net.sf.jasperreports.engine.JRDataSource` object or that the connection expression will return a `java.sql.Connnection` object—whichever is present.

To see how subreports work, check the `/demo/samples/subreport` sample provided with the project distribution.

Returning Values from Subreports

Values calculated by a subreport can be returned to the parent report. More specifically, after a subreport is filled, values of the subreport variables can be either copied or accumulated (using an incrementer) to variables of the caller report.

The <returnValue> element is used inside <subreport> to specify values to be returned from the subreport. Listing 11-2 gives the structure of the <returnValue> element.

Listing 11-2. *JRXML Syntax*

```
<!ELEMENT returnValue EMPTY>

<!ATTLIST returnValue
    subreportVariable CDATA #IMPLIED
    toVariable CDATA #IMPLIED
    calculation (Nothing | Count | DistinctCount | Sum | Average | Lowest | Highest
        | StandardDeviation | Variance | First) "Nothing"
    incrementerFactoryClass CDATA #IMPLIED
>
```

Subreport Variable

The subreportVariable attribute specifies the name of the subreport variable whose value is to be returned. At fill time, the name is checked to ensure it is an existing variable name of the report specified by the subreport expression.

Master Report Variable

The toVariable attribute specifies the name of the parent report variable whose value is to be copied/incremented with the value from the subreport. The name is checked at compile time to ensure it is an existing variable name of the master report. At fill time, the system checks that the types of the subreport and master variables are compatible.

Using Returned Values

A value returned from a subreport can simply be copied into the target master report variable, or it can be subject to a certain type of calculation made on the variable. The type of the operation performed with the returned value is specified by the calculation attribute, which works like the homonym attribute of the <variable> element (see the "Calculations" section of Chapter 8). The default value is Nothing, which means that the value returned from the subreport will be simply copied into the master report variable.

Custom Incrementers

Just as for report variables, the engine lets users customize how they want the returned subreport values handled. The incrementerFactoryClass attribute specifies the factory class for creating the incrementer instance. The attribute is equivalent to the same attribute of the <variable> element (see the "Incrementers" section of Chapter 8).

A variable of the master report used when returning values from subreports should be declared with System calculation because its value is not calculated by the main calculation engine. The variable could declare a reset type, for example, when the sum of a subreport total is to be calculated per one of the master's groups. The same value can be returned more than once from a subreport, for example, if different calculations are required.

Note that the value from the subreport is not returned on a column or page break, but only when the subreport filling is done. Also note that the calculation is a two-level process—that is, if the subreport computes a total average and the master accumulates values from the subreports using calculated averages, then the master result will be the average of the subreport averages, not the average of the combined subreport records.

The `/demo/samples/subreport` sample contains two examples of values returned from subreports.

Subreport Runners

By default, JasperReports uses multiple threads to render subreports. There is a separate thread for the master report and one thread for each subreport element found in the report template hierarchy. Each of these threads deals with the filling of its associated report template, which is either a master report or an embedded subreport. Even though multiple threads are involved when subreports are present, those threads do not actually run simultaneously; rather, they pass the control from one another at specific moments, usually when page breaks occur. At any one moment, there is only one report or subreport-filling thread in execution, the others being in wait state.

Using multiple threads was the easiest way to add subreporting functionality in JasperReports. It allowed the reuse of the existing report-filling logic. However, while initially easy to implement, the solution proved to have some drawbacks due to the heavy use of threads. One of the most important limitations was that J2EE containers discourage any use of threads. Also, some operating systems manage threads poorly, which resulted in decreased performance and heavy memory usage.

There was no alternate solution to this for a long time, but then one was found in a concept called *Java continuations*. For those not familiar with continuations, I'll quote Paul Graham's *On Lisp*:

> *A continuation is a program frozen in action: a single functional object containing the state of a computation. When the object is evaluated, the stored computation is restarted where it left off. In solving certain types of problems it can be a great help to be able to save the state of a program and restart it later. In multiprocessing, for example, a continuation conveniently represents a suspended process. In nondeterministic search programs, a continuation can represent a node in the search tree.*[1]

This seemed to be exactly the way JasperReports used threads to render subreports, and Java continuations proved to be the perfect solution to replace them. From among several third-partly libraries implementing this concept that were available at the time, JasperReports proved to work well with Jakarta Commons Javaflow (still a sandbox project at the time of this writing).

---

1. Paul Graham, *On Lisp* (Upper Saddle River, NJ: Prentice Hall, 1993).

In order to avoid breaking any existing functionality and also allow users to turn off multithreading when working with subreports in JasperReports, the solution was to isolate subreport-filling logic into a separate abstract class called `net.sf.jasperreports.engine.fill.JRSubreportRunnable`, which would have two interchangeable implementations:

- `net.sf.jasperreports.engine.fill.JRThreadSubreportRunner`: The initial thread-based implementation
- `net.sf.jasperreports.engine.fill.JRContinuationSubreportRunner`: A Javaflow-based implementation

Switching between the preceding subreport runner implementation is not done through direct instantiation, but rather through a configuration property called `net.sf.jasperreports.subreport.runner.factory`. This configuration property should point to a `net.sf.jasperreports.engine.fill.JRSubreportRunnerFactory` implementation able to produce the needed `JRSubreportRunnable` objects at runtime. That could be one of the following two:

- `net.sf.jasperreports.engine.fill.JRContinuationSubreportRunnerFactory`
- `net.sf.jasperreports.engine.fill.JRThreadSubreportRunnerFactory`

The default value for the factory configuration property is `JRThreadSubreportRunnerFactory`, for backward-compatibility reasons.

Note A special JasperReports JAR file built using Javaflow byte code instrumentation is available for download with each JasperReports release and should be used when Java Continuations support during subreport filling is needed. In such cases, the Jakarta Commons Javaflow library is required; it can be found in the `/lib` directory of the JasperReports project distribution package.

CHAPTER 12

■ ■ ■

Datasets

A *dataset* is a concept that lies somewhere between a data source and a subreport. Datasets allow the engine to iterate through some virtual records, just as data sources do, but they also enable calculations and data grouping during this iteration using variables and groups. Because dataset declarations contain parameters, fields, variables, and groups, they closely resemble subreports, but they completely lack any visual content (i.e., they have no sections or layout information at the dataset level).

Datasets are useful for chart and crosstab generation when you need to iterate through data that is not the main report data source itself, in order to gather data for the chart or perform data bucketing for the crosstab. Before datasets, the use of subreports was the only way to iterate through virtual records that were nested collections of virtual records rather than part of the current report data source. However, subreports come with unwanted visual settings and tend to complicate layout and report template structure.

Main Dataset

The report data source, along with the parameters, fields, variables, and groups declared at the report level, represent the building blocks of the *main dataset* for the report. All report templates implicitly declare and use this main dataset.

The main dataset is responsible for iterating through the data source records, calculating variables, filtering out records, and estimating group breaks during the report-filling process.

Subdatasets

User-defined datasets are declared in JRXML using the `<subDataset>` tag, as shown in the Listing 12-1.

Listing 12-1. *JRXML Syntax*

```
<!ELEMENT subDataset (property*, parameter*, queryString?, field*, sortField*,
variable*, filterExpression?, group*)>

<!ATTLIST subDataset
    name CDATA #REQUIRED
    scriptletClass CDATA #IMPLIED
```

```
    resourceBundle CDATA #IMPLIED
    whenResourceMissingType (Null | Empty | Key | Error) "Null"
>
```

The engine does not necessarily use a declared dataset. Datasets are instantiated and iterate through the supplied data source to calculate dataset variable values only if they are referenced by a chart or crosstab *dataset run*.

Just like subreports, datasets, when instantiated, expect to receive parameter values and a data source to iterate through. As a convenience, datasets can have an associated SQL query that is executed by the engine if a `java.sql.Connection` object is supplied to them instead of the usual data source.

Datasets can also have scriptlets associated with them to allow making callbacks to user-defined business logic during the dataset iteration, if further data manipulation is needed.

Dataset Runs

Once a dataset is declared inside a report template, it can be used only if it's actually referenced by a chart or crosstab. Simply declaring a dataset at the report level does not have any effect.

When a dataset is referenced by a chart or crosstab, a dataset run is instantiated, meaning the dataset runs through the supplied data source performing all the variable calculations and required data grouping (see Listing 12-2).

Listing 12-2. *JRXML Syntax*

```
<!ELEMENT datasetRun (parametersMapExpression?, datasetParameter*,
(connectionExpression | dataSourceExpression)?)>
<!ATTLIST datasetRun
    subDataset CDATA #REQUIRED
>

<!ELEMENT datasetParameter (datasetParameterExpression?)>
<!ATTLIST datasetParameter
    name CDATA #REQUIRED
>

<!ELEMENT datasetParameterExpression (#PCDATA)>
```

A dataset run declaration supplies the values for the dataset parameters as well as the data source through which the dataset will iterate. Optionally, a `java.sql.Connection` can be passed to the dataset instead of a `JRDataSource` instance, when there is a SQL query associated with the dataset. This query is executed by the engine using the supplied Java Database Connectivity (JDBC) connection and the `java.sql.ResultSet` object obtained is iterated through.

Dataset runs resemble subreports in the way parameters and the data source/connection are passed in. Please refer to Chapter 11 for more details.

Both charts and crosstabs can reference datasets by instantiating and configuring dataset runs. If no dataset run is specified for a chart or crosstab, the main dataset of the report is used.

CHAPTER 13

Charts

JasperReports now has built-in support for charts using the new chart component, which greatly simplifies the way charts are included inside reports. Previously, users had to completely rely on scriptlets to gather the chart data and render the chart using an image element in the report template.

Note Users can still render charts by making direct API calls to a particular charting library, which allows them to fully control the appearance and content of their charts, as demonstrated in the `jcharts` and `jfreechart` samples. The former sample uses the jCharts library and the latter sample uses the JFreeChart library for rendering the charts as images.

The new chart component uses the JFreeChart library and exposes a limited set of visual properties that the charting package actually supports. This limited set should be sufficient for the majority of users, and in the future it will be extended to accommodate community feedback and requests.

With the new chart component, users only have to apply the desired visual settings and define the expressions that will help the engine build the chart dataset incrementally during the iteration through the report data source.

When including and configuring a chart component, three entities are involved:

- The overall chart component
- The chart dataset (which groups chart data–related settings)
- The chart plot (which groups visual settings related to the way the chart items are rendered)

JasperReports currently supports the following types of charts: Pie, Pie 3D, Bar, Bar 3D, XY Bar, Stacked Bar, Stacked Bar 3D, Line, XY Line, Area, XY Area, Scatter Plot, Bubble, Time Series, High-Low-Open-Close, and Candlestick.

For each type of chart there is a special JRXML tag that groups various chart settings, including the dataset and the plot.

Chart Properties

All chart types have a common set of properties. Charts are normal report elements, so they share some of their properties with all the other report elements, as explained in Chapter 10.

Charts are also box elements and can have hyperlinks associated with them (see the "Box Elements" section and the "Hyperlinks, Anchors, and Bookmarks" section of Chapter 10).

Special chart-specific settings that apply to all types of charts are grouped under a special JRXML tag called <chart>, as shown in Listing 13-1.

Listing 13-1. *JRXML Syntax*

```
<!ELEMENT chart (reportElement, box?, chartTitle?, chartSubtitle?, chartLegend?,
anchorNameExpression?, hyperlinkReferenceExpression?, hyperlinkAnchorExpression?,
hyperlinkPageExpression?, hyperlinkTooltipExpression?, hyperlinkParameter*)>
<!ATTLIST chart
    isShowLegend (true | false) "true"
    evaluationTime (Now | Report | Page | Column | Group | Band) "Now"
    evaluationGroup CDATA #IMPLIED
    hyperlinkType CDATA "None"
    hyperlinkTarget (Self | Blank) "Self"
    bookmarkLevel NMTOKEN "0"
    customizerClass CDATA #IMPLIED
>

<!ELEMENT chartTitle (font?, titleExpression?)>

<!ATTLIST chartTitle
    position (Top | Bottom | Left | Right) "Top"
    color CDATA #IMPLIED
>

<!ELEMENT titleExpression (#PCDATA)>

<!ELEMENT chartSubtitle (font?, subtitleExpression?)>

<!ATTLIST chartSubtitle
    color CDATA #IMPLIED
>

<!ELEMENT subtitleExpression (#PCDATA)>

<!ELEMENT chartLegend (font?)>

<!ATTLIST chartLegend
    textColor CDATA #IMPLIED
    backgroundColor CDATA #IMPLIED
>
```

Chart Evaluation

Charts resemble text fields and images in that they can postpone their actual rendering until all the data needed for this operation becomes available to the reporting engine.

Data needed by a chart is gathered by the associated dataset during iteration through the report data. However, you might want to display charts at the beginning of a document, where the required data is not yet available given the way the engine process data and renders the final document.

In such cases, you can postpone chart evaluation using the `evaluationTime` and `evaluationGroup` attributes, which work in the same manner as for text fields and images, as explained in previous chapters.

Chart Title and Subtitle

All charts can have one title and one subtitle. Both are optional and can be customized for color, font, and position.

The title of a chart can be placed at the top of the chart, at the bottom of the chart, or on the left or right side of the chart, depending on the value of the `position` attribute of the `<chartTitle>` tag.

Chart Legend

All chart types can display a legend that explains the values represented by the chart. By default all charts display the legend, but you can suppress this display by setting the `isShowLegend` flag to `false`.

You can control the font-related properties as well as the text color and the background color of the chart legend using the optional `<chartLegend>` tag and its nested `<font>` tag.

Chart Customizer

Although the JFreeChart library is a fairly complete charting package that offers great flexibility and a comprehensive range of settings to fully customize the appearance and the content of the charts it renders, the built-in chart component offered by JasperReports exposes only a subset of the library's original charting functionality. This ensures that JasperReports charts are easily embeddable into reports and that the basic set of properties exposed through JRXML and the object model is enough for the majority of use cases.

In time, other JFreeChart settings will be exposed through the built-in chart component, but certainly JasperReports will never be able to expose all the JFreeChart settings through JRXML tags or the API.

To provide full control over chart customization even when using the built-in chart component, JasperReports can make use of a `net.sf.jasperreports.engine.JRChartCustomizer` implementation associated with the chart element using the `customizerClass` attribute.

We recommend extending the `net.sf.jasperreports.engine.JRAbstractChartCustomizer` class instead of directly implementing the chart customizer interface, because the supplied abstract implementation gives access to parameters, fields, and variables, and allows more flexible chart customization based on report data.

Chart Datasets

One of the most important considerations when putting a chart element into a report template is the data mapping. The chart will need to extract its data from whatever data is available inside the report at runtime.

In the sections that follow, we first present an overview of the chart dataset, and then we detail each of the available datasets.

Chart Dataset Overview

Charts rely on a data-oriented component called the *chart dataset* for mapping report data and retrieving chart data at runtime.

A chart dataset is an entity that somewhat resembles a report variable because it gets initialized and incremented at specified moments during the report-filling process and iteration through the report data source. Like a report variable, at any moment a chart dataset holds a certain value, which is a complex data structure that gets incremented and will be used for rendering the chart at the appropriate moment.

Several types of chart datasets are available in JasperReports because each type of chart works with certain datasets: Pie, Category, XY, Time Series, Time Period, XYZ, and High-Low.

The JasperReports object model uses the `net.sf.jasperreports.engine.JRChartDataset` interface to define chart datasets. There are implementations of this interface for each of the aforementioned dataset types.

All chart datasets initialize and increment in the same way, and differ only in the type of data or data series they map.

Common dataset properties are grouped under the `<dataset>` tag in JRXML format, as shown in Listing 13-2.

Listing 13-2. *JRXML Syntax*

```
<!ELEMENT dataset (incrementWhenExpression?, datasetRun?)>

<!ATTLIST dataset
    resetType (None | Report | Page | Column | Group) "Report"
    resetGroup CDATA #IMPLIED
    incrementType (None | Report | Page | Column | Group) "None"
    incrementGroup CDATA #IMPLIED
>

<!ELEMENT incrementWhenExpression (#PCDATA)>
```

Resetting and Incrementing Chart Datasets

As previously mentioned, chart datasets resemble variables in that they are used to calculate a certain value in an incremental fashion. In the case of the chart dataset, this value is a complex data structure that will be used by the charting library to render the chart. This data structure is built incrementally during iteration through the report data source by adding values to it.

At certain moments, the chart dataset must be reinitialized because it has probably already been used for rendering a chart during report filling and must be prepared for further incrementation for later reuse.

All four attributes—`resetType`, `resetGroup`, `incrementType`, and `incrementGroup`—have the same meaning and work exactly as previously explained for report variables.

Filtering Out Data

The way a chart dataset is incremented can be further customized by filtering out unwanted data through the use of the `<incrementWhenExpression>` tag. The chart dataset is incremented in accordance with the specified `incrementType` and `incrementGroup` attributes, but only if the mentioned expression returns `Boolean.TRUE` (or is not present). The expression returning `null` is equivalent to `Boolean.FALSE`, so incrementation does not occur at that particular moment.

Using Report Subdatasets Through Dataset Runs

The `<datasetRun>` tag is optional for a chart dataset declaration. This means that by default, the engine will use the main dataset of the report. In such a case, all chart expressions make use of report-level parameters, fields, and variables, and the group level resets or increments are performed based on the report data-grouping structure.

Charts that use the main dataset of the report gather their data during iteration through the data source of the report itself and can be rendered only when this process is completed. This is why charts that use the main dataset of the report are usually placed at the end of the report or the end of a certain group. If the chart precedes the data it used inside the overall document, then the `evaluationTime` attribute must be used to postpone rendering of the chart after the iteration through that data has completed.

Sometimes charts and crosstabs need to gather data by iterating through virtual records that are not part of the report data source, but are instead virtual records nested inside complex data structures that are part of the current record inside the report data source. To iterate through such nested data structures, use subdatasets as explained in the previous chapter.

A chart dataset can instantiate a dataset run by referencing a subdataset declared at the report level and by supplying parameter values to it, as well as a data source or a connection.

Using a chart coupled with a dataset run is equivalent to putting a chart inside a subreport and doing all the required wiring for passing the data from the master report to the subreport. Datasets were introduced to simplify this procedure and to remove the need to use subreports that do not have visual content but are used only for iterating through data and performing calculations.

We'll now take a closer look at the dataset types to see what kind of data mapping they require.

Pie Dataset

This dataset is useful for rendering Pie or Pie 3D charts. Data required for such charts comes in the form of key-value pairs. Each pair represents a slice in the pie chart. Listing 13-3 gives the JRXML syntax for the Pie dataset.

Listing 13-3. *JRXML Syntax*

```
<!ELEMENT pieDataset (dataset?, keyExpression?, valueExpression?, labelExpression?,
sectionHyperlink?)>
```

Key Expression

Values of this expression represent the categories that will make up the slices in the pie chart. This expression can return any `java.lang.Comparable` object.

Value Expression

This expression produces the values that correspond to each category/key in the dataset. Values are always `java.lang.Number` objects.

Label Expression

If this expression is missing, the chart will display default labels for each slice in the pie chart. Use this expression, which returns `java.lang.String` values, to customize the item labels for the pie chart.

Category Dataset

This dataset accommodates one or more data series consisting of values associated with categories. It is used to render Bar, Bar 3D, Stacked Bar, Line, Area, and Stacked Area charts, and its JRXML syntax is given in Listing 13-4.

Listing 13-4. *JRXML Syntax*

```
<!ELEMENT categoryDataset (dataset?, categorySeries*)>

<!ELEMENT categorySeries (seriesExpression?, categoryExpression?, valueExpression?,
labelExpression?, itemHyperlink?)>
```

Series Expression

This expression indicates the name of the series. The value of this expression can be any `java.lang.Comparable` object.

Note that this expression may return different values with each iteration, which in turn will result in the dataset having multiple category series, even though a single `<categorySeries>` tag was used inside `<categoryDataset>`. However, this expression usually returns a `java.lang.String` constant, and there are several `<categorySeries>` tags that introduce multiple category series in the dataset.

Category Expression

This expression returns the name of the category for each value inside the series specified by the series expression. Categories are `java.lang.Comparable` objects and not necessarily `java.lang.String` objects.

Value Expression

This expression returns the `java.lang.Number` values for each category in the specified series.

Label Expression

If present, this expression allows customization of the item labels in the chart.

XY Dataset

This dataset is a wrapper for data series made of (x, y) value pairs and is used for rendering XY Bar, XY Line, XY Area, and Scatter Plot charts. Its JRXML syntax is given in Listing 13-5.

Listing 13-5. *JRXML Syntax*

```
<!ELEMENT xyDataset (dataset?, xySeries*)>

<!ELEMENT xySeries (seriesExpression?, xValueExpression?, yValueExpression?,
labelExpression?, itemHyperlink?)>
```

Series Expression

This expression returns the `java.lang.Comparable` object that identifies a certain data series in the overall dataset. Because it is an expression, it can return different values, which will result in the dataset containing multiple series even when a single `<xySeries>` tag is used inside the `<xyDataset>` tag.

X Value Expression

This expression returns the `java.lang.Number` value representing the X value from the (x, y) pair that will be added to the current data series.

Y Value Expression

This expression returns the `java.lang.Number` value representing the Y value from the (x, y) pair that will be added to the current data series.

Time Series Dataset

This dataset wraps one or multiple time series. A time series consists of (time period, numeric value) pairs. The Time Series dataset can be used with Times Series and XY Bar charts, and its JRXML syntax is given in Listing 13-6.

Listing 13-6. *JRXML Syntax*

```
<!ELEMENT timeSeriesDataset (dataset?, timeSeries*)>

<!ATTLIST timeSeriesDataset
    timePeriod (Year | Quarter | Month | Week | Day | Hour | Minute | Second |
Millisecond ) "Day"
>

<!ELEMENT timeSeries (seriesExpression?, timePeriodExpression?, valueExpression?,
labelExpression?, itemHyperlink?)>
```

Time Period

The `timePeriod` attribute, available inside the `<timeSeriesDataset>` tag, is for specifying the type of the data series inside the dataset. Time series can contain numeric values associated with days, months, years, or other predefined time periods.

Series Expression

As for all other series-based datasets, this expression specifies the series to which to add the current value pair when incrementing the dataset. Any `java.lang.Comparable` object can be used to identify a series.

Time Period Expression

This expression returns a `java.util.Date` value from which the engine will extract the corresponding time period depending on the value set for the `timePeriod` attribute mentioned earlier in the Time Series dataset. For instance, if the chart is about yearly data, the engine will extract only the year from the date value, or if you are gathering monthly data, the engine will use only the month value from the date object returned by this expression.

Value Expression

This expression returns the `java.lang.Number` value to associate with the corresponding time period value when incrementing the current series of the dataset.

Label Expression

This expression should return `java.lang.String` values and, if present, it helps customize the item labels inside charts.

Time Period Dataset

The Time Period dataset is very much like the Time Series dataset in that it wraps series consisting of (time period, numeric value) pairs. The only difference is that in this case the time periods are not chosen from a predefined list but can be arbitrary time intervals. This kind of dataset is for use only with XY Bar charts, and its JRXML syntax is given in Listing 13-7.

Listing 13-7. *JRXML Syntax*

```
<!ELEMENT timePeriodDataset (dataset?, timePeriodSeries*)>

<!ELEMENT timePeriodSeries (seriesExpression?, startDateExpression?,
endDateExpression?, valueExpression?, labelExpression?, itemHyperlink?)>
```

Series Expression

Multiple series can be put inside the dataset, and this expression returns a `java.lang.Comparable` object that identifies each series. This tag is common for all series-based datasets, as explained in the "Category Dataset" section earlier in this chapter.

Start Date and End Date Expressions

These two expressions specify the date interval with which the numeric value will be associated when it is added to the time period series.

Value Expression

This expression returns the `java.lang.Number` value to associate with the current date interval specified by the start date and end date expressions.

Label Expression

If the label expression is present, its values will be used to customize item labels in the resulting chart.

XYZ Dataset

The XYZ dataset wraps series consisting of (x, y, z) items. It is used only by the Bubble chart, and its JRXML syntax is given in Listing 13-8.

Listing 13-8. *JRXML Syntax*

```
<!ELEMENT xyzDataset (dataset?, xyzSeries*)>

<!ELEMENT xyzSeries (seriesExpression?, xValueExpression?, yValueExpression?,
zValueExpression?, itemHyperlink?)>
```

Series Expression

This expression identifies the series in multiseries datasets. See the "Time Period Dataset" section for more details about this tag.

X, Y, and Z Value Expressions

These expressions return a `java.lang.Number` value that will form the (x, y, z) item to add to the current series when incrementing the dataset.

High-Low Dataset

Although the name of this dataset is "High-Low," it can actually hold a series of (x, high, low, open, close, volume) items. It is used in combination with either a High-Low or a Candlestick chart. Listing 13-9 gives the JRXML syntax for High-Low datasets.

Listing 13-9. *JRXML Syntax*

```
<!ELEMENT highLowDataset (dataset?, seriesExpression?, dateExpression?,
highExpression?, lowExpression?, openExpression?, closeExpression?,
volumeExpression?, itemHyperlink?)>
```

Series Expression

Currently only one series is supported inside a High-Low or Candlestick chart. This limitation is documented inside JFreeChart, the library we are using for the built-in chart support. However, this single series must be identified by a `java.lang.Comparable` value returned by this expression, and it must also be used as the series name in the chart's legend.

Date Expression

This expression returns the date to which the current (high, low, open, close, volume) item refers.

High, Low, Open, and Close Expressions

Each one of these expressions returns a `java.lang.Number` value, which will be part of the data item added to the series when the dataset gets incremented.

Volume Expression

This is a numeric expression that returns the volume value to use for the current data item. It is used only for Candlestick charts.

Value Dataset

This is a special chart dataset implementation that contains a single value and is used for rendering Meter and Thermometer charts. Its JRXML syntax is given in Listing 13-10.

Listing 13-10. *JRXML Syntax*

```
<!ELEMENT valueDataset (dataset?, valueExpression )>
```

Chart Item Hyperlinks

Individual chart items, such as a slice in a pie chart or a bar in a bar chart, can have associated hyperlinks to allow navigation to another document or section within the same document, providing a certain degree of interactivity with the end user in the form of drill-down and drill-through reports.

Chart item hyperlinks can be specified for charts that rely on the following types of datasets: Pie, Category, XY, XYZ, Time Series, Time Period, and High-Low. Pie datasets hold item hyperlink information in the `<sectionHyperlink>` tag, while all other datasets use a tag called `<itemHyperlink>`. Listing 13-11 gives the JRXML syntax for chart item hyperlinks.

Listing 13-11. *JRXML Syntax*

```
<!ELEMENT sectionHyperlink (hyperlinkReferenceExpression?,
hyperlinkAnchorExpression?, hyperlinkPageExpression?, hyperlinkTooltipExpression?,
hyperlinkParameter*)>

<!ATTLIST sectionHyperlink
    hyperlinkType CDATA "None"
    hyperlinkTarget (Self | Blank) "Self"
>

<!ELEMENT itemHyperlink (hyperlinkReferenceExpression?, hyperlinkAnchorExpression?,
hyperlinkPageExpression?, hyperlinkTooltipExpression?, hyperlinkParameter*)>

<!ATTLIST itemHyperlink
    hyperlinkType CDATA "None"
    hyperlinkTarget (Self | Blank) "Self"
>
```

The hyperlinks can be associated with the chart items by putting hyperlink-related information in the chart dataset. Each chart dataset can contain one or more hyperlink definitions (depending on the dataset type), with each definition corresponding to a series of chart items generated by the dataset. Hyperlink expressions are evaluated each time the chart dataset gets incremented, and the resulting hyperlinks are associated with the chart items generated during the increment operation.

When a chart contains item hyperlinks, the generated hyperlinks are kept as part of the renderer responsible for drawing the chart. In this case, the renderer would implement the `net.sf.jasperreports.engine.JRImageMapRenderer` interface. The report exporters can then detect whether an image has an image area map and enable the hyperlinks on specific image areas. Using this mechanism, you could also create your own `net.sf.jasperreports.engine.JRImageMapRenderer` custom implementation and use it as image expression. This mechanism has one limitation, though: the image area hyperlinks are lost when a report is exported to XML, because the XML exporter saves the image data and not the image renderer.

The built-in Swing report viewer and the HTML exporter detect images with hyperlink area maps and use the saved information to enable hyperlinks on image areas. The HTML exporter will produce standard `<map>` elements for such images, and the built-in viewer will register Swing listeners to handle image area hyperlinks.

More details about how hyperlinks work can be found in the "Hyperlinks, Anchors, and Bookmarks" section of Chapter 10.

Chart Plots

The *chart plot* is the area of the chart on which the axes and items are rendered. Plots differ based on the type of chart. Some plots specialize in drawing pies; others specialize in drawing bar items or lines.

In this section, we first present an overview of the chart plot, and then we detail each of the various plot types.

Chart Plot Overview

Each type of plot comes with its own set of properties or attributes for customizing the chart's appearance and behavior.

There is, however, a subset of plot properties common to all plot types. They are grouped under the `<plot>` tag in JRXML and can be part of any chart/plot definition in the report template. Listing 13-12 provides the complete syntax.

Listing 13-12. *JRXML Syntax*

```
<!ELEMENT plot (seriesColor*) >

<!ATTLIST plot
    backcolor CDATA #IMPLIED
    orientation (Horizontal | Vertical) "Vertical"
    backgroundAlpha NMTOKEN "1"
    foregroundAlpha NMTOKEN "1"
    labelRotation CDATA "0.0"
>

<!ELEMENT seriesColor EMPTY>

<!ATTLIST seriesColor
    seriesOrder CDATA #REQUIRED
    color CDATA #REQUIRED
>
```

Plot Background Color

You can use the `backcolor` attribute to specify the color used for drawing the plot's area background.

Plot Orientation

Some types of plots can draw their items either vertically or horizontally. For instance, Bar charts can display either vertical or horizontal bars. Pie charts do not use this setting, but since the majority of charts do have a concept of orientation, the attribute was included among the common plot settings.

Plot Transparency

When filling up the background with a specified color or drawing items on the target device, the plot can use a customizable degree of transparency, which you can control using the `backgroundAlpha` and `foregroundAlpha` attributes. These attributes accept numeric values ranging from 0 to 1. The default for both attributes is 1, which means drawings on the plot area are opaque.

Label Rotation

The text labels on the x axis of a chart can be rotated clockwise or counterclockwise by setting a positive or a negative numeric value representing the number of degrees to the `labelRotation` attribute of the plot. This attribute applies only to charts for which the x axis is not numeric or does not display dates.

Series Colors

To control the color of each series in a chart displaying multiple series, you can use the `<seriesColor>` tag available at the chart-plot level. If only one `<seriesColor>` tag is specified, it becomes the color of the first series. If more than one `<seriesColor>` tag is specified, the chart will cycle through the supplied colors.

Pie charts do not have multiple series, but they do need different colors for each slice, so the specified colors will be used. Meter and Thermometer charts do not have series and will ignore any `<seriesColor>` settings.

When used in a chart that is part of a Multi-axis chart, the series colors are treated a bit differently. The default color series to cycle through is defined in the plot of the Multi-axis chart, and the color series for the nested charts define series colors for that chart only. This is useful when a Multi-axis chart contains several line charts, each with one series. By default every line will be the first in its plot and will have the first color defined in the Multi-axis plot, so every line will be the same color. To solve this, you can set a `<seriesColor>` for each nested chart to override the default colors.

All series colors are sorted by the value of the `seriesOrder` attribute and appear in that order when coloring the series.

Pie Plot

This type of plot is used for rendering Pie charts. There is no special setting for this type of plot other than the common settings just presented. Listing 13-13 provides the JRXML syntax.

Listing 13-13. *JRXML Syntax*

```
<!ELEMENT piePlot (plot)>
```

Pie 3D Plot

As its name suggests, this type of plot is used only for rendering Pie 3D charts. Its JRXML syntax is given in Listing 13-14.

Listing 13-14. *JRXML Syntax*

```
<!ELEMENT pie3DPlot (plot)>

<!ATTLIST pie3DPlot
    depthFactor CDATA "0.2"
>
```

Depth Factor

The only special setting that the Pie 3D plot exposes is the depth factor, a numeric value ranging from 0 to 1 that represents the depth of the pie as a percentage of the height of the plot area.

Bar Plot

This type of plot can be used to render Bar, Stacked Bar, and XY Bar charts, and its JRXML syntax is given in Listing 13-15.

Listing 13-15. *JRXML Syntax*

```
<!ELEMENT barPlot (plot, categoryAxisLabelExpression?, categoryAxisFormat?,
valueAxisLabelExpression?, valueAxisFormat?)>

<!ATTLIST barPlot
    isShowLabels (true | false ) "false"
    isShowTickMarks (true | false) "true"
    isShowTickLabels (true | false) "true"
>

<!ELEMENT categoryAxisFormat (axisFormat)>

<!ELEMENT valueAxisFormat (axisFormat)>
```

Axis Labels

Bar plots display two axes: one for categories and another for the values associated with those categories. Both axes can display labels if `<categoryAxisLabelExpression>` and `<valueAxisLabelExpression>` are used. These two expressions are supposed to return `java.lang.Comparable` values.

Showing Item Labels

By default, this plot does not display labels for the items it draws on the plot area. By setting `isShowLabels` to `true`, default or customized labels should appear. Check the corresponding dataset used by the chart to see how the item can be customized.

Showing Tick Marks and Tick Labels

There are two Boolean attributes, `isShowTickMarks` and `isShowTickLabels`, for controlling the display of tick marks and labels on the chart axes. Both are set to `true` by default.

Bar 3D Plot

Only the Bar 3D and the Stacked Bar 3D charts make use of the Bar 3D plot.

Like the aforementioned Bar plot, the Bar 3D plot allows customization of the labels for both of its axes and the display of the item labels. Listing 13-16 gives the JRXML syntax for the Bar 3D plot.

Listing 13-16. *JRXML Syntax*

```
<!ELEMENT bar3DPlot (plot, categoryAxisLabelExpression?, categoryAxisFormat?,
valueAxisLabelExpression?, valueAxisFormat?)>

<!ATTLIST bar3DPlot
    isShowLabels (true | false ) "false"
    xOffset CDATA #IMPLIED
    yOffset CDATA #IMPLIED
>
```

3D Effect

This plot exposes two special attributes, `xOffset` and `yOffset`, that allow users to control the 3D effect. Both accept numeric values representing the number of pixels in the 3D effect on the two axes.

Line Plot

This plot is used by the Line and XY Line charts. Its JRXML syntax is given in Listing 13-17.

Listing 13-17. *JRXML Syntax*

```
<!ELEMENT linePlot (plot, categoryAxisLabelExpression?, categoryAxisFormat?,
valueAxisLabelExpression?, valueAxisFormat?)>

<!ATTLIST linePlot
    isShowLines (true | false) "true"
    isShowShapes (true | false) "true"
>
```

Axis Labels

The Line plot also has two axes. Their labels can be controlled by using the `<categoryAxisLabelExpression>` and `<valueAxisLabelExpression>` tags to return `java.lang.Comparable` values to use as labels.

Show Lines

The Line plot draws lines between the points that represent the chart items inside the plot area. Those lines can be suppressed if the `isShowLines` attribute is set to `false`.

Show Shapes

The Line plot also marks each item point with a small graphical shape that is different for each series in the underlying dataset. This small shape can be hidden by setting the `isShowShapes` flag to `false`.

Area Plot

Area charts and Stacked Area charts rely on this plot to render their axes and items. This kind of plot allows users to specify only the labels for both axes and their format. Currently no other settings are permitted, as shown in the Listing 13-18, where the complete JRXML syntax for the Area plot is given.

Listing 13-18. *JRXML Syntax*

```
<!ELEMENT areaPlot (plot, categoryAxisLabelExpression?, categoryAxisFormat?,
valueAxisLabelExpression?, valueAxisFormat?)>
```

Scatter Plot

Scatter plots are used only with Scatter Plot charts. They render items as points on a two-axis plot area. This plot closely resembles the Line plot just described, in that it lets users configure the labels for both axes, the rendering of lines to unite the item points, and the rendering of the small shapes that mark each item point on the target plot area. Listing 13-19 gives the JRXML syntax for the Scatter plot.

Listing 13-19. *JRXML Syntax*

```
<!ELEMENT scatterPlot (plot, xAxisLabelExpression?, xAxisFormat?,
yAxisLabelExpression?, yAxisFormat?)>

<!ATTLIST scatterPlot
    isShowLines (true | false) "true"
    isShowShapes (true | false) "true"
>

<!ELEMENT xAxisFormat (axisFormat)>

<!ELEMENT yAxisFormat (axisFormat)>
```

Bubble Plot

Only Bubble charts use this type of plot. Like all other two-axis plots, it lets users control the labels displayed for each axis. Listing 13-20 gives the JRXML syntax for the Bubble plot.

Listing 13-20. *JRXML Syntax*

```
<!ELEMENT bubblePlot (plot, xAxisLabelExpression?, xAxisFormat?,
yAxisLabelExpression?, yAxisFormat?)>

<!ATTLIST bubblePlot
    scaleType (BothAxes | DomainAxis | RangeAxis) "RangeAxis"
>
```

Bubble Scale Type

The plot draws an ellipse for each item present in the dataset for a given series. Usually this is a circle whose radius is specified by the Z value in that chart item. However, the plot needs to know whether the Z value is proportional to its corresponding X value or to its corresponding Y value in order to calculate the actual size of the bubble.

The type of bubble scaling is specified by the `scaleType` attribute that the plot exposes:

- *Range axis scaling*: The bubble is a circle with the radius proportional to the Y value for each item (`scaleType="RangeAxis"`).
- *Domain axis scaling*: The bubble is a circle with the radius proportional to the X value for each item (`scaleType="DomainAxis"`).
- *Scaling on both axes*: The bubble is an ellipse with the height proportional to the Y value and the width proportional to the X value for each item (`scaleType="BothAxes"`).

By default, bubbles scale on the range axis.

Time Series Plot

This type of plot is similar to the Line plot and Scatter plot in that it lets users configure the labels for both axes, the rendering of lines to unite the item points, and the rendering of the small shapes that mark each item point on the target plot area. It is used only in combination with Time Series charts, and its JRXML syntax is given in Listing 13-21.

Listing 13-21. *JRXML Syntax*

```
<!ELEMENT timeSeriesPlot (plot, timeAxisLabelExpression?, timeAxisFormat?,
valueAxisLabelExpression?, valueAxisFormat?)>

<!ATTLIST timeSeriesPlot
    isShowLines (true | false) "true"
    isShowShapes (true | false) "true"
>

<!ELEMENT timeAxisFormat (axisFormat)>
```

High-Low Plot

Used only in combination with High-Low charts, this type of plot lets users customize the labels for both axes, like all the other axis-oriented plots. The JRXML syntax of this type of plot is given in Listing 13-22.

Listing 13-22. *JRXML Syntax*

```
<!ELEMENT highLowPlot (plot, timeAxisLabelExpression?, timeAxisFormat?,
valueAxisLabelExpression?, valueAxisFormat?)>

<!ATTLIST highLowPlot
    isShowCloseTicks (true | false) "true"
    isShowOpenTicks (true | false) "true"
>
```

Show Tick Marks

This special type of plot draws the items as vertical lines that start at the high value and go downward to the low value. On each line the plot displays by default small ticks to indicate the open and close values corresponding to the current item. To suppress these ticks, set to `false` the two flags available inside the plot definition: `isShowCloseTicks` and `isShowOpenTicks`.

Candlestick Plot

The Candlestick plot is also an axis-oriented plot and allows you to customize axis labels using expressions. It can be used only in combination with a Candlestick chart, and its JRXML syntax is given in Listing 13-23.

Listing 13-23. *JRXML Syntax*

```
<!ELEMENT candlestickPlot (plot, timeAxisLabelExpression?, timeAxisFormat?,
valueAxisLabelExpression?, valueAxisFormat?)>

<!ATTLIST candlestickPlot
    isShowVolume (true | false) "true"
>
```

Show Volume

The Candlestick chart uses a High-Low dataset, but unlike the High-Low chart, the Candlestick chart can make use of the volume value inside each dataset item.

The volume value is displayed as the body of the candlestick figure rendered for each item. The volume is displayed by default in a Candlestick chart but can be suppressed by setting the `isShowVolume` flag to `false`.

Meter Plot

This type of plot can be used only for Meter charts, and its syntax is given in Listing 13-24.

Listing 13-24. *JRXML Syntax*

```
<!ELEMENT meterPlot (plot, valueDisplay?, dataRange, meterInterval*)>

<!ATTLIST meterPlot
    shape (chord | circle | pie) "pie"
    angle CDATA "180"
    units CDATA #IMPLIED
    tickInterval CDATA "10.0"
    meterColor CDATA #IMPLIED
    needleColor CDATA #IMPLIED
    tickColor CDATA #IMPLIED
>

<!ELEMENT valueDisplay (font?)>

<!ATTLIST valueDisplay
    color CDATA #IMPLIED
    mask CDATA #IMPLIED
>

<!ELEMENT dataRange (lowExpression, highExpression)>

<!ELEMENT meterInterval (dataRange)>

<!ATTLIST meterInterval
    label CDATA #IMPLIED
    color CDATA #IMPLIED
    alpha CDATA "1.0"
>
```

Meter Angle and Shape

The angle attribute of the plot represents the extent of the meter in degrees. By default the meter dial is a semicircle.

The shape attribute is used only if the angle of the dial is over 180 degrees. In such cases, the space between the start and end of the meter can be filled in several different ways. The best way to visualize this is to think of a 12-hour clock face. If the angle of the meter is 240 degrees, the meter will start at 8, and then sweep up past 12 and down to 4. This attribute specifies how to fill the area between 4 o'clock and 8 o'clock, and there are three possibilities:

- chord: A straight line is drawn between the start point and the end point, and the area bounded by the meter and this line is shaded with the background color (shape="chord").
- circle: The unused portion of the circle that describes the meter is shaded with the background color (shape="circle").
- pie: The unused portion of the circle that describes the meter is not shaded at all (shape="pie").

The last option is also the default.

Units and Value Display Options

The meter chart displays a single value, and the optional `units` attribute can be used to describe this value. The text will be appended to the value.

When displayed, the value of the meter chart can use a specified font and color, and can have a formatting pattern. All these are introduced by the nested `<valueDisplay>` tag.

Date Range and Intervals

The dial of the meter chart has a minimum and a maximum value that can be specified using the `<dataRange>` tag.

In addition, the dial can be divided into sections such as "normal," "warning," and "critical," which can be color-coded to help interpret the value. You can do so by using additional `<meterInterval>` tags, which introduce data ranges with their labels and colors.

Meter Colors

The Meter plot also lets you specify the background color of the dial (which will be masked by individual interval colors), the color of the needle, and the color of the ticks on the dial.

Thermometer Plot

This type of plot can be used only for Thermometer charts, which display a single value on a thermometer. In addition to the value being plotted, three ranges can be specified to help interpret the value as shown in Listing 13-25, where the complete JRXML syntax is given.

Listing 13-25. *JRXML Syntax*

```
<!ELEMENT thermometerPlot (plot, valueDisplay?, dataRange, lowRange?,
mediumRange?, highRange?)>

<!ATTLIST thermometerPlot
    valueLocation ( none | left | right | bulb ) "bulb"
    isShowValueLines ( true | false) "false"
    mercuryColor CDATA #IMPLIED
>

<!ELEMENT valueDisplay (font?)>

<!ATTLIST valueDisplay
    color CDATA #IMPLIED
    mask CDATA #IMPLIED
>

<!ELEMENT dataRange (lowExpression, highExpression)>

<!ELEMENT lowRange (dataRange)>
```

```
<!ELEMENT mediumRange (dataRange)>

<!ELEMENT highRange (dataRange)>
```

Value Location

`valueLocation` specifies where to display the textual representation of the value being displayed, relative to the thermometer outline. The possible values are as follows:

- `none`: The text value is not displayed (`valueLocation="none"`).
- `left`: The text value is displayed to the left of the thermometer outline (`valueLocation="left"`).
- `right`: The text value is displayed to the right of the thermometer outline (`valueLocation="right"`).
- `bulb`: The text value is displayed in the bulb at the bottom of the thermometer (`valueLocation="bulb"`).

The last option is also the default.

Value Display Options

Besides specifying the font, color, and pattern to use when rendering the chart value using the `<valueDisplay>` tag options, this plot also allows suppressing the lines on the thermometer or changing the color of the liquid.

Multi-axis Plot

This plot is for Multi-axis charts. It groups all the common plot options shared by the charts inside the Multi-axis chart. The JRXML syntax for this type of plot is given in Listing 13-26.

Listing 13-26. *JRXML Syntax*

```
<!ELEMENT multiAxisPlot (plot, axis+)>

<!ELEMENT axis (barChart | bar3DChart | xyBarChart | stackedBarChart
| stackedBar3DChart| lineChart | xyLineChart | areaChart | xyAreaChart
| scatterChart | bubbleChart | timeSeriesChart | highLowChart | candlestickChart
| stackedAreaChart)>

<!ATTLIST axis
    position (leftOrTop | rightOrBottom) "leftOrTop"
>
```

The nested charts are specified via the `<axis>` tags. All nested charts must share the same type of domain axis: category, numeric (XY), or time based.

Axis Format

Chart plots that display axes also provide a way to customize these axes and specify how to draw the axis line, its label, and the label tick marks. Listing 13-27 gives the JRXML syntax for specifying an axis format.

Listing 13-27. *JRXML Syntax*

```
<!ELEMENT axisFormat (labelFont?, tickLabelFont?)>

<!ATTLIST axisFormat
    labelColor CDATA #IMPLIED
    tickLabelColor CDATA #IMPLIED
    tickLabelMask CDATA #IMPLIED
    axisLineColor CDATA #IMPLIED
>

<!ELEMENT labelFont (font?)>

<!ELEMENT tickLabelFont (font?)>
```

Depending on the types of values displayed by the axis, `tickLabelMask` can be a number format pattern (`<valueAxisFormat>`, `<xAxisFormat>`, `<yAxisFormat>`), a date/time format pattern (`<timeAxisFormat>`), or simply ignored (`<categoryAxisFormat>`).

Chart Types

JasperReports offers built-in support for several chart types. The JFreeChart library used to render the charts supports an even wider range of chart types, but the subset offered through the chart element available in JasperReports should be sufficient for the majority of reporting requirements.

Note You can still render special charts by making direct calls to the charting API inside a generic image element placed inside the report template.

Each of the predefined chart types in JasperReports is a combination of a dataset and a plot. These types are described in the sections that follow. Listings 13-28 through 13-47 present the JRXML syntax for each.

Pie Chart

This chart is a combination of a Pie dataset and a Pie plot.

Listing 13-28. *JRXML Syntax*

```
<!ELEMENT pieChart (chart, pieDataset, piePlot)>
```

Pie 3D Chart

This chart groups a Pie dataset and a Pie 3D plot.

Listing 13-29. *JRXML Syntax*

```
<!ELEMENT pie3DChart (chart, pieDataset, pie3DPlot)>
```

Bar Chart

This chart is a basic combination of a Category dataset and a Bar plot.

Listing 13-30. *JRXML Syntax*

```
<!ELEMENT barChart (chart, categoryDataset, barPlot)>
```

Bar 3D Chart

This chart wraps a Category dataset and a Bar 3D plot.

Listing 13-31. *JRXML Syntax*

```
<!ELEMENT bar3DChart (chart, categoryDataset, bar3DPlot)>
```

XY Bar Chart

This chart supports Time Period datasets, Time Series datasets, and XY datasets, and uses a Bar plot to render the axis and the items.

Listing 13-32. *JRXML Syntax*

```
<!ELEMENT xyBarChart (chart, (timePeriodDataset | timeSeriesDataset | xyDataset ),
barPlot)>
```

Stacked Bar Chart

Just like the Bar chart, the Stacked Bar chart uses data from a Category dataset and renders its content using a Bar plot.

Listing 13-33. *JRXML Syntax*

```
<!ELEMENT stackedBar3DChart (chart, categoryDataset, bar3DPlot)>
```

Stacked Bar 3D Chart

This type of chart is very similar to the Bar 3D chart in that it wraps together a Category dataset and a Bar 3D plot.

Listing 13-34. *JRXML Syntax*

```
<!ELEMENT stackedBar3DChart (chart, categoryDataset, bar3DPlot)>
```

Line Chart

Line charts are made of a Category dataset and a Line plot.

Listing 13-35. *JRXML Syntax*

```
<!ELEMENT lineChart (chart, categoryDataset, linePlot)>
```

XY Line Chart

This chart groups an XY dataset and a Line plot.

Listing 13-36. *JRXML Syntax*

```
<!ELEMENT xyLineChart (chart, xyDataset, linePlot)>
```

Area Chart

Items from a Category dataset are rendered using an Area plot.

Listing 13-37. *JRXML Syntax*

```
<!ELEMENT areaChart (chart, categoryDataset, areaPlot)>
```

Stacked Area Chart

Similar to the Area chart, the items from a Category dataset are rendered using an Area plot.

Listing 13-38. *JRXML Syntax*

```
<!ELEMENT stackedAreaChart (chart, categoryDataset, areaPlot)>
```

XY Area Chart

This chart uses data from an XY dataset and renders it through an Area plot.

Listing 13-39. *JRXML Syntax*

```
<!ELEMENT xyAreaChart (chart, xyDataset, areaPlot)>
```

Scatter Plot Chart

This chart wraps an XY dataset with a Scatter plot.

Listing 13-40. *JRXML Syntax*

```
<!ELEMENT scatterChart (chart, xyDataset, scatterPlot)>
```

Bubble Chart

This chart is usable only with an XYZ dataset and only in combination with a Bubble plot.

Listing 13-41. *JRXML Syntax*

```
<!ELEMENT bubbleChart (chart, xyzDataset, bubblePlot)>
```

Time Series Chart

This chart is usable only with a Time Series dataset and a Time Series plot.

Listing 13-42. *JRXML Syntax*

```
<!ELEMENT timeSeriesChart (chart, timeSeriesDataset, timeSeriesPlot)>
```

High-Low-Open-Close Chart

This chart is a combination of a High-Low dataset and a High-Low plot.

Listing 13-43. *JRXML Syntax*

```
<!ELEMENT highLowChart (chart, highLowDataset, highLowPlot)>
```

Candlestick Chart

This chart uses data from a High-Low dataset but with a special Candlestick plot.

Listing 13-44. *JRXML Syntax*

```
<!ELEMENT candlestickChart (chart, highLowDataset, candlestickPlot)>
```

Meter Chart

A Meter chart displays a single value from a Value dataset on a dial, using rendering options from a Meter plot.

Listing 13-45. *JRXML Syntax*

```
<!ELEMENT meterChart (chart, valueDataset, meterPlot)>
```

Thermometer Chart

This chart displays the single value in a Value dataset using rendering options from a Thermometer plot.

Listing 13-46. *JRXML Syntax*

```
<!ELEMENT thermometerChart (chart, valueDataset, thermometerPlot)>
```

Multi-axis Chart

A Multi-axis chart has multiple range axes, all sharing a common domain axis.

Listing 13-47. *JRXML Syntax*

```
<!ELEMENT multiAxisChart (chart, multiAxisPlot)>
```

The domain is determined by the dataset of each nested report, and they must all use the same type of dataset. The time period datasets (High-Low, Candlestick, and Time Series) are considered the same and can be mixed.

Each nested chart has its own range, so you can combine charts with significantly different scales. Each chart will have its own axis showing its range, and it is highly recommended that you match the color of the data series and the axis.

The plot options of the nested charts are ignored—the plot is configured via the Multi-axis plot. The only exception to this is any series color specified in the plot of a nested report, which will be used to color a specific series in that report. In this case, the `seriesOrder` attribute in `<seriesColor>` is an absolute specification of a series to color, not a relative ordering.

CHAPTER 14

Crosstabs

A crosstab is a special type of report element that summarizes data into a two-dimensional grid. Crosstabs usually display the joint distribution of two or more variables in the form of a table in which both rows and columns are dynamic, and in which the table cells use these variables to display aggregate data such as sums, counts, minimums, and maximums.

Crosstab Overview

Crosstabs are useful because they are easy to understand, can be used with any level of data (nominal, ordinal, interval, or ratio), and provide greater insight than single statistics. Listing 14-1 gives the JRXML syntax for crosstabs.

Listing 14-1. *JRXML Syntax*

```
<!ELEMENT crosstab (reportElement, crosstabParameter*, parametersMapExpression?,
crosstabDataset?, crosstabHeaderCell?, rowGroup*, columnGroup*, measure*,
crosstabCell*, whenNoDataCell?)>

<!ATTLIST crosstab
    isRepeatColumnHeaders (true | false) "true"
    isRepeatRowHeaders (true | false) "true"
    columnBreakOffset NMTOKEN "10"
    runDirection (LTR | RTL) "LTR"
>
```

Repeating Row and Column Headers

When a crosstab does not fit entirely on the current page and either a column or row break occurs, the crosstab is split into multiple pieces and continues on the same page or overflows onto a new page. By default, the subsequent crosstab pieces redisplay the column and rows headers, in order to recreate the context for the values displayed inside the crosstab cells. To suppress this behavior, set the `isRepeatColumnHeaders` and `isRepeatRowHeaders` attributes to `false`.

Column Break Offset

When a column break occurs and there is still enough space on the current page, the subsequent crosstab piece is placed below the previous one at a controlled offset that you can specify with the `columnBreakOffset` attribute.

Run Direction

Crosstabs can either be filled from left to right (the default) or from right to left (mainly for reports in right-to-left languages). When a crosstab is filled from right to left, the crosstab contents will start from the right extremity of the crosstab element area and grow toward the left.

Crosstab Parameters

Crosstabs use an internal calculation engine for bucketing and preparing the aggregated data they display. However, sometimes it is useful to pass single values from the containing report and display them inside the crosstab. This would be the case for some crosstab header titles.

Any number of crosstab parameters can be declared inside the crosstab element. Each parameter has its own name and type, as well as its own expression used at runtime to obtain the value to pass into the crosstab.

Listing 14-2 gives the JRXML syntax for crosstab parameters.

Listing 14-2. *JRXML Syntax*

```
<!ELEMENT crosstabParameter (parameterValueExpression?)>

<!ATTLIST crosstabParameter
    name CDATA #REQUIRED
    class CDATA "java.lang.String"
>

<!ELEMENT parameterValueExpression (#PCDATA)>
```

All parameters must be declared explicitly using the corresponding `<crosstabParameter>` tag, even when no expression is associated with the parameter and all parameter values are passed from the parent report using a single `java.util.Map` instance through the `<parametersMapExpression>` tag.

Tip Inside a `<parameterValueExpression>` tag, you can reference parameters, fields, and variables from the parent report.

Crosstab parameters can be referenced only from crosstab cell expressions using the `$P{}` syntax, so they can participate only in the displayed values.

Crosstab Datasets

The crosstab calculation engine aggregates data by iterating through an associated dataset. This can be the parent report's main dataset or a dataset run that uses one of the report's declared subdatasets.

Listing 14-3 gives the JRXML syntax for crosstab datasets.

Listing 14-3. *JRXML Syntax*

```
<!ELEMENT crosstabDataset (dataset?)>

<!ATTLIST crosstabDataset
    isDataPreSorted (true | false) "false"
>
```

Crosstab dataset resetting, incrementing, and filtering out data work the same as for chart datasets (explained in the "Chart Datasets" section of Chapter 13).

Using Presorted Data

The calculation engine of a crosstab works faster if the data in its associated dataset is already sorted in accordance with the row and column groups (buckets) declared by the crosstab, in this order: row buckets, and then column buckets.

If data is not already sorted in the dataset before the iteration starts, then the crosstab calculation engine can sort it during the data aggregation process using supplied comparators (explained in Chapter 15). However, this will result in some performance loss.

Data Grouping (Bucketing)

The original dataset data through which the crosstab calculation engine iterates to make the required data aggregation must be grouped in accordance with the declared rows and columns of the crosstab. Row and column groups in a crosstab rely on group items called *buckets*. A bucket definition consists of the following:

- An expression evaluated at runtime that obtains the group items (buckets) in which to place the aggregated information
- A comparator to sort the group items (buckets) in case the natural ordering of the values is not acceptable or even possible

For example, if you want to group by city, the expression would be the city name (provided that it's unique) and the comparator expression could be a `java.text.Collator` to perform locale-sensitive ordering.

A bucket is an expression that is evaluated at runtime in order to obtain the data buckets in which to place the aggregated information and also a comparator to sort the buckets in case the natural ordering of the bucket values is not acceptable or even possible.

Listing 14-4 gives the JRXML syntax for buckets.

Listing 14-4. *JRXML Syntax*

```
<!ELEMENT bucket (bucketExpression?, comparatorExpression?)>

<!ATTLIST bucket
    order (Ascending | Descending) "Ascending"
>

<!ELEMENT bucketExpression (#PCDATA)>

<!ATTLIST bucketExpression
    class CDATA #REQUIRED
>

<!ELEMENT comparatorExpression (#PCDATA)>
```

Bucket Expression

Crosstab data grouping is similar to report data grouping. Both require that an expression be evaluated to obtain a series of distinct values that will identify the data groups. Crosstabs have both row grouping and column grouping, but there is no distinction between the two as far as data is concerned. The only difference is in the crosstab layout and the way it flows. Both row and column group declarations have a nested data bucket, which introduces the mentioned expression as the bucket expression using the `<bucketExpression>` tag.

■ **Note** Both the `<bucketExpression>` and the `<comparatorExpression>` tags can contain only parameter, field, and variable references from the associated dataset. If the crosstab dataset uses a dataset run associated with a subdataset declared at report level, then all those references inside the expression will point to parameters, fields, and variables declared in that subdataset. For crosstab datasets that run on the main dataset of the report, the references inside expressions point to the parent report parameters, fields, and variables as expected.

Bucket Comparator and Sort Order

The row and column groups are always sorted in the final crosstab layout. Bucket values usually make it into the row or column headers, which are always sorted either by their natural order (when `java.lang.Comparable` values are used for those buckets) or through the use of a custom `java.util.Comparator` that is supplied using the `<comparatorExpression>`.

Row Groups

Crosstabs can have any number of row groups, nested according to the order in which they were declared.

Listing 14-5 gives the JRXML syntax for row groups.

Listing 14-5. *JRXML Syntax*

```
<!ELEMENT rowGroup (bucket, crosstabRowHeader?, crosstabTotalRowHeader?)>

<!ATTLIST rowGroup
    name CDATA #REQUIRED
    width NMTOKEN #REQUIRED
    totalPosition (Start | End | None) "None"
    headerPosition (Top | Middle | Bottom | Stretch) "Top"
>

<!ELEMENT crosstabRowHeader (cellContents?)>

<!ELEMENT crosstabTotalRowHeader (cellContents?)>
```

Row Group Name

All groups require a unique name, specified using the `name` attribute. This name is used to reference the group when declaring the content of its corresponding cells or when referencing the bucket values of the group to display them in the group headers.

Row Group Headers

A row group can have one header for introducing the rows that correspond to each distinct bucket value and a special header for introducing the totals of the group when the crosstab ends or when a higher-level row group breaks due to a changing bucket value.

Both header areas are optional. If present, they have a free-form layout. You can place almost any kind of report element inside, except for subreports, charts, and crosstabs.

Note Inside a row header area, put only information that the crosstab calculation engine produced during the aggregation and bucketing process, as well as crosstab parameter values. The `$P{}` syntax used inside the header expressions points to crosstab parameter values, and the `$V{}` syntax points to either a bucket value (if the name of a group is mentioned between the brackets) or to a measure value (if a measure is referenced by name).

Note that measures and groups cannot have the same name—this is to avoid naming conflicts when using the `$V{}` syntax.

Row Header Width

For each row header, specify the width in pixels using the `width` attribute. This value is used by the engine to render the headers that introduce bucket values. For the totals header, the width comes as a sum of the row headers it wraps.

Position of Totals Row

The `totalPosition` attribute controls the appearance of the row that displays the totals for the row group:

- *Start*: The row that displays the totals for the group precedes the rows corresponding to the group's bucket values (`totalPosition="Start"`).
- *End*: The row that displays the totals for the group is rendered after the rows corresponding to the group's bucket values (`totalPosition="End"`).
- *None*: The row that displays the totals for the group is not displayed (`totalPosition="None"`).

Row Header Stretch Behavior

When multiple nested row groups are used in the crosstab, the height of the row headers for the higher-level groups grows in order to wrap the rows of the nested groups. The `headerPosition` attribute determines how the row header content should adapt to the increased height. The possible values for this attribute are as follows:

- *Top*: The content of the row header does not stretch and remains at the top of the header area (`headerPosition="Top"`).
- *Middle*: The content of the row header does not stretch and moves to the middle of the header area (`headerPosition="Middle"`).
- *Bottom*: The content of the row header does not stretch and moves to the bottom of the header area (`headerPosition="Bottom"`).
- *Stretch*: The content of the row header adapts its height proportionally to the newly increased row header height (`headerPosition="Stretch"`).

By default, the row header content stays at the top of the row header area.

Column Groups

As previously mentioned for the row groups, a crosstab can contain any number of nested columns. The order of column groups is also important.

Listing 14-6 gives the JRXML syntax for column groups.

Listing 14-6. *JRXML Syntax*

```
<!ELEMENT columnGroup (bucket, crosstabColumnHeader?, crosstabTotalColumnHeader?)>

<!ATTLIST columnGroup
    name CDATA #REQUIRED
    height NMTOKEN #REQUIRED
```

```
    totalPosition (Start | End | None) "None"
    headerPosition (Left | Center | Right | Stretch) "Left"
>

<!ELEMENT crosstabColumnHeader (cellContents?)>

<!ELEMENT crosstabTotalColumnHeader (cellContents?)>
```

Column Group Name

Column groups are also uniquely identified by the `name` attribute, typically to reference the column group (when declaring the content of its corresponding cells) or the bucket values of the group (for display in the group headers).

Column Group Headers

Any column group can have two optional header regions, one at the top of the bucket columns and the other at the top of the column displaying the totals of the column group.

These column header regions have a free-form layout and can contain any kind of report element, except subreports, charts, and crosstabs.

Note Inside a column header area, only the `$P{}` and `$V{}` references are valid for expressions. They point to crosstab parameters, bucket values, and measures, as already explained for row headers.

Column Header Height

The `height` attribute specifies the height of the column headers in pixels. The header for the group totals column takes its height from the total height of the column headers it wraps.

Position of Totals Column

The `totalPosition` attribute controls the appearance of the column that displays the totals for the column group:

- *Start*: The column that displays the totals for the group precedes the columns corresponding to the group's bucket values (`totalPosition="Start"`).
- *End*: The column that displays the totals for the group is rendered after the columns corresponding to the group's bucket values (`totalPosition="End"`).
- *None*: The column that displays the totals for the group is not displayed (`totalPosition="None"`).

Column Header Stretch Behavior

The column headers of crosstabs with multiple nested column groups must adapt their content to the increased width caused by the nested columns they wrap. There are four possibilities as specified by the values of the headerPosition attribute:

- *Left*: The content of the column header does not stretch and remains to the left of the header area (headerPosition="Left").
- *Center*: The content of the column header does not stretch and moves to the center of the header area (headerPosition="Center").
- *Right*: The content of the column header does not stretch and moves to the right of the header area (headerPosition="Right").
- *Stretch*: The content of the column header adapts its width proportionally to the newly increased column header width (headerPosition="Stretch").

By default, the column header content stays to the left of the column header area.

Measures

The crosstab calculation engine aggregates data, called a *measure*, while iterating through the associated dataset. A measure is typically displayed in the crosstab cells. For each thing that the crosstab needs for accumulating data during bucketing, a corresponding measure must be declared.

Listing 14-7 gives the JRXML syntax for measures.

Listing 14-7. *JRXML Syntax*

```
<!ELEMENT measure (measureExpression?)>

<!ATTLIST measure
    name CDATA #REQUIRED
    class CDATA #IMPLIED
    calculation (Nothing | Count | DistinctCount | Sum | Average | Lowest | Highest
        | StandardDeviation | Variance | First) "Nothing"
    incrementerFactoryClass CDATA #IMPLIED
    percentageOf (None | GrandTotal) "None"
    percentageCalculatorClass CDATA #IMPLIED
>

<!ELEMENT measureExpression (#PCDATA)>
```

Measure Name

Crosstab measures are identified by a unique name. The value of the name attribute of a measure cannot coincide with any row or column group names.

Measure Type

Just like report variables, crosstab measures have an associated type specified by the `class` attribute.

Measure Expression

The `<measureExpression>` specifies the expression that produces the values used by the calculation engine to increment the measure during the data aggregation process.

Note All the parameter, field, and variable references used inside a measure expression point to the references declared in the crosstab dataset definition. If the crosstab does not use a subdataset run, then all these references point to the report's main dataset. Therefore, they are actually parameters, fields, and variables of the parent report.

Measure Calculation and Custom Incrementers

Crosstab measures behave just like report variables. They store a value that is incremented with each iteration through the crosstab dataset. The supported types of calculations are the same for measure as for report variables, except for the calculation type `System`, which does not make sense for measures.

Furthermore, custom-defined calculations can be introduced using implementations of the `net.sf.jasperreports.engine.fill.JRExtendedIncrementer` interface, as explained in the discussion of the `incrementerFactoryClass` attribute in the "Incrementers" section of Chapter 8.

Percentages and Second-Pass Types of Calculations (Deprecated)

Note The crosstab functionality described in the following two paragraphs is now considered deprecated. The introduction of the built-in crosstab total variables helps displaying percentage like types of values in a simpler manner. See the following section for details.

In addition to the calculations supported by the report variables and mentioned in the preceding paragraph, you can use crosstabs to calculate and display percentage values for numerical measurements that have calculation type `Sum` or `Count`. To do this, set the `percentageOf` attribute to a value other than `None`. Currently, only percentages of the grand total of the crosstab are supported.

The percentage calculation is a type of calculation that requires at least a second pass through the data after the totals are calculated. However, there may be other custom-made calculations that require a similar second pass. To enable users to define their own types of calculations that require a second pass, implement the `net.sf.jasperreports.crosstabs.fill.JRPercentageCalculator` interface and associate it with the measure using the `percentageCalculatorClass` attribute.

Built-In Crosstab Total Variables

The value of a measure is available inside a crosstab cell through a variable bearing the same name as the measure. In addition to the current value of the measure, totals of different levels corresponding to the cell can be accessed through variables named according to the following scheme:

- `<Measure>_<Column Group>_ALL`: Yields the total corresponding to a column group (i.e., the total for all the entries in the column group from the same row)
- `<Measure>_<Row Group>_ALL`: Yields the total corresponding to a row group (i.e., the total for all the entries in the row group from the same column)
- `<Measure>_<Row Group>_<Column Group>_ALL`: Yields the combined total corresponding to the row and column groups (i.e., the total corresponding to all the entries in both row and column groups)

For example, if one creates a crosstab having `Year` and `Month` column groups, a `City` row group, and a `Sales` measure, the following variables can be used:

- `Sales`: The current measure value
- `Sales_Month_ALL`: The total for all the months (one year) corresponding to the current cell
- `Sales_Year_ALL`: The total for all the years
- `Sales_City_ALL`: The total for all the cities
- `Sales_City_Month_ALL`: The total for all the cities and all the months (one year)
- `Sales_City_Year_ALL`: The grand total

These variables can be used in both detail and total cells. In total cells, such a variable can be used to access a total corresponding to a higher-level group of the same dimension (e.g., in a `Month` total cell, `Sales_Year_ALL` can be used as the total for all the years) or a total corresponding to a group on the other dimension (e.g., in a `Month` total cell, `Sales_City_ALL` can be used as the total for all the cities and one year).

A typical usage of these variables is to show measure values as percentages out of arbitrary level totals.

Crosstab Governor

The crosstab calculation engine performs all calculations in memory. In case large volumes of data are processed, it could be possible to run out of memory due to the large number of totals and aggregation variables that the engine keeps track of.

To avoid the situation in which the JVM raises an `OutOfMemory` error, and thus triggers memory reclaim procedures with potentially serious effects on the application's overall behavior, a crosstab governor has been put in place. This is basically a simple memory consumption test that the engine performs when filling a crosstab, to check whether a given memory threshold has been reached. When the limit is reached, the program raises an exception that can be caught and dealt within the caller program, preventing a more serious `OutOfMemory` error from occurring.

The governor threshold is given as an integer number representing the maximum number of cells multiplied by the number of measures in the generated crosstab. It can be set using the `net.sf.jasperreports.crosstab.bucket.measure.limit` configuration property. This property defaults to `-1`, meaning that the crosstab governor is disabled by default.

Crosstab Cells

A crosstab cell is a rectangular area at the intersection of a crosstab row and a crosstab column. The cell is a free-form element that can contain any kind of report element except subreports, charts, and crosstabs.

Crosstab cells are of two types:

- *Detail crosstab cell*: Both the row and the column correspond to bucket values, not totals.
- *Total crosstab cell*: Either the row or the column or both correspond to a group total.

Listing 14-8 gives the JRXML syntax for crosstab cells.

Listing 14-8. *JRXML Syntax*

```
<!ELEMENT crosstabCell (cellContents?)>

<!ATTLIST crosstabCell
    width NMTOKEN #IMPLIED
    height NMTOKEN #IMPLIED
    rowTotalGroup CDATA #IMPLIED
    columnTotalGroup CDATA #IMPLIED
>

<!ELEMENT cellContents (box?, (line | rectangle | ellipse | image | staticText
| textField | elementGroup | frame)*)>

<!ATTLIST cellContents
    backcolor CDATA #IMPLIED
    mode (Opaque | Transparent) #IMPLIED
    style CDATA #IMPLIED
>

<!ELEMENT crosstabHeaderCell (cellContents)>

<!ELEMENT whenNoDataCell (cellContents)>
```

Cell Backcolor And Border

All crosstab cells can have a background color and a border, specified by the `background` attribute and the nested `<box>` tag, respectively. In the resulting document, each crosstab cell is transformed into a frame element containing all the nested elements of that cell.

Crosstab Header Cell

The optional `<crosstabHeaderCell>` tag defines the content of the region found at the upper-left corner of the crosstab where column headers and row headers meet. The size of this cell is calculated automatically based on the defined row and column widths and heights.

Detail Cell

The crosstab cell at the intersection of a row bucket value and a column bucket value (called the detail crosstab cell) can be declared using a `<crosstabCell>` tag in which both the `rowTotalGroup` and `columnTotalGroup` attributes are empty. For the detail crosstab cell, both the `width` and the `height` attributes are mandatory, specifying the size of the cell in pixels.

Total Cells

Total crosstab cells are those declared using a `<crosstabCell>` tag for which at least one of the two `rowTotalGroup` and `columnTotalGroup` attributes are present and point to a row group or a column group, respectively.

If the `rowTotalGroup` attribute is present, then the crosstab cell displays column totals for the mentioned row group. For such total crosstab cells, only the `height` is configurable, and the `width` is forced by the detail cell.

If the `columnTotalGroup` attribute is present, then the cell displays row totals for the specified column group. For these cells, only the `width` is configurable, and the cell inherits the value of the `height` attribute from the detail cell.

■ **Note** Crosstab cell expression can only reference crosstab parameters using the `$P{}` syntax and bucket and measure values using the `$V{}` syntax.

No Data Cell

The optional `<whenNoDataCell>` defines a pseudo–crosstab cell used by the engine to display something when the crosstab does not have any data. The crosstab dataset might not have any virtual records to iterate through, raising the question of what to display in the parent report.

If this pseudo-cell is declared, its content is rendered if the crosstab data is missing, allowing users to view messages such as “No data for the crosstab!” instead of only empty space.

CHAPTER 15

Scriptlets

All the data displayed in a report comes from the report parameters and report fields. This data can be processed using the report variables and their expressions. Some variables are initialized according to their reset type when the report starts, or when a page or column break is encountered, or when a group changes. Furthermore, variables are evaluated every time new data is fetched from the data source (for every row).

But simple variable expressions cannot always implement complex functionality. This is where scriptlets come in. Scriptlets are sequences of Java code that are executed every time a report event occurs. Through scriptlets, users can affect the values stored by the report variables. Since scriptlets work mainly with report variables, it is important to have full control over the exact moment the scriptlet is executed.

JasperReports allows the execution of custom Java code *before* or *after* it initializes the report variables according to their reset type: `Report`, `Page`, `Column`, or `Group`.

In order to make use of this functionality, users need only create a scriptlet class, by extending one of the following two classes:

```
net.sf.jasperreports.engine.JRAbstractScriptlet
net.sf.jasperreports.engine.JRDefaultScriptlet
```

The complete name of this custom scriptlet class (including the package) must be specified in the `scriptletClass` attribute of the `<jasperReport>` element, and must be available in the classpath at report filling time so that the engine can instantiate it on the fly. If no value is specified for the `scriptletClass` attribute, the engine instantiates the `JRDefaultScriptlet` class.

When creating a JasperReports scriptlet class, there are several methods that developers should implement or override, including `beforeReportInit()`, `afterReportInit()`, `beforePageInit()`, `afterPageInit()`, `beforeGroupInit()`, and `afterGroupInit()`. The report engine calls these methods at the appropriate time when filling the report.

For more complex reports containing very complicated report expressions for grouping or displaying data, create a separate class to which you then make calls from simplified report expressions. The scriptlet class is ideal for this. This is because the reporting engine supplies you with a reference to the scriptlet object it creates on the fly using the built-in `REPORT_SCRIPTLET` parameter.

Check the `/demo/samples/scriptlet` sample provided with the project source files to see this type of functionality used.

CHAPTER 16

Internationalization

JasperReports lets you associate a java.util.ResourceBundle with the report template, either at design time (by using the new resourceBundle attribute) or at runtime (by providing a value for the built-in REPORT_RESOURCE_BUNDLE parameter).

If the report needs to be generated in a locale that is different from the current one, use the built-in REPORT_LOCALE parameter to specify the runtime locale when filling the report. To facilitate report internationalization, a special syntax is available inside report expressions to reference java.lang.String resources placed inside a java.util.ResourceBundle object associated with the report. The $R{} syntax is for wrapping resource bundle keys to retrieve the value for that key.

For formatting messages in different languages based on the report locale, a built-in method inside the report's net.sf.jasperreports.engine.fill.JRCalculator offers functionality similar to the java.text.MessageFormat class. This method, msg(), has three convenient signatures that allow you to use up to three message parameters in the messages.

Also provided is the built-in str() method (the equivalent of the $R{} syntax inside the report expressions), which gives access to the resource bundle content based on the report locale.

For date and time formatting, the built-in REPORT_TIME_ZONE parameter can be used to ensure proper time transformations.

In the generated output, the library keeps information about the text run direction so that documents generated in languages that have right-to-left writing (like Arabic and Hebrew) can be rendered properly.

If an application relies on the built-in Swing viewer to display generated reports, then it too must be internationalized by adapting the button tooltips or other texts displayed. This is very easy to do since the viewer relies on a predefined resource bundle to extract locale-specific information. The base name for this resource bundle is net.sf.jasperreports.view.viewer. Check the /demo/samples/i18n and /demo/samples/unicode samples for details.

CHAPTER 17

Report Exporters

The proprietary document format used by JasperReports to generate and store final documents is represented by a net.sf.jasperreports.engine.JasperPrint object, which can be serialized for transfer over the network or permanent storage. However, when these documents must be sent to third-party consumers who do not have the proper tools to view and print them in the JasperReports proprietary format, the best solution is to export those documents to more popular formats like PDF, HTML, RTF, XLS, ODT, or CVS, for which there are specialized viewers available on almost all platforms.

JasperReports tries to expose its exporting functionality in a flexible way and allow users to fully customize how documents are exported, as well as extend the existing functionality if needed. All document exporting in JasperReports is done through a very simple interface called net.sf.jasperreports.engine.JRExporter. Every document format that JasperReports currently supports has an implementation of this interface. When a report must be exported, an instance of the desired exporter implementation is created and configured before the export method is called to launch the actual export process on that exporter.

All the input data the exporter might need is supplied by the so-called exporter parameters before the exporting process is started. This is because the exporting process is always invoked by calling the exportReport() method of the net.sf.jasperreports.engine.JRExporter interface, and this method does not receive any parameters when called. The exporter parameters must have already been set using the setParameter() method on the exporter instance you are working with before the export task is launched.

You might also choose to bulk set all the exporter parameters using the setParameters() method, which receives a java.util.Map object containing the parameter values. The keys in this map should be instances of the net.sf.jasperreports.engine.JRExporterParameter class, as they are supplied when individually calling the setParameter() method for each of the exporter parameters.

Note that no matter what type of output your exporter produces, you will be using parameters to indicate to the exporter where to place or send this output. Such parameters might be called OUT parameters. For example, if you want your exporter to send the output it produces to an output stream, supply the java.io.OutputStream object reference to the exporter using a parameter, probably identified by the net.sf.jasperreports.engine.JRExporterParameter.OUTPUT_STREAM constant.

All the supported exporter parameters are identified by an instance of the net.sf.jasperreports.engine.JRExporterParameter class or one of its subclasses. All have predefined constants that are used as keys to store and retrieve the parameter values from the internal map that each exporter uses behind the scenes to keep all parameter values. Each exporter can recognize and use its own parameters, but some predefined parameters are common to all exporters. These are identified by constants in the JRExporterParameters base class. They are described in the following section.

Exporter Input

The input data for an exporter comes in the form of one or more JasperPrint documents that must be exported to some other document format. These JasperPrint objects may be already in memory, come from the network through an input stream, or reside in files on disk.

An exporter should be able to handle such a wide range of document sources. In fact, all the exporter implementations that are shipped inside the library already do this. They all extend the net.sf.jasperreports.engine.JRAbstractExporter class, which holds all the logic for dealing with the source documents that need to be exported inside its defined setInput() method.

Batch Mode Export

The first thing an exporter needs to know is whether it is acting on a single JasperPrint document or a list with several such generated documents. Exporting multiple JasperPrint objects to a single resulting document is called *batch mode exporting*.

Not all exporters can work in batch mode, but those that do first look into the supplied parameter values to see whether a java.util.List of JasperPrint object has been supplied to them using the JASPER_PRINT_LIST exporter parameter. If so, the exporter loops through this list of documents and produces a single document from them.

If the exporters act on a single document, then they check whether a value is supplied to the JASPER_PRINT parameter, representing a single in-memory JasperPrint document that must be exported. If no value is found for this parameter, then the input for the exporter is a single JasperPrint document to be loaded from an input stream, an URL, a file object, or a file name. The exporter checks the following exporter parameters in this exact order, stopping at the first that has a non-null value: INPUT_STREAM, INPUT_URL, INPUT_FILE, and INPUT_FILE_NAME. If it does not find any of these parameters being set, then the exporter throws an exception telling the caller that no input source was set for the export process.

Exporter Output

There are at least three types of exporters, depending on the type of output they produce:

- Exporters that export to text- or character-based file formats (HTML, RTF, CSV, TXT, and XML exporters)
- Exporters that export to binary file formats (PDF and XLS exporters)
- Exporters that export directly to graphic devices (Graphics2D and Java Print Service exporters)

The first two categories of exporters reuse generic exporter parameters for configuring their output. A text- or character-oriented exporter first looks into the OUTPUT_STRING_BUFFER parameter to see whether it needs to output the text content it produces to a supplied `java.lang.StringBuffer` object. If no value has been supplied for this parameter, then it will subsequently try to identify the output destination for the content by checking the following exporter parameters in this order: `OUTPUT_WRITER`, `OUTPUT_STREAM`, `OUTPUT_FILE`, and `OUTPUT_FILE_NAME`. If none of these OUT parameters have been set, then the exporter throws an exception to inform the caller.

A binary exporter uses similar logic to find the output destination for the binary content it produces. It checks generic exporter parameters in this exact order: `OUTPUT_STREAM`, `OUTPUT_FILE`, and `OUTPUT_FILE_NAME`.

Special exporters that do not produce character or binary output but rather render the document directly on a target device have special export parameters to configure their output. These special parameters are explained in the following sections.

When not working in batch mode, all exporters allow users to export only parts of the single document received as input. To export a single page or a range of pages from this source document, set the `PAGE_INDEX` or the `START_PAGE_INDEX` and the `END_PAGE_INDEX` exporter parameters. Page indexes are zero-based, and `PAGE_INDEX` overrides both `START_PAGE_INDEX` and `END_PAGE_INDEX` if all are set for any given exporter.

The page content can be moved horizontally and vertically by using the `OFFSET_X` and `OFFSET_Y` parameters. This is useful especially for printing, when the page content doesn't always fit with the printer page margins.

All text-based exporters except the RTF one (RTF is a 7-bit ASCII format) support the `CHARACTER_ENCODING` exporter parameter, which can be used to force the encoding of the generated text files.

Monitoring Export Progress

Some applications need to display a progress bar to show the user how much has been already processed from the supplied document and how much remains to be exported. All exporters can inform the caller program of their progress through a simple interface called `net.sf.jasperreports.engine.export.JRExportProgressMonitor`. To monitor the exporter's progress, implement this interface and supply an instance of its export progress monitor class as the value for the `PROGRESS_MONITOR` parameter, which is recognized by almost all built-in exporters.

The interface has only one method, `afterPageExport()`, which gets called by the exporter on the monitor object after exporting each page from the supplied document. The monitor object can keep track of the number of pages already exported and the total number of pages to be exported by checking the number of pages in the source `JasperPrint` object.

The supplied `/demo/samples/scriptlet` sample shows how a simple export monitor can be used to track exporter progress.

Grid Exporters

The main goal of the JasperReports library is to produce high-quality, pixel-perfect documents for printing. The documents it produces can have rich content, and all the elements on a given page are positioned and sized absolutely. The library tries to keep the same document quality throughout all supported export formats, but there are some limitations for each of these formats. All existing exporters fall into one of two categories, depending on the way the content of the documents they produce can be structured:

- The exporters that target document formats that support free-form page content. These are the `Graphics2D`, PDF, RTF, and XML exporters.
- Exporters that target document formats that only support relative positioning of elements on a page or a grid-based layout. In this category are the HTML, XLS, and CSV exporters.

Exporters from this second category are also known as *grid exporters* because the layout of the documents they produce is formed by a grid. For instance, the HTML exporter will generate a `<table>` element for each page and try to put each element on that page inside a `<td>` tag. Likewise, the XLS exporter must put each element inside a sheet cell.

These grid exporters have an obvious limitation: a built-in algorithm for transforming an absolutely positioned page layout into a grid-based layout. This algorithm analyzes each page and tries to build a virtual table in which to place elements so that the overall layout of the document remains intact. However, since a table cell can contain only a single element, elements that overlap in the initial absolutely positioned layout will not display correctly in a grid-based layout. In fact, when two elements overlap, the element behind will not even appear in the grid-based layout.

Creating Grid-Friendly Report Layouts

When the report templates are very complex or agglomerated, passing from absolute positioning to grid or table layout produces very complex tables with many unused rows and columns, in order to make up for the empty space between elements or their special alignment. Here are a few very simple guidelines for obtaining optimized HTML, XLS, or CSV documents when using the built-in JasperReports grid exporters:

1. Minimize the number of rows and columns in the grid-oriented formats (the number of "cuts"). To do this, align your report elements as often as you can, both on the horizontal and the vertical axes, and eliminate the space between elements.

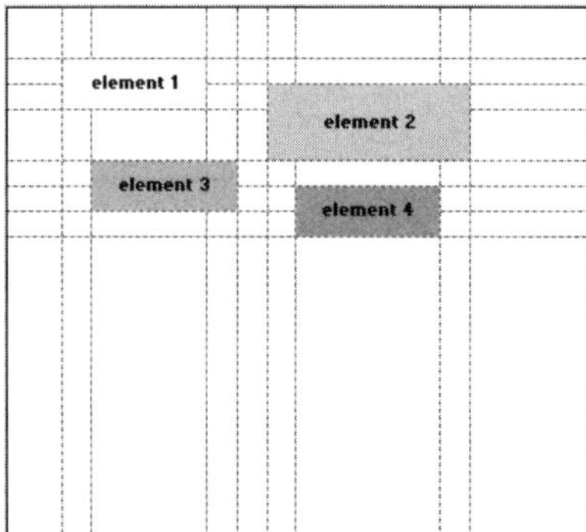

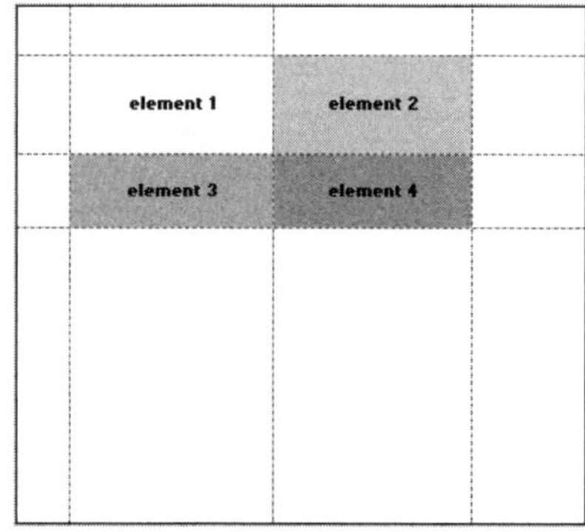

Figure 17-1. *Inefficient layout (left) and grid-friendly layout (right)*

2. Make sure report elements will not overlap when the report is generated. If two elements share a region, they cannot share the same cell in the resulting grid structure. Overlapping elements might lead to unexpected results.

Font Mappings

Since exported documents will probably be transferred and viewed on other systems and platforms, be especially careful with fonts. In the "Fonts and Unicode Support" section of Chapter 10, we already talked about fonts, how they work, and what needs to be done with them when exporting to PDF format. We have explained how the PDF font mappings are made using the attributes `pdfFontName`, `pdfEncoding`, and `isPdfEmbedded`. However, the font mapping issue is not specific to PDF, and similar mappings are required when exporting to other formats, like HTML or RTF.

The three PDF-related font attributes are present in JRXML and in the object model today only for historical reasons, because JasperReports started with support for PDF export, and at the time we did not realize that this would be a common issue for various export formats. Even though the three original PDF font attributes specified inside the report template are still supported and are not deprecated yet, we recommend making all the required font mappings at export time using the `FONT_MAP` exporter parameter, which is recognized by all the exporters that work with fonts.

For more details about export-time font mappings, please refer to the later sections in this chapter that present exporters individually, because the same exporter parameter is used differently by each of the exporters.

Graphics2D Exporter

JasperReports relies on AWT for text measurements and all sorts of layout calculations during report filling, so documents created using AWT will certainly look perfect when rendered with AWT on a `java.awt.Graphics2D` context. For this reason, the `net.sf.jasperreports.engine.export.JRGraphics2DExporter` is the perfect exporter. The output it produces is considered to be the reference in terms of layout capabilities and element styling.

Generally speaking, the document quality produced by all the other exporters is only an approximation of the perfect output that the `Graphics2D` exporter can produce. As its name indicates, this exporter is special because it does not produce files or send character or binary data to an output stream. Instead, its only target for rendering the content of a page is a `java.awt.Graphics2D` object. This exporter is also special because it can export only one page at a time.

This exporter is used by the built-in Swing viewer to render the content of each page, and it is also used when printing the documents. The documents are printed page by page, and the exporter is invoked to draw each document page on the graphic context associated with the selected printer job.

Because we are relying on the same code (same exporter) when viewing the documents using the built-in viewer and when printing them, JasperReports is a perfect WYSIWYG tool. The document quality on paper is the same as on the screen.

In terms of exporter input, note that this exporter does not work in batch mode. If a `java.util.List` of `JasperPrint` documents is supplied to it using the `JASPER_PRINT_LIST` parameter, it considers only the first one for exporting and ignores all the others.

Furthermore, this exporter can export only a single page at a time. The index of the page to be exported can be set using either the START_PAGE_INDEX parameter or the PAGE_INDEX parameter. Note that if present, PAGE_INDEX overrides the value of START_PAGE_INDEX. Therefore, this exporter actually exports only the first page from the specified page range, no matter how the page range is specified.

As already mentioned, this exporter needs a target java.awt.Graphics2D object onto which to render the specified page. This Graphics2D object can be set using the special exporter parameter GRAPHICS_2D. If this parameter is not set, the exporter will throw an exception signaling to the caller program that no output target was specified for the export process.

By default, the exporter renders the content of the page at normal proportions. However, it can also render it at different proportions if needed. For instance, when used inside the Swing viewer, the Graphics2D exporter must render the page using the user-defined zoom ratio. To set the zoom ratio for the exporter, supply a java.lang.Float value ranging from 0 to 1 as the value for the ZOOM_RATIO exporter parameter.

The Graphics2D exporter is also used when printing directly from Java. The Java Print Service exporter, presented in the following section, relies on the Graphics2D exporter and delegates to it all the rendering that needs to be performed on the printer's graphic context. Some of the existing JVM implementations have problems related to the huge size of the printer spool jobs that are created even for small documents. To avoid this, a bug fix was introduced in the Graphics2D exporter to minimize the impact of this problem and reduce the size of print spool jobs, while preserving document quality when printing. However, the bug fix itself is not perfect, and users might experience problems when printing bidirectional writing texts such as Arabic and Hebrew.

This is why the special JRGraphics2DExporterParameter.MINIMIZE_PRINTER_JOB_SIZE exporter parameter was introduced, along with a configuration property called net.sf.jasperreports.export.graphics2d.min.job.size, to allow users to turn on and off this rendering optimization, depending on their actual needs. The configuration property value is used only in the absence of the exporter parameter.

Java Print Service Exporter

In the "Printing Reports" section of Chapter 4 we explained how to print generated reports in JasperReports. As mentioned there, JDK 1.4 added a new printing API called the Java Print Service API, which gives Java applications better control over selecting a printer based on its capabilities or when printing documents in specific formats.

Access to this new printing API is available in JasperReports through a special exporter implementation called the net.sf.jasperreports.engine.export.JRPrintServiceExporter.

There are four ways of using the Java Print Service with the Java 2D API:

- Printing 2D graphics using PrinterJob
- Streaming 2D graphics using PrinterJob
- Printing 2D graphics using DocPrintJob and a service-formatted DocFlavor
- Streaming 2D graphics using DocPrintJob and a service-formatted DocFlavor

The `net.sf.jasperreports.engine.export.JRPrintServiceExporter` implementation takes the first approach and uses some of the new methods added to the `java.awt.print.PrinterJob` class:

- Static convenience methods to look up print services that can image 2D graphics, which are returned as an array of `PrintService` or `StreamPrintServiceFactory` objects depending on the method
- Methods to set and get a `PrintService` on a `PrinterJob`
- A `pageDialog()` method that takes a `PrintRequestAttributeSet` parameter
- A `printDialog()` method that takes a `PrintRequestAttributeSet` parameter
- A print method that takes a `PrintRequestAttributeSet` parameter

Looking Up a Printing Service

This exporter tries to find a print service that supports the necessary attributes. The set of attributes can be supplied to the exporter in the form of a `javax.print.attribute.PrintServiceAttributeSet` object that is passed as the value for the special `PRINT_SERVICE_ATTRIBUTE_SET` exporter parameter. For more details about the attributes that can be part of such an attribute set, check the Java Print Service API documentation.

The lookup procedure might return one or more print services able to handle the specified print service attributes. If so, the exporter uses the first one in the list. If no suitable print service is found, then the exporter throws an exception. As an alternative, a `javax.print.PrintService` instance can be passed in using the `PRINT_SERVICE` exporter parameter when users do not want the Java Print Service to search for an available print service.

Configuring the Printer Job

Once a print service has been located, it is associated with a `PrinterJob` instance. Further customization is made by passing a `javax.print.attribute.PrintRequestAttributeSet` instance when calling the `print()` method on the `PrinterJob` object to start the printing process.

To supply the `javax.print.attribute.PrintRequestAttributeSet` object containing the desired `javax.print.attribute.PrintRequestAttribute` values to the exporter, set the special `PRINT_REQUEST_ATTRIBUTE_SET` exporter parameter.

Displaying Print Dialogs

If this exporter is invoked by a desktop or client-side Java application, you can offer the end user a final chance to customize the printer job before the printing process actually starts. The exporter has two other predefined parameters: `DISPLAY_PAGE_DIALOG` and `DISPLAY_PRINT_DIALOG`, both receiving `java.lang.Boolean` values, which show or suppress the page dialog and/or the print dialog associated with the `PrinterJob` instance.

The two dialogs are cross-platform. They enable users to alter the print service attributes and the print request attributes that are already set for the current print service and printer job. They also allow canceling the current printing procedure altogether. When batch printing a set of documents, if DISPLAY_PAGE_DIALOG or DISPLAY_PRINT_DIALOG are set to true, a dialog window will pop up each time a document in the list is to be printed. This is very useful if you intend to set different printing options for each document. However, setting the same page/printing options each time would quickly become cumbersome. If same settings are intended for all documents in the list, the exporter provides two additional predefined parameters: DISPLAY_PAGE_DIALOG_ONLY_ONCE and DISPLAY_PRINT_DIALOG_ONLY_ONCE. These are only effective if the corresponding DISPLAY_PAGE_DIALOG or DISPLAY_PRINT_DIALOG parameter is true.

If DISPLAY_PAGE_DIALOG_ONLY_ONCE is true, then the page dialog will open only once, and the export options set within will be preserved for all documents in the list. The same thing happens when DISPLAY_PRINT_DIALOG_ONLY_ONCE is set to true—the print dialog will open only once.

The JRPrintServiceExporter can be used only with JRE 1.4 or later. The supplied /demo/samples/printservice sample shows you how.

PDF Exporter

Exporting to PDF was among the initial requirements for the JasperReports library. As its name indicates, PDF is a very precise and complex document format that ensures documents will look and print the same on all platforms.

This is why the PDF exporter implemented by the net.sf.jasperreports.engine.export.JRPdfExporter class in JasperReports is one of the best exporters. The output it produces is almost of the same quality as that produced by the net.sf.jasperreports.engine.export.JRGraphics2DExporter, which is always the reference.

The JRPdfExporter implementation uses iText, which is a specialized PDF-generating library. PDF is a binary document format that allows absolute positioning of the elements inside a page, so the existing PDF exporter does not have the limitations of a grid exporter.

It also works very well in batch mode because it allows concatenation of multiple documents within the same PDF file, even if the files have different page sizes.

Font Mappings

As discussed in the "Fonts and Unicode Support" section of Chapter 10, exporting to PDF requires mapping the fonts using three attributes: pdfFontName, pdfEncoding, and isPdfEmbedded. Even though these three attributes are still supported in JRXML and the API, we recommend making the PDF font mappings at export time using the FONT_MAP exporter parameter.

When exporting documents to PDF, for each combination of the three fontName, isBold, and isItalic font attributes, there must be an equivalent combination of the PDF-related font attributes pdfFontName, pdfEncoding, and isPdfEmbedded.

Equivalent combination means one that causes the text elements to be rendered exactly the same (or at least as closely as possible) in PDF and the built-in Graphics2D exporter, which is the reference.

If a value is supplied for the FONT_MAP exporter parameter, the PDF exporter expects it to be a java.util.Map instance that contains net.sf.jasperreports.engine.export.FontKey objects as keys and net.sf.jasperreports.engine.export.PdfFont objects as corresponding values. It then uses those key-value pairs as font mappings to render text elements in PDF.

In some cases, there is no font file available to use with the pdfFontName attribute in order to render bold and italic text exactly like the Graphics2D exporter renders it in AWT. Those fonts might only have a normal style variant and no variants for bold and italic. In such cases, the PDF exporter (the iText library, to be more precise) is able to simulate those styles by applying transformations to the normal font glyphs.

This feature can be turned on by using the Boolean isPdfSimulatedBold and isPdfSimulatedItalic parameters in the constructor of the PdfFont objects that are part of the font mapping construct.

Batch Mode Bookmarks

When several JasperPrint documents must be concatenated in the same PDF file by batch export, you can introduce PDF bookmarks in the resulting PDF document to mark the beginning of each individual document that was part of the initial document list. These bookmarks have the same name as the original JasperPrint document as specified by the jasperPrint.getName() property. However, users can turn on and off the creation of those bookmarks by setting the IS_CREATING_BATCH_MODE_BOOKMARKS exporter parameter to Boolean.TRUE or Boolean.FALSE. The exporter does not create such bookmarks by default.

The supplied /demo/samples/batchexport sample shows how this parameter works.

Encrypted PDF

In some cases, users might want to encrypt the PDF documents generated by JasperReports so that only authorized viewers can have access to those documents.

There are five exporter parameters for this:

IS_ENCRYPTED: When set to Boolean.TRUE, this parameter instructs the exporter to encrypt the resulting PDF document. By default PDF files are not encrypted.

IS_128_BIT_KEY: The PDF exporter can encrypt the files using either a 40-bit key or a 128-bit key. By default, it uses a 40-bit key, but if you set this flag to Boolean.TRUE, it can be configured to use a 128-bit key for stronger encryption.

USER_PASSWORD: This parameter specifies the password required from a normal PDF file user to access the document.

OWNER_PASSWORD: This parameter specifies the password required from the owner of the PDF file to access the document. The owner usually has more permissions. If this password is not set, an arbitrary string will be used when encrypting so that access is denied to all would-be owners.

PERMISSIONS: This exporter parameter accepts java.lang.Integer values representing the PDF permissions for the generated document. The open permissions for the document can be AllowPrinting, AllowModifyContents, AllowCopy, AllowModifyAnnotations, AllowFillIn, AllowScreenReaders, AllowAssembly, and AllowDegradedPrinting (these are all in the PdfWriter class of the iText library). Permissions can be combined by applying bitwise OR to them.

A special sample, /demo/samples/pdfencrypt, is supplied with the project to show how to use all these exporter parameters.

PDF Version and Compression

Some applications require marking the generated files with a particular PDF specifications version.

The `PDF_VERSION` exporter parameter accepts `java.lang.Character` values, but only a few values are recognized as valid, so users have to use the constants defined in the `JRPdfExporterParameter` class to point to the PDF specification version (from 1.2 to 1.6).

Since version 1.5, the PDF format supports compression. By default, the PDF exporter in JasperReports does not create compressed PDF documents, but this feature can be turned on using the `IS_COMPRESSED` exporter parameter. Note that because compressed PDFs are available only since PDF version 1.5, the PDF version of the resulting document is set to 1.5 automatically if compression is turned on.

Word Wrap and Line Break Policy

By default, the PDF exporter does not guarantee that text with the same style properties will be rendered exactly as it is using AWT. The word wrap and line break policy is slightly different, and in some cases it might cause portions of text to disappear at the end of longer text paragraphs.

To make sure this does not happen, you can configure the PDF exporter to use the AWT word wrap and line break policy by setting the `FORCE_LINEBREAK_POLICY` parameter to `Boolean.TRUE`. Note that this feature is not turned on by default, because it affects the exporter performance. This default behavior that applies in the absence of the mentioned export parameter can be controlled using the `net.sf.jasperreports.export.pdf.force.linebreak.policy` configuration property (see Chapter 18 for more details).

JavaScript Actions

The PDF specifications provide a means for the automation of various processes, such as the automatic printing of the document when it is opened. PDF viewer applications are able to execute Acrobat JavaScript code that is embedded in the PDF and associated with different events.

JasperReports only allows inserting Acrobat JavaScript code. This code gets executed when the PDF document is opened in the viewer. This can be achieved using the `JRPdfExporterParameter.PDF_JAVASCRIPT` parameter, which takes the Acrobat JavaScript source code as value. Note that Acrobat JavaScript is a programming language based on JavaScript, originally developed by Netscape Communications. More details about this can be found in the iText documentation.

Metadata Information

PDF documents can store metadata information such as the author of the document, its title, and keywords. JasperReports exposes this feature of PDF through special exporter parameters having the `METADATA` prefix and found in the `JRPdfExporterParameter` class. They are all listed following:

```
METADATA_TITLE
METADATA_AUTHOR
METADATA_SUBJECT
METADATA_KEYWORDS
METADATA_CREATOR
```

Rendering SVG Using Shapes

The `JRPdfExporterParameter.PDF_FORCE_SVG_SHAPES` flag is used to force the rendering of SVG images using shapes on the PDF `Graphics2D` context. This allows fonts to be rendered as shapes, thus avoiding any font mapping issues that might cause Unicode text to not show up properly; however, it has the disadvantage of producing larger PDF files.

By default, the flag is set to `true`, mainly due to backward-compatibility reasons. To reduce PDF file size for documents containing SVG images such as charts, this flag should be set to `false`. However, in such a case, the accuracy of the text content rendered by the SVG element in PDF depends on the correct PDF font information being available in the SVG implementation itself.

In JasperReports, SVG elements are rendered using `JRRenderable` implementations, which are most likely subclasses of the `JRAbstractSvgRenderer` class (like the `JFreeChartRenderer` class used to draw charts when the built-in chart element is used in the report). SVG renderer implementations should be concerned only with implementing the `public void render(Graphics2D grx, Rectangle2D rectangle) throws JRException;` method, which should contain all the code required for rendering the SVG on a `Graphics2D` context. Correct PDF font information means that the `java.awt.Font` objects used to draw text on the `Graphics2D` context should have PDF-related text attributes embedded so that when rendered on a PDF `Graphics2D` context, the exporter can make use of them. Embedding PDF-related text attributes into the SVG means using the following text attributes when creating `java.awt.Font` to render text in the SVG renderer implementation:

```
JRTextAttribute.PDF_FONT_NAME
JRTextAttribute.PDF_ENCODING
JRTextAttribute.IS_PDF_EMBEDDED
```

The built-in chart component in JasperReports hides this complexity of dealing with fonts in a SVG renderer by exposing to the end user the usual three PDF-specific font attributes (`pdfFontName`, `pdfEncoding`, and `isPdfEmbedded`) to be set along with the normal font attributes every time a font setting is made for the chart title, subtitle, chart legend, or axis. This feature can be controlled system-wide using the `net.sf.jasperreports.export.pdf.force.svg.shapes` configuration property.

The `PDF_FORCE_SVG_SHAPES` export parameter overrides the configuration property value, if present.

RTF Exporter

The `net.sf.jasperreports.engine.export.JRRtfExporter` implementation is a recent addition to the JasperReports library. It helps to export `JasperPrint` documents in RTF format using

RTF Specification 1.6. This means that the RTF files produced by this exporter are compatible with Microsoft Word 6.0, 2003, and XP.

However, users might experience some problems when opening those RTF files with OpenOffice or StarOffice, as these products are not perfectly compatible with the RTF specifications from Microsoft.

RTF is a character-based file format that supports absolute positioning of elements, which means that this exporter produces output very similar to that of the Graphics2D and PDF exporters. There are no special parameters for this exporter.

Almost all the provided samples show how to export to RTF.

Font Mappings

The RTF exporter expects to find a java.util.Map instance as the value for the FONT_MAP exporter parameter. If such a value is supplied at export time, then this exporter assumes that this map contains key-value pairs where both the keys and the values are java.lang.String values. The key represents the name of the font as specified by the fontName attribute in JRXML. The value represents the name of the font to use when generating the corresponding RTF font tags in the destination file.

This font mapping capability is particularly useful when the report template uses Java logical fonts as values for the fontName attribute (Serif, Sans-Serif, Monospaced, etc.) and these need to be translated into real TTF font names during the RTF export process.

XML Exporter

The discussion of the ways to store generated JasperPrint objects in the "Loading and Saving Generated Reports" section of Chapter 4 mentioned the net.sf.jasperreports.engine.export.JRXmlExporter as a possible way to transform documents into a text-based format. As report templates are defined using the special XML syntax JRXML, the JasperReports library also has a special XML structure for storing generated documents in XML format. This format is called JRPXML because the files produced by the JRXmlExporter usually have the *.jrpxml extension. These XML files can be loaded back into the JasperPrint object using the net.sf.jasperreports.engine.xml.JRPrintXmlLoader utility class. Their structure is validated against an internal DTD file called jasperprint.dtd. This document does not provide the details of the JRPXML structure. Valid JRPXML files should point to the internal DTD file using a public ID, as follows:

```
<!DOCTYPE jasperPrint PUBLIC "-//JasperReports//DTD JasperPrint//EN"
"http://jasperreports.sourceforge.net/dtds/jasperprint.dtd">
```

The root element of a JRPXML document is <jasperPrint>, which contains a list of report font definitions (<reportFont> tags) that are reused by text elements throughout the document, and a list of pages (<page> tags), each of which contains a nested list of elements like lines, rectangles, ellipses, images, and texts.

The quality of this exporter is equal to the Graphics2D exporter because it preserves 100% of the initial document content and properties. There is no loss in document quality when exporting to XML because the resulting XML content can be loaded back into a JasperPrint object that will look the same as the original one.

The built-in viewers can display documents exported in JRPXML format because they actually rely on the `JRPrintXmlLoader` to load the document back into a `JasperPrint` object before rendering it on the screen.

Embedding Images

When exporting XML, pay special attention to how images are stored. The two ways are as follows:

- If the exporter outputs to a file on disk, it stores the images contained by the source document in separate files that accompany the main JRPXML file. The image files are put in a directory that takes its name from the original destination file name plus the `_files` suffix, the same directory as the JRPXML file.
- The exporter can embed images in the JRPXML file itself by encoding their binary data using a Base64 encoder. This simplifies transfer over the network or by direct output to streams.

To determine how to handle images, set the `IS_EMBEDDING_IMAGES` exporter parameter, which expects a `java.lang.Boolean`. By default, the images are embedded in the resulting XML.

Overriding the DTD Location

For various reasons, you might need to handle the generated JRPXML content with special XML viewers or even browsers. To prevent these tools from complaining about not finding the public DTD mentioned in the header of the document when Internet access is not available, have your files point to a local DTD file instead of the public location previously mentioned in this guide. In such cases, use the `DTD_LOCATION` exporter parameter to override the default DTD location used by the exporter and point to the local DTD file.

HTML Exporter

Among the first export formats supported by JasperReports was HTML. This is because HTML is a very popular document format and browsers are available on all platforms. Also, many Java applications requiring reporting functionality are web-based applications.

The `net.sf.jasperreports.engine.export.JRHtmlExporter` tries to produce high-quality HTML output by using the most common tags to ensure that the documents are compatible with the great majority of browsers, and that they look almost the same on all platforms. It is a grid-based exporter because it structures the layout of each document page using a `<table>` element, so all the limitations mentioned about grid exporters are applicable to this exporter, too (see the "Grid Exporters" section, earlier in this chapter).

Since JasperReports version 1.2.0, the built-in HTML exporter produces output that is compatible with the XHTML standard.

Perfect Element Alignment

As previously mentioned, regardless of the output format, the JasperReports exporters try to produce documents that are as close as possible to their `Graphics2D` representation. This is also true for HTML. In HTML, elements are placed inside <td> tags, which are part of a <table> component associated with each document page. In older browsers, to have full control over a table cell in HTML, a 1×1 pixel transparent image had to be used as a spacer to ensure that the browser preserved the specified width and height for each component and did not adapt them to the size of the window.

Recent browser versions no longer have this problem, or at least they no longer make it so obvious. Also, the JRHtmlExporter implementation relies more and more on CSS for element sizing and styling, so the spacer is no longer needed. The Boolean IS_USING_IMAGES_TO_ALIGN parameter can be used to turn off the use of spacer images inside the generated HTML content, which greatly simplifies the handling of the output, especially if the original documents do not contain images of their own. By default, the HTML exporter still uses the spacer image for alignment.

Flow-Oriented Output

The JasperPrint documents can contain one or more pages and the HTML exporter can export either one page or several pages at a time. Because all exporters try to adhere as closely as possible to the Graphics2D or PDF representation of the source document's quality and layout, the page breaks are visible in HTML format in case multiple pages are exported in the same HTML document. Sometimes, however, this is not desirable. One way to make page breaks less obvious is to suppress all the blank space left between cells on the vertical axis to achieve a more flow-based layout. When set to Boolean.TRUE, the IS_REMOVE_EMPTY_SPACE_BETWEEN_ROWS exporter parameter ensures that all empty rows on the resulting HTML table are collapsed. By default, the exporter preserves all the whitespace for precise page layout.

Furthermore, between two consecutive pages rendered as two separate <table> components inside the generated HTML, the exporter places two <br /> tags by default to display the pages separately. To alter the default behavior, specify the HTML chunk to be used as a page separator in the resulting HTML. The BETWEEN_PAGES_HTML exporter parameter accepts a java.lang.String to replace the default page separator when exporting to HTML format.

The provided /demo/samples/nopagebreak sample uses this parameter when exporting to produce a more flow-based document layout.

To completely ignore pagination, use the built-in fill-time parameter IS_IGNORE_PAGINATION, as explained in the "Built-In Report Parameters" section of Chapter 8.

HTML Header

Since HTML content is usually sent directly to the browser as an individual document or stored on disk, the HTML exporter wraps the result inside document-level tags like <html> and <body>.

The default HTML header used by the JRHtmlExporter class is as follows:

```
<html>
<head>
  <meta http-equiv="Content-Type" content="text/html; charset=UTF-8">
  <style type="text/css">
    a {text-decoration: none}
  </style>
```

```
</head>
<body text="#000000" link="#000000" alink="#000000" vlink="#000000">
<table width="100%" cellpadding="0" cellspacing="0" border="0">
<tr><td width="50%"> </td><td align="center">
By default, the HTML result ends with this chunk:
</td><td width="50%"> </td></tr>
</table>
</body>
</html>
```

You can customize both the header and the footer chunks used for wrapping the document pages by setting the desired HTML chunks as values for the HTML_HEADER and HTML_FOOTER exporter parameters. These two parameters enable you to make references to other resources, such as style sheet files, or even to suppress the header and footer completely if the resulting HTML content is used only for embedding into another web page that is part of a portal-like application.

Font Mappings

When working with fonts in JasperReports, the engine relies on the fontName attribute and uses the metrics of the fonts with AWT to make all layout calculations during the report-filling process. Once exported to HTML, however, it's likely that the documents will either be viewed on systems that don't have these fonts installed or on browsers that don't recognize the fonts as specified by the original fontName values. For example, say the report templates use the Arial font for rendering a text element. A report is generated and exported to HTML on a Windows machine that has the Arial font installed and available to the current JVM. Then the HTML output produced by JasperReports is displayed on a browser that runs on a client Linux/UNIX machine and does not have the Arial font installed. In this case, the HTML will look different because the client browser will use a default font instead of Arial.

To solve this issue, the HTML exporter can be configured to use font mappings. These mappings can replace the original font name as specified by the fontName attribute with a sequence of font names separated by commas. This provides a safer fallback mechanism—rendering the text using the closest font possible if the original one is not available on the client machine.

If a value is supplied to the FONT_NAME exporter parameter, then the HTML exporter expects it to be a java.util.Map value with both keys and values of type java.lang.String. The key should be the original fontName value and the value should be the sequence of substitute fonts described in the preceding paragraph.

Background Color

Empty space found on each page in the source JasperPrint document normally results in empty cells inside the corresponding HTML <table> component. The background color of these empty cells is specified by a browser configuration or by a container component of a higher level if the HTML is embedded inside a web page and is not a standalone page. This causes the cells to appear transparent. However, if you set the IS_WHITE_PAGE_BACKGROUND exporter parameter to Boolean.TRUE, then the exporter can make the cell content appear as if printed on white paper.

Text Wrapping

The text wrap policy can vary with the document format. This is the main reason that document output may vary slightly when viewing or printing the same document with the `JRGraphics2DExporter`.

By default, browsers try not to break long words. The only way to force them to do so is to use a CSS attribute that specifies the text wrap policy to use for a given text element in HTML. Long words are broken into multiple lines if they do not fit the width of their container if the `IS_WRAP_BREAK_WORD` is set to `Boolean.TRUE` for the exporter.

Pixels or Points

All positioning and sizing in JasperReports templates and generated documents is performed using the default Java resolution of 72 dpi. The built-in Swing viewer used to display `JasperPrint` documents can detect the screen resolution at runtime and adapt the size of one point drawn on the screen so that the document can keep its normal size even when viewed on high-resolution devices.

The PDF, XLS, and RTF viewers can also do that, so at 100% zoom ratio a document maintains the same size throughout all mentioned document formats.

However, in HTML, dimensions can be specified using several different length measurement units. The width of a table cell can be specified either in pixels or in points. If specified in pixels, the document will look smaller when viewed with the browser on high-resolution screens, because the size of a pixel is smaller. Measuring all sizes in points (a point being the CSS equivalent of 1/72 of an inch) is not perfect either, because the browser cannot scale up images that are rendered at their normal size in pixels rather than points, especially if they are lazy loaded.

Because there is no perfect solution for measurement units used in the resulting HTML, choose the unit that best suits your needs by setting the `SIZE_UNIT` exporter parameter to one of the values predefined as a constant in the `JRHtmlExporterParameter` (`SIZE_UNIT_PIXEL` or `SIZE_UNIT_POINT`).

Working with Images

Because HTML is a character-based format, the `JRHtmlExporter` can send HTML content to a `java.lang.StringBuffer`, `java.io.Writer` or `java.io.OutputStream`, as described in the "Exporter Output" section, earlier in this chapter. However, in HTML format, image elements get special treatment because they cannot be embedded into the HTML content itself; they must be delivered to the browser using different techniques depending on the type of deployment.

If the HTML content produced by the exporter is to be stored in a file on disk, then it is easier to handle the images because they can be placed as individual image files inside a separate folder that accompanies the main HTML file. This closely resembles how browsers save HTML pages on disk. It is the exporter's default behavior when its output is directed to a file using either the `OUPUT_FILE` or `OUTPUT_FILE_NAME` parameters.

But even in this case, the creation of a separate folder for the images can be suppressed if the `IS_OUTPUT_IMAGES_TO_DIR` exporter parameter is set to `Boolean.FALSE`.

If the images folder is created, it has by default the same name as the target HTML file plus the _files suffix. To change this default name for the images folder, supply a value for either the IMAGES_DIR exporter parameter, which expects a java.io.File value, or the IMAGES_DIR_NAME parameter, which expects the name of the folder as java.lang.String.

A special scenario occurs when the HTML content does not get directed to files on disk, but must be delivered to an output stream. Saving the images as files on disk would not make much sense because the HTML consumer (most likely a web browser) would have no way to retrieve those files from the local disk at HTML-rendering time.

Regardless of the output destination set for the generated HTML, the exporter always gives each image a name with the form of img_x_y_z[_z_z], where

- x is the index of a document within the list of documents to export in batch mode.
- y is the page index.
- z values are a series of one or more element indexes that locate the image on the page, looping through nested frames if needed.

Lazy loaded images are not given a name, because they are supposed to be loaded by the browser from a public URL available at HTML-rendering time.

In the URLs for each <img> tag inside the generated HTML content, images are referenced using their export time–calculated name, which is img_x_y_z[_z_z], as explained previously. In those URLs, the name of the image is prefixed with a path (URI), which is automatically calculated by the exporter when the HTML is directed to a file and the images are stored in a separate folder. This prefix is actually the name of the images folder. This URI prefix can be supplied to the exporter using the IMAGES_URI exporter parameter in case the HTML is sent over the network to a browser and the images are supposed to be delivered to that browser by calling a special image servlet. The IMAGES_URI parameter can point to that servlet, and the image name that gets appended to it in order to construct a fully formatted URL can be the value for a servlet parameter that will help identify the image that needs to be sent out.

For more details about the HTML exporter, see the "Using JasperReports in Web Environments" section of Chapter 19.

XLS Exporters

For generating XLS files, there are currently two different exporter implementations available in JasperReports. The first to appear was the net.sf.jasperreports.engine.export.JRXlsExporter implementation, which uses the POI library. Because the POI library does not handle images very well, or at least not in a transparent way, this exporter implementation completely ignores the image elements present in the source documents that need to be exported.

This was the main reason to try to come up with a new XLS exporter that would support images. The new solution is the net.sf.jasperreports.engine.export.JExcelApiExporter implementation, which makes use of the JExcelApi library.

Because in XLS all document content is placed inside cells, the XLS exporters are considered typical grid exporters, and have the limitations mentioned previously (see the "Grid Exporters" section earlier in this chapter).

Configuring Sheets

An XLS file is structured in multiple sheets, and both exporters can be configured either to put all pages inside the source JasperPrint document on one sheet (one after the another), or to put each page on a separate sheet in the resulting XLS file. The choice is made by setting the IS_ONE_PAGE_PER_SHEET exporter parameter, which is set to Boolean.FALSE by default.

When IS_ONE_PAGE_PER_SHEET is set to Boolean.TRUE, or when you have to execute a batch export to XLS, multiple sheets are created in the worksheet. The JasperReports XLS exporters provide a simple but efficient sheet-naming mechanism. They use the SHEET_NAMES export parameter to read custom sheet names from the String array passed as value. This exporter parameter can hold an array of strings, which are passed as sheet names in order. If no value is supplied for the SHEET_NAMES parameter or if the value contains fewer sheet names than actually needed by the final document, then the sheets are named by default Page i (where i represents the one-based sheet index).

Flow-Oriented Output

The JasperPrint documents are page-oriented. When they are exported to a single-sheet XLS document, all the pages are rendered consecutively. Because all exporters try to adhere as closely as possible to the quality and layout of the source document's Graphics2D or PDF format, the page breaks are visible in XLS format. Sometimes this is not desirable. One way to make page breaks less obvious and the layout more flow-based is to suppress all the remaining blank space between cells on the vertical axis. When set to Boolean.TRUE, the IS_REMOVE_EMPTY_SPACE_BETWEEN_ROWS exporter parameter ensures that all empty rows on the resulting XLS sheet are collapsed. By default, the exporter preserves all the whitespace for a precise page layout.

The provided /demo/samples/nopagebreak sample shows you how to use this parameter when exporting to XLS to produce a more flow-based document layout.

To completely ignore pagination, use the built-in fill-time parameter IS_IGNORE_PAGINATION (explained in the "Built-In Report Parameters" section of Chapter 8).

Cell Types

Inside the proprietary document format that JasperReports uses (represented by a JasperPrint object), all text elements are considered alphanumeric values. This means that if a numeric text field of type java.lang.Double is placed in the report template at design time, all the text elements inside the JasperPrint object resulting from it will hold java.lang.String values, even though they are actually numbers. Therefore, in a sense, data type information is lost during report filling. This is because the main goal of JasperReports is to create documents for viewing and printing, not necessarily for further data manipulation inside tools like Excel, where formulas could be added to numeric cells.

However, these resulting text elements found in the generated documents nowadays hold enough data type information (in addition to the alphanumeric content) for the original value of the text element to be re-created, if needed.

Both XLS exporters support the IS_DETECT_CELL_TYPE parameter, which forces the re-creation of the original cell value in accordance with its declared data type, as specified in the report template. This new exporter parameter deprecates the former IS_AUTO_DETECT_CELL_TYPE exporter parameter, which dealt only with numeric cells, ignored date and time cells, and had the disadvantage of transforming into numbers all text cells that would successfully parse into numeric values, regardless of their initial data type.

Cell type detection is turned off by default.

Format Pattern Conversions

When using the POI library–based implementation, it is important to keep in mind that standard Java format patterns are not completely supported by the POI APIs. There are only a few data patterns that make a perfect match between Java and POI.

In the case that the Java pattern stored in the generated report does not match any of the supported POI cell patterns, there is still a way to choose an appropriate POI format pattern. The solution is to use the `FORMAT_PATTERNS_MAP` export parameter and supply a `java.util.Map` as value. This map should contain Java format patterns as keys and corresponding proprietary format patterns as values.

Font Mappings

Font mappings for the XLS exporter work exactly as they do for the RTF exporter. Both keys and values in the supplied `FONT_MAP` exporter parameter should be of type `java.util.String`. Font mappings are especially useful when the report templates rely on logical Java font names that must be translated into physical font names at export time.

Font Size Correction

Currently, there is no way to control the line spacing in a spreadsheet cell, which results in the cell text not fitting exactly within the cell boundaries. As a workaround, in order to force the cell text to fit, you can use the `IS_FONT_SIZE_FIX_ENABLED` exporter parameter to decrease the font size by one point when generating the cell format.

Background Color

Empty space found on each page in the source `JasperPrint` document normally results in empty cells on the corresponding sheet inside the XLS file. The background color of these empty cells is specified by the configuration of the XLS viewer itself. This makes the cells appear transparent. To force the document's background to be white, set the `IS_WHITE_PAGE_BACKGROUND` exporter parameter to `Boolean.TRUE`.

Excel Color Palette

In JasperReports, any color can be used for the background or the foreground of a report element. However, when exporting to XLS format, only a limited set of colors is supported, through what is called a *color palette*.

If the colors used in a report template do not match the colors in the color palette, then the XLS exporter will use a special algorithm to determine the closest matches by comparing the RGB levels. However, the results might not always be what you'd expect.

ODT Exporter

Open Document Format (short for OASIS Open Document Format for Office Applications) describes electronic documents such as memos, spreadsheets, books, charts, presentations, and word processing documents. `.odt` is the file extension used for the word processing documents in the Open Document Format, and JasperReports now has a grid exporter for this type of file in the `net.sf.jasperreports.engine.export.oasis.JROdtExporter` class.

So far, the ODT exporter does not have any special parameters, and has the known limitations of grid exporters (see the "Grid Exporters" section earlier in this chapter). It can work in batch mode and supports all types of exporter input and output as well as font mappings.

CSV Exporter

Initially, exporting to CSV files was not a goal or requirement of the JasperReports library. Because CSV is a data-oriented file format, exporting rich content documents to CSV results in a tremendous loss of quality. However, community feedback has shown that this is often a requirement for applications. Thus, the `net.sf.jasperreports.engine.export.JRCsvExporter` was eventually implemented and shipped with the library.

However, users should still think twice before deciding to use JasperReports, a very complex visual tool, to generate data files in a simple format like CSV. It would probably require too much overhead to use JasperReports just for that.

It is obvious that the CSV exporter will completely ignore graphic elements present in the source document that needs to be exported. It will only deal will text elements, and from those, it will only extract the text value, completely ignoring the style properties.

CSV is a character-based file format whose content is structured in rows and columns, so the `JRCsvExporter` is a grid exporter because it must transform the free-form content of each page from the source document into a grid-like structure using the special algorithm mentioned in the "Grid Exporters" section, earlier in this chapter.

By default, the CSV exporter uses commas to separate column values and newline characters to separate rows in the resulting file. However, you can redefine the delimiters using the two special exporter parameters `FIELD_DELIMITER` and `RECORD_DELIMITER`, which both accept `java.lang.String` values.

Plain Text Exporter

The `net.sf.jasperreports.engine.export.JRTextExporter` implementation represents a plain text exporter that tries to convert the JasperReports document into a simple text document with a fixed page width and height, measured in characters. Users can specify the desired page width and height, and the engine will make the best effort to fit text elements into the corresponding text page. The basic idea of the algorithm is to convert pixels to characters (find a pixel/character ratio). To achieve this, use the following parameters:

- `CHARACTER_WIDTH` *and* `CHARACTER_HEIGHT` *parameters*: These specify how many pixels in the original report should be mapped onto a character in the exported text.

- `PAGE_WIDTH` *and* `PAGE_HEIGHT` *parameters*: These specify the text page width and height in characters.

Note that both width and height must be specified and that character sizes have priority over page sizes.

Since the algorithm causes loss of precision, a few precautions should be taken when creating templates that will eventually be exported to plain text:

- Report sizes and text page sizes should be divisible (e.g., specify a template width of 1,000 pixels and a page width of 100 characters, resulting in a character width of 10 pixels).
- Text element sizes should also follow the preceding rule (e.g., if the character height is 10 pixels and a particular text element is expected to span two rows, then the text element should be 20 pixels tall).
- For best results, text elements should be aligned in a grid-like fashion.
- Text fields should not be too small. Following are two examples of problems that this can cause:
  - If the element height is smaller than the character height, then the element will not appear in the exported text file.
  - If the character width is 10 and the element width is 80, then only the first eight characters will be displayed.

Users can specify the text that should be inserted between two subsequent pages by using the `BETWEEN_PAGES_TEXT` parameter. The default value is two blank lines.

The line separator to be used in the generated text file can be specified using the `LINE_SEPARATOR` exporter parameter. This is most useful when you want to force a particular line separator, knowing that the default line separator is operating system dependent, as specified by the `line.separator` system property of the JVM.

Check the supplied `/demo/samples/text` sample to see the kind of output this exporter can produce.

CHAPTER 18

Configuration Files

The configuration properties of the JasperReports library can be specified using a properties file. The file can be read from the file system, accessed as a resource from the classpath, or loaded from an URL. The default name of the properties file is `jasperreports.properties`. The `net.sf.jasperreports.properties` system property can be used to specify a different file name or location. The default or custom name is successively interpreted as a file name, a resource name, and an URL; the properties are read from the first succeeding source.

Most of the configuration properties have default values hard-coded in the library. These values act as defaults for the properties read from the file. Therefore, the properties file can contain only properties whose values differ from the default.

To access and set configuration properties at runtime, use the `net.sf.jasperreports.engine.util.JRProperties` static methods. This class contains constants for all the configuration properties.

These are the most useful methods:

- `String getProperty(String key)`: Returns the value of a property as a `String`
- `boolean getBooleanProperty(String key)`: Returns the value of a property as a `boolean`
- `void setProperty(String key, String value)`: Sets the value of a property
- `void setProperty(String key, boolean value)`: Sets the value of a Boolean property

Prior to version 1.0.0, some of the configuration properties were specified by way of system properties. This has been deprecated in version 1.0.0 in favor of using a properties file. The names of the properties have also changed.

Using system properties to configure JasperReports is still partially supported for backward compatibility. If the system properties are set, their values are used when initializing the corresponding configuration properties. Setting and changing the configuration properties via `java.lang.System.setProperty` after the configuration properties are initialized is no longer supported; use the `JRProperties` methods instead. Table 18-1 shows the configuration properties currently used by the library, along with the old (pre-1.0.0) property names.

Table 18-1. *JasperReports Configuration Properties*

Property Name	Former System Property Name
net.sf.jasperreports.compiler.class	jasper.reports.compiler.class
net.sf.jasperreports.compiler.xml.validation	jasper.reports.compile.xml.validation
net.sf.jasperreports.compiler.keep.java.file	jasper.reports.compile.keep.java.file
net.sf.jasperreports.compiler.classpath	jasper.reports.compile.class.path
net.sf.jasperreports.compiler.temp.dir	jasper.reports.compile.temp
net.sf.jasperreports.crosstab.bucket.measure.limit	None
net.sf.jasperreports.default.font.name	None
net.sf.jasperreports.default.font.size	None
net.sf.jasperreports.default.pdf.font.name	None
net.sf.jasperreports.default.pdf.encoding	None
net.sf.jasperreports.default.pdf.embedded	None
net.sf.jasperreports.ejbql.query.hint.*	None
net.sf.jasperreports.ejbql.query.page.size	None
net.sf.jasperreports.export.graphics2d.min.job.size	None
net.sf.jasperreports.export.pdf.font.*	None
net.sf.jasperreports.export.pdf.fontdir.*	None
net.sf.jasperreports.export.pdf.force.linebreak.policy	None
net.sf.jasperreports.export.pdf.force.svg.shapes	None
net.sf.jasperreports.export.xml.validation	jasper.reports.export.xml.validation
net.sf.jasperreports.file.buffer.os.memory.threshold	None
net.sf.jasperreports.hql.clear.cache	None
net.sf.jasperreports.hql.field.mapping.descriptions	None
net.sf.jasperreports.hql.query.list.page.size	None
net.sf.jasperreports.hql.query.run.type	None
net.sf.jasperreports.jdbc.fetch.size	None
net.sf.jasperreports.properties	None
net.sf.jasperreports.query.executer.factory.*	None
net.sf.jasperreports.subreport.runner.factory	None
net.sf.jasperreports.viewer.render.buffer.max.size	None
net.sf.jasperreports.virtualizer.files.delete.on.exit	None

The meaning of each property can be found in the related chapters of this guide.

In the future, more configuration properties will be supported by the JasperReports library to reduce its reliance on hard-coded constant values for various internal settings.

CHAPTER 19

Advanced JasperReports

Previous chapters have presented the core functionality that most people will use when working with the JasperReports library. However, some complex requirements of your specific applications might force you to dig deeper into the JasperReports functionality. The following sections provide a closer look at those aspects that can help you make fuller use of the JasperReports library.

Implementing Data Sources

The JasperReports library comes with several default implementations of the `net.sf.jasperreports.engine.JRDataSource` interface. This interface supplies the report data when invoking the report-filling process, as explained in the previous chapters of this book.

These default implementations let you generate reports using data from relational databases retrieved through JDBC, from Java Swing tables, or from collections and arrays of JavaBeans objects.

However, your application data might have a special structure or an organization that prevents you from using any of the default implementations of the data source interface that come with the library. In such situations, you will have to create custom implementations for the `net.sf.jasperreports.engine.JRDataSource` interface to wrap your special report data so that the reporting engine can understand and use it when generating the reports.

Creating a custom implementation for the `net.sf.jasperreports.engine.JRDataSource` interface is not very difficult since you have to implement only two methods. The first one, the `next()` method, is called by the reporting engine every time it wants the current pointer to advance to the next virtual record in the data source. The other, the `getFieldValue()` method, is called by the reporting engine with every iteration through the data source to retrieve the value for each report field.

If your custom data source is also supposed to work with subreports that are placed inside bands that cannot split due to the `isSplitAllowed="false"` property, you can implement the `JRRewindableDataSource` interface. This interface contains an extra method that lets the record pointer move back before the first virtual record in the data source if the subreport needs to restart on a new page.

Customizing Viewers

The JasperReports library comes with built-in viewers that enable you to display the reports stored in the library's proprietary format or to preview your report templates when you create them.

These viewers are represented by the following two classes:

- `net.sf.jasperreports.view.JasperViewer`: Use this class to view generated reports, either as in-memory objects or serialized objects on disk or even stored in XML format.
- `net.sf.jasperreports.view.JasperDesignViewer`: Use this class to preview report templates, either in JRXML or compiled form.

However, these default viewers might not suit everybody's needs. You may want to customize them to adapt to certain application requirements. If you need to do this, be aware that these viewers actually use other, more basic visual components that come with the JasperReports library.

The report viewers mentioned previously use the visual component represented by the `net.sf.jasperreports.view.JRViewer` class and its companions. It is in fact a special `javax.swing.JPanel` component that is capable of displaying generated reports. It can be easily incorporated into other Java Swing–based applications or applets.

If the functionality of this basic visual component does not meet your needs, you can adapt it by subclassing it. For example, to create an extra button on the toolbar of this viewer, extend the component and add that button yourself in the new visual component you obtain by subclassing.

This is shown in the `/demo/samples/webapp` sample, where the "Printer Applet" displays a customized version of the report viewer with an extra button in the toolbar.

Another very important issue is that the default report viewer that comes with the library does not know how to deal with document hyperlinks that point to external resources. It deals only with local references by redirecting the viewer to the corresponding local anchor.

However, JasperReports lets you handle the clicks made on document hyperlinks that point to external documents. To do this, simply implement the `net.sf.jasperreports.view.JRHyperlinkListener` interface and add an instance of this listener class to register with the viewer component, using the `addHyperlinkListener()` method exposed by the `net.sf.jasperreports.view.JRViewer` class. By doing this, you ensure that the viewer will also call your implementation of the `gotoHyperlink()` method in which you handle the external references yourself.

There are two ways of rendering the current document page on the viewer component:

- Creating an in-memory buffered image and displaying that image
- Rendering the page content directly to the `Graphics2D` context of the viewer component

The first approach has the advantage of smoother scroll operations, since the page content is rendered only once as an image, after which the scroll operations occur within the view port of that image. The drawback is that at high zoom ratios, the image could become so large that an out-of-memory error could occur.

The second approach avoids any potential memory problems at high zoom ratios by rendering page content directly onto the view component, but this results in a drop of performance that can be seen when scrolling the page.

Switching between the two rendering methods can be controlled by setting the `net.sf.jasperreports.viewer.render.buffer.max.size` configuration property. The value of this property represents the maximum size (in pixels) of a buffered image that would be used by the JRViewer component to render a report page (the first rendering technique). If rendering a report page requires an image larger than this threshold (i.e., image width × image height > maximum size), then the report page will be rendered directly on the viewer component.

By default, this configuration property is set to 0, which means that only direct rendering is performed, no matter what the zoom ratio.

Using JasperReports in Web Environments

Recent surveys indicate that JasperReports is usually used inside web-based applications to render dynamic content.

When using JasperReports inside such applications, keep in mind how to handle report templates, reference report resources, and deal with images when exporting to HTML.

A small web application that does these things is included as one of the samples. The `/demo/samples/webapp` directory inside the project distribution package contains the source files of a simple web application that uses JasperReports for rendering a report. This report can be viewed in HTML and PDF format, or even directly as a `JasperPrint` object using the built-in Swing viewer as an applet inside the browser.

Compiling Report Templates

Any Java application that needs reporting functionality can use the JasperReports library in two ways:

- To generate documents out of static report templates that get compiled at development time and are distributed in the compiled form as part of the application distribution files
- To generate documents out of dynamically built or so-called ad hoc report templates that are the result of some user input at runtime

In the first case, `*.jasper` files containing compiled report templates are deployed as resources inside the application distribution package, just as images or normal Java `*.class` files are distributed and deployed. The compilation of the static report templates should be part of the application build system, taking into account that the library is shipped with a ready-to-use Ant task for bulk-compiling multiple report template files at once.

The second scenario assumes that static report templates cannot be used, or at least are subject to some runtime modifications based on user feedback. Runtime-created or runtime-modified report templates must be compiled on the fly. Report compilation in a web environment can be a challenge if JDK-based report compilers are used, because they require a temporary working directory and an explicitly set classpath. However, recent versions of JasperReports use the JDT-based compiler by default, which is both faster and easier to use because it does not require any configuration. To use it, make sure the `jdt-compiler.jar` file distributed with the JasperReports project source files inside the `/lib` directory is part of the web application classpath.

Deploying Report Templates and Resources

Report templates can reference other resources such as images, fonts, or other report templates used as nested subreports. In any Java application, but especially inside web applications where locating files on disk is more challenging, the best way to locate static resources is by means of classpath. All the resources that need to be loaded using a relative location at runtime should be part of the application's classpath. Images, fonts, and subreports should be referenced inside a report template using their relative location within the classpath. By doing this, you ensure that links between those resources are still valid regardless of how the application is actually deployed.

Delivering Images in HTML Format

Since images cannot be embedded in the HTML output directly, but are supposed to be retrieved by the browser from their specified public URL, a web application using JasperReports for generating reports in HTML must be specially configured for the `JRHtmlExporter`.

JasperReports is now shipped with a ready-to-use servlet implementation that can deliver images from a `JasperPrint` document or a list of `JasperPrint` documents placed on the HTTP session.

The HTML exporter can be configured so that all the images point to this servlet in their URLs. To do this, supply the URL prefix to use for all the images as the value for the `IMAGES_URI` exporter parameter.

The image servlet is implemented by the `net.sf.jasperreports.j2ee.servlets.ImageServlet` class. An example is in the supplied `/demo/samples/webapp` sample inside the project distribution.

Page-by-Page HTML Viewer

The `JRHtmlExporter` can be configured to export one page at a time. With the source `JasperPrint` document kept on the HTTP session, an application can simulate a viewer that allows users to view the document page by page, as we do with the built-in Swing viewer, instead of viewing all the pages at the same time, one after the other.

The provided `/demo/samples/webapp` sample shows how such a simple HTML viewer can be implemented inside a web application.

Sending PDF Content to the Browser

Although it can send binary PDF content directly into an output stream, the PDF exporter must be used in combination with an in-memory `java.io.ByteArrayOutputStream` when used inside a web application to send output to the browser on the client side. It must measure the length of the binary output that it produces before even attempting to send that output directly to the browser because some browsers need to know the size of the binary content they will receive in order to work properly.

The downside is that you consume extra memory by temporarily storing PDF content instead of sending it directly to the consumer.

Applet Viewer

If a web-based application is used only or mainly inside an intranet, and it is acceptable to use Java applets for enhanced usability, generated reports can be viewed with the built-in Swing viewer. The server application would no longer need to export the `JasperPrint` objects to more popular formats such as HTML or PDF, but can instead send the objects over the network in serialized form to an applet that can display them natively.

Among the files available for download on the JasperReports web site is one called `jasperreports-x.x.x-applet.jar`. This JAR file is smaller than the complete `jasperreports-x.x.x.jar` because it contains only the class interfaces that the viewer needs to display documents in the proprietary `JasperPrint` format, making it more appropriate for an applet.

An applet making use of this smaller JAR file is in the supplied `/demo/samples/webapp` sample provided with the project's source files.

Index

J

S

T